Writers in Crisis

THE AMERICAN NOVEL, 1925–1940

Books by Maxwell Geismar

AMERICAN MODERNS: From Rebellion to Conformity
REBELS AND ANCESTORS: The American Novel, 1890–1915
THE LAST OF THE PROVINCIALS: The American Novel, 1915–1925
WRITERS IN CRISIS: The American Novel, 1925–1940

Editor

THE VIKING PORTABLE THOMAS WOLFE
THE POCKET BOOK WHITMAN READER
JACK LONDON: SHORT STORIES
SHERWOOD ANDERSON: SHORT STORIES

Writers in Crisis

THE AMERICAN NOVEL, 1925–1940

By MAXWELL GEISMAR

'Long, too long America,
Traveling roads all even and peaceful
   you learn'd from joys and prosperity only,
But now, ah now, to learn from crises of anguish...'

RING LARDNER · ERNEST HEMINGWAY

JOHN DOS PASSOS · WILLIAM FAULKNER

THOMAS WOLFE · JOHN STEINBECK

HILL AND WANG NEW YORK

To Anne

Still the Christina of Crisis

FIRST AMERICAN CENTURY SERIES EDITION MARCH 1961
SECOND PRINTING OCTOBER 1963

Acknowledgment is made to *The Virginia Quarterly Review,* in which a condensation of the Hemingway chapter first appeared. Acknowledgment is also made to the following publishers for their courteous permission to quote illustrative passages: to Charles Scribner's Sons, for passages from the works of Ring Lardner, Ernest Hemingway, and Thomas Wolfe; to Houghton Mifflin Company, for passages from the works of John Dos Passos; to Random House, for passages from the works of William Faulkner; to Harper and Brothers, for passages from Thomas Wolfe's 'The Web and the Rock' and 'You Can't Go Home Again'; to The Viking Press, for passages from the works of John Steinbeck.

MANUFACTURED IN THE UNITED STATES OF AMERICA
BY THE COLONIAL PRESS, INC., CLINTON, MASS.

Preface

A RETAKE FROM THE SIXTIES

THIS PREFACE marks the fourth printing of *Writers in Crisis* and a new paperback edition. My first book, it has done well enough through the years, and I look back upon it with a certain feeling of nostalgia. I see its faults. There are some curious sentences in this narrative, as though the typist of the manuscript had suffered from spells of vertigo—as indeed he did. But the book has survived for almost twenty years; it has kept its personality intact. I have no great desire to change anything in it now. Let it stand: as a mark of its own period, and of a younger author who possessed both the illusions of his time and of his own temperament then.

What has changed more, that earlier critic or his society and culture, I don't know. It is a sort of triumph just to maintain oneself on the purely bio-psychic level—simply to not be fragmented by life—in the best of times. The world we are now in can hardly be called that; and I have seen both older and younger writers hard-pressed by its demands, or shattered, or retreating to some soothing nonobjective nirvana. I have seen a few of them violating elementary concepts of human decency (so I thought) in order to secure their own place or power or prestige; or perhaps they were simply fighting for their own survival—something that the earlier author of *Writers* could hardly have known, or hoped for.

Well, it was different in the early 'forties. I was writing a study of the changing beliefs of the contemporary American novelist in a period of domestic crisis which itself was filled with faith. Or perhaps that high period of our national letters from the 'twenties to the 'forties was the real subject of this book, and the writers were the witnesses at this investigation; just as the artist always is, whatever his personal school or credo, the Biblical 'witness' to the conditions of human existence. I used Ring Lardner to summarize the values of the 1920's. With some reservations, I used John Steinbeck to illustrate the social values of the late 'thirties which were in such complete contrast to those of the decade before.

Between Lardner and Steinbeck, I said then, we shall study what happened to the work of Hemingway and Dos Passos, William Faulkner and Thomas Wolfe. Each of these writers is viewed in some, or large, detail against both the epoch of prosperity and that of the depression. I was attempting, as I still am in the later books of this series, to describe the full growth of the modern American novelist in his own terms and in his culture's. Even then I was not unaware of the problems of literary 'Technique,' which our New Criticism stresses so absolutely today, and which my own books mention more discreetly. I only thought that any study of Technique for its own sake, without the primary and driving forces of history and of the individual alike—was merely a pedantic exercise.

I still think, today, that a writer's technique reveals his inner personality, or that his personality *makes* his technique, just as it makes his tone, his central vision of life, or—in short—his books. It is this literary personality that I am after, situated as it is in a certain period of time, using a certain literary craft to express itself, and at its best producing, at rare moments, those works of art which do stand by themselves, and which have their own inner logic and organic development. Thus *Writers in Crisis*, like its companion volumes, concentrates on the key figures of its epoch, and through their histories it shows the shifting values of the 'twenties and 'thirties, the creative conflicts, the social impact of these periods, and the individual responses.

And that was a particularly interesting time in which to study art. Never before, I said then, had the American writer been subject to so many changing pressures within so short a space: but this, as it turned out, was only the prelude to what followed.

"The bias of the book is democratic, its belief is in the potential of democratic society, and especially American society, as the only mature form of communal life." So the original preface to *Writers* stated, amidst the shifting ideological travail of the late 'thirties and early 'forties, and so I am impelled to say again today, when the need for dissent and variety in the democracy is even more urgent. The prevailing point of view in the book is critical but not negative. We shall notice, to be sure, the familiar distaste of the American writer for the commercial epoch of the later 'twenties, this high noon of frantic finance. The age of prosperity ends up in the red. The Lardnerian cosmos, in whose gaudy heaven glowed only the mystic dollar sign, in which every pen was golden, alienated its central literary talents. The dazzling materialism of 1929 led only to spiritual frustration on the part of the American writer.

But the depression of the 1930's, apparently so destructive and so despairing, was actually a time of regeneration for the typical American literary talents who are studied here. The social and cultural crisis of the new decade brought to our writers a set of spiritual positives based, as it were, on the actual collapse of their own society. The 'American conversion' of Hemingway, however late or imperfect; the apparent fusion, however hesitant, of Dos Passos' 'two nations'; the slow, groping, awkward and provincial, but finally quite admirable growth of Tom Wolfe; the typical evolution of John Steinbeck—all this points to the same conclusion. Too long we had traveled roads 'all even and peaceful,' as Walt Whitman declared at the outset of our Civil War. Once more we were learning from crises of anguish. But in crisis the American writer had gained moral stature, a sense of his own cultural connection, a series of new meanings and new values for his work.

Does art always oscillate, as Otto Rank believed, between the two poles of the individual and community—the community and the individual? At least the typical, the most representative American fiction writers of the 'thirties had discarded the exiled, the outraged 'I' of the later 'twenties, and had moved to the suffering, the searching 'we' of the depression years. Or so at least I felt, I wrote, when this book first appeared in the early 'forties, though even then I held no blithe or fanatical thesis: no 'single view' of either life or literature. "The world-wide ills of modern civilization are also deeply rooted in our own country. These studies will attempt to estimate both the corrosive and the creative strains in the national temperament as they are reflected by our literary spokesmen." All the same, why is it today, looking back across the abyss, one feels so much less sanguine or satisfied, not only with the later work of the surviving authors in this volume, but with the whole development of our literary scene—our creative vein in general—since the early 'forties?

The Second World War, of course, cut across the hopeful democratic vistas of that time. But even at the war's end, there was confidence in our literary achievement; there was an expectation, indeed, that we might witness another postwar revival to match the famous generation of the 'twenties. Perhaps that hope was our first mistake. Very slowly we came to realize that the flowering in our literature both before and after the First World War was the climax of that larger movement of modern American realism (called Naturalism at its inception) which began to stir up the blood in our writers as early as the 1890's. Our great literary figures of the 'twenties had behind them almost three decades of pioneering and rebellious literature. These artists were themselves the high esthetic individuals who mark the peak of all such artistic movements; and these peaks do not recur, historically speaking, within brief intervals.

There were some fine and promising new talents in the late 'forties and early 'fifties (John Hersey, Nelson Algren, Ira Wolfert, William Styron, James Jones, Norman Mailer, John Howard Griffin, Saul Bellow, to mention a few of them). During this period both Hemingway and Faulkner received their 'official' world recognition, the Nobel prize. But the decade of the 1950's —concerned with its stress on 'normalcy' and on material advantages, private possessions and private pleasure; but also with its own aversion to any show of social conflict, to any deep concern with world affairs, to any manifestation of public spirit, in truth, when it might conflict with personal comfort: that decade was only an ironical, or perhaps macabre, retake on the 'twenties. And over it hovered always the increasingly ominous storm clouds of the Cold War, the nuclear bomb and rocket, and of that large part of the outside world which was absorbed in revolutionary ferment rather than in new ice-boxes.

So here at home the age of Mencken and Dreiser (which had opened the way for Hemingway, Dos Passos, and Faulkner) became the age of Marquand and Wouk. The 'fifties became, indeed, mainly an age of Revivals, in which that talented and perplexing master in fictional entertainment, Henry James himself, was hailed not only as the greatest but almost as the only American novelist, while, at the other pole of the national letters, the great social realists of our literature were practically excluded from the lexicon of art. (Oh well, I mean at least from the authoritarian guidebooks of the New Criticism.) It was not a happy period, with all its 'pleasures'; but then, how could it be? "The social atmosphere was heavy and dense, if not oppressive. The esthetic air was so thin, pure and abstract." So I said in another book (*American Moderns,* in 1958) which described the post–World-War-II period of our literature, and which traced the later careers of the four surviving writers in the group studied in the present volume.

What really happened to them? Among other things we discovered that the glittering rebellion of the 'twenties was based on inadequate human values. The great charm of the Lost Generation lay indeed in its youth: in that high-handed, arbitrary, confident, entertaining rejection of so many traditional norms of society, which was embodied so well again in the early verse of Edna Millay. There is something exhilarating in the cutting of all ties, the breaking of all bonds, the rejection of roots. And conversely there was the breathing of a new literary air, it seemed, the discovery of so many forbidden artistic subjects and themes, the forging of that new literary language in which the best books of the 'twenties were written. But the delight of being young and gifted in the arts holds no solution for the necessity of growing older and (maybe) wiser.

When I left my group of American novelists in *Writers* in the early 'forties, four of them were just at this critical juncture in their careers. When you return to them now, in the 'sixties, you feel (I hope wrongly) they are at the point of no return. With a heavy heart I have watched their work meanwhile, for in their decline has been dissipated a part of my own earlier faith and confidence. To a certain degree I had identified my own career with them; they were my generation, critically speaking, and my own best hope. Isn't it true, too, that both the biological and the social theories which may be advanced in explanation of their later work are inadequate? What really went wrong with them? Why is it that the major European authors, faced often with a more desperate set of personal or social circumstances, seem to have survived with, on the whole, a better tone? "Grace under pressure," as the grand old man of our modern fictionalists has so often proclaimed, scenting the true dangers of his time. And that is precisely what is lacking in the maturity of this present group of contemporary American novelists, even when compared with the Middle and Older generation of our native writers who prepared the way for them.

What was the real failure? One of character or of culture? But meanwhile one returns to their achievement in this book not only with nostalgia, but also with a certain elation—an exhilaration to match their own, artistically, when they were at their best. In those days, they were bold and fresh; they were brilliant and serious and exciting; they were master craftsmen exulting in their discoveries and penetrations; they were the magicians of new life in the arts, and true voices of the best and highest creative strain in the national temperament. So let it all stand.

MAXWELL GEISMAR

Harrison, New York
November 1960

Contents

Chapter One

Ring Lardner: LIKE SOMETHING WAS GOING TO HAPPEN

◇

1. SUCCESS STORY, '29   2. PARADISE BY PULLMAN
3. O KEEP YOUR MOUTH SHUT   4. LIKE SOMETHING
WAS GOING TO HAPPEN BUT IT DON'T

Chapter One

Ring Lardner : LIKE SOMETHING WAS GOING TO HAPPEN

---

1. SUCCESS STORY, '29.   The popular humorist is the genuine historian. As our jokes reveal our intentions, in the wit of a culture we may find its basic beliefs. The funnyman of the nineteen-twenties, Ring Lardner is an authentic commentator on American capitalism in its frantic flowering. Though neither the era nor the author realized it, Lardner became the mordant chronicler of a moribund social order. The diversions of a period bent so grimly on pleasure, Lardner recorded and made into a new literature — this age of speculation and crossword puzzles, of Mah-Jong, Teapot Dome, and Halitosis, of rising skirts and rising stocks, Pyorrhea and Peaches Browning, of Mencken and Cabell, and of highballs, which for the Lardnerian protagonist became a vocation rather than a diversion.

So particularly its native product, how could Lardner not portray the epoch of finance? His own history is the Jazz Age's myth. Did any small-town boy rise faster, higher? Reporter on the *South Bend Times* in 1905, Lardner went to St. Louis, Boston; and in Chicago started his celebrated sports column. An entire generation began to follow 'The Wake of the News' in the *Tribune*, entranced by Lardner's new language which made most of the previous attempts at an American style sound rather like the diction of an Oxford don. Lardner was in the big money, for Lardner knew Al, and Al was worth a million. Who wants knowledge, who thinks of sorrow, there was only Success in the America of the twenties.

In 1919 we dispensed with our radicals, solved the evils of liquor by decree in a strange burst of righteousness which inaugurated the era of entertainment. Lardner gave up his newspaper routine. Writing feature articles, stories when he felt like it, he came East to the provincial's golden aspiration, The Big Town. Long Island estate, metropolitan society, literary figures, theatrical figures (Lardner always loved the stage): money, friends, fame all tumbled on the boy from Niles, Michigan. Life was all joy in the age of first mortgages, and our Lardner seemed to have everything. The intellectuals hailed 'How to Write Short Stories,' recalling Shakespeare in his popularity and immortality alike. Lardner had before him not only material success, living the best life of the age in the wealthiest nation of the world; he was also a 'great indigenous artist.'

He was, at any rate, the big humorist of his era, and in the tradition of Artemus Ward, Mr. Dooley, and Sam Slick, inferior only to Mark Twain. Yet thus given the rewards of a culture unsurpassed in material splendor; sketching in, as Lardner did, the most wonderful fragments of contemporary satire; such a writer, in fact, as may come along once in a generation, Lardner came into a sorry fruition. Though he annihilated Babbitt, while Sinclair Lewis merely (and somewhat uneasily) took off our social prototype, Lardner could never have written a 'Main Street.' Before Dos Passos, Lardner blasted the American Success Myth, but he could never have written 'The Big Money.' A score of other figures have been influenced by him (with Hemingway he helped to change the currents of our literature), and yet with lesser talent they have often done more than Lardner with such great gifts. For the factors which contributed to the tragic climax of this fabulous Success Story of '29, we must now consider Ring Lardner's history, his age, and what he tells us about it. Lardner wrote what he saw, and what did he see?

2. PARADISE BY PULLMAN.　Busying itself so passionately with the here-and-now even while it was in fact momentarily dissolving, Lardner's era, like its protagonists whom he so brilliantly described, had little sense of time, or the strange, or of truth. To itself it was unparalleled, unique and eternal. Under the mysterious heavens there was only a Stutz in every garage, now and forever, always and amen. Here was the blossoming of American materialism, the strange adolescence of a frontier nation. Everything that could be done, Uncle Sam would do it. Terms: cash. Fixed and immutable, the rising sun of the post-war decade, glowed the mystic sign of the dollar, and around it the world of the twenties gyrated breathlessly, bigger, better, faster than any world that had ever been.

Was there need for a nobler view of man's activity? What could be more inspiring than Chrysler's glistening tower? If you wanted new feelings, you voyaged to new vistas, with General Motors. What institution was solider than Prudential Life, with its Rock of Gibraltar embedded in mortuary statistics? At the identical moment American Tel and Tel could line your purse and transmit your joy to the corners of the universe. It was the playtime of streamlining capitalism, evening would never come, and under this bright, artificial sunlight (by General Electric) Lardner and his U.S.A. saw no shadow in its passing of Time's ancient chariot.

Yet what Lardner did gave evidence of the facts his period defied. In the older tradition of the artist, he was the vessel through which the folk-heroes of the Jazz Age poured their elations and depressions to make the history they ignored. In a Keefe, the busher poet of this busher society, in the anonymous but astounding American adolescent of 'I Can't Breathe,' in the detective Fred Gross, whose symbolic frustration it was to own his own home, Lardner has traced the *mores* of a nation jolting to its Florida paradise by Pullman. The name of his hero was unimportant to Lardner. He, in fact, usually discarded nomenclature for the generalized but omnipotent 'I.' Is there any distinction between the facile Lou Gregg of Modern Pictures,

Inc., and Broadway's Conrad Green? They are brothers in those more dubious qualities of the human temperament which unite us all. Fragmentary and inchoate as the expression of Lardner's talent was, the various parts of his writing have thus their underlying unity. <u>Lardner wrote in effect the outline of a single work, this history of America in her boom period, and the work has a single hero.</u> In a variety of guises, and for the first time so completely, Lardner presents the unknown 'Mr.' of the U.S.A. The boxing champ who scores his first knockout off his lame brother, the rich man who cheats his dead secretary, the society golfer who 'don't tip his caddy unless he wins' — these are the Lardnerian supermen. But they merely dare to do what Lardner's Mr. U.S.A. dreams of.

As there is no distinction of name in the Lardnerian personages, there is also no hierarchy of class. His American aristocracy — the 'highpolloi' he called them — are simply the extension of his middle class. Lady Perkins of the Long Island society whose members had children if they couldn't afford dogs, Mrs. Garrett of the bridge élite who, refinement cracking, disgorges a quite plebeian yowl, the Thayers who imprison their guests in the calculating cordiality of 'Liberty Hall' — these are souls who, climbing a little faster, are a little more ostentatious, but no more cultivated than those who are climbing after them. And Lardner's workers are simply the appendages of the rich; the underprivileged who, struggling to better themselves, succeed, in fact, merely in revealing their betters. Lardner's America was the true classless society, for the America of the twenties was middle-class throughout, always in its beliefs, if not always in its bank account. As the historian of this society, Lardner marvelously reports its values: its love relationships, business ethics, sports, dinner conversation, education, and society. He presents its ballplayers, boxers, song-writers, executives, rotarians, policemen, poets, caddies, soldiers, crooners, the young, and the dying. And in Lardner's 'bushers' he reaches the core of '29's motivation.

Manager Nate of 'Frameup,' we are told, handled a lot of

boxers, but he 'never seen one yet that despised himself.' In the entire range of his writing Lardner also handled a lot of Americans, but he too never saw one that defied Manager Nate's dictum. This is the Lardnerian refrain, always implicit and usually expressed, which runs through his studies of America in affluence. This conceit is the center of Lardner's humanity. The U.S. champion, master of one field, believed himself master of all, and the U.S. mediocrity believed himself a champion. In Lardner's view, the bombastic American ego always aspired to exceed its own potentialities, and all other potentialities too. Beside this contemporary conqueror, Marlowe's mighty Tamburlaine was an Elizabethan ne'er-do-well. Private Keefe, actually a good ballplayer, and in his own fantasies a great lover, artist, 'poultry writer,' soldier and tactician, plans to advise Pershing on 'military stragety' and learns French so that he in person can win the First World War —

> ... if I am an officer by that time which it looks like a cinch I will be one by that time at the outside why suppose I was standing by 1 of our genls. and a French genl. wanted to tell him what was what and etc. but couldn't talk nothing but French and our genl. couldn't make head or tales of it then I could act like and interpreter between the both of them and the first thing you know all the high monkey monks when they want to talk back and forth will be pageing Capt. Keefe or Major Keefe or whatever officer I am by that time.

To Major Keefe or 'Genl. Keefe' or whatever officer he is by this time at the outside, the war was simply another occasion to exhibit his own manifold talents — this moronic Da Vinci of the Dollar! Just this way, the last busher, the Danny of 'Lose with a Smile,' knows he will become a great 'grooner' like Rudy Vallee. The bellowing amateur Elliott will be, he is equally positive, a sensation on the stage. The caddy Dick is certain, along with all the countless would-be geniuses whom Lardner addresses so suavely in 'How to Write Short Stories,' that he will instantaneously learn the 'nag of writeing.' Stealing his melodies from the masters, the popular composer Harry Hart

persuades himself he is a Yankee Beethoven, and Follies comedian Ralston of 'The Big Town' views himself as the supreme
playwright of the twentieth century. Don Quixote is the pale
archetype of Lardner's commercial supermen, enthusiastic
visionaries of the pocketbook, pursuing a lofty but impractical
materialism, utterly regardless of their spiritual interests, tilting
at Packards.

This overwhelming narcissism destroys all sense of proportion.
Because they are forever trying to be something else, Lardner's
people can never accept themselves as they are. Quick to suspect danger to their swollen vanity, they are quicker to resent
the most casual of incidents. 'Flatfoot' Gross passes his life
plotting a cheap revenge on the wrong person for an imaginary
insult. This egotism stifles the generosity of Lardner's characters, their sense of identification with life. In their desire to be
unique individuals (most absurd and terrifying of desires), they
are astounded when their neighbors do to them what they are
continually doing to their neighbors. They break the links binding them to humanity; in their conceit they grossly break even
the apparent links of their own individual life. For logic and
truth, the outer-world, their given word, have no existence to
them apart from their changing desires. What the Lardnerian
hero says today will contradict what he said yesterday, and tomorrow's pledge today's. Thus Keefe's famous lease on his
love nest will vary according to the state of his amorous affairs.
When the love nest's landlord (coarse and plebeian spirit) holds
Keefe to his contract, the landlord becomes a villain and the
lease a gigantic plot against Keefe, or so the busher reasons.
Paranoia has replaced probity.

The tremendous moral transformation brought about by the
impact of the Fascist states on modern life is simply a variation
of this. While for centuries we have preached ethics *in ab-
sentia*, the preaching being civilizational, it was not too much
to hope that eventually we might act ethically. But the modern
dictator has elevated immorality into a moral virtue, and with
this he has given up the pretense of civilization — the pretense

which, as the record of evolution shows, must always come in man's history some hundreds of years before the fact of civilization, but whose symbolic arrival hints at its literal advent, the breath of it invoking its flesh and blood. That poor pretense of morality, indeed, which is perhaps all that we have ever had, but which is the one thing we must continue to have. Before '29 Lardner saw this, or, at least partly seeing, he showed that American speech and even the written contract, like the objective morality they signified, had little meaning to the genuine desires of the individual. The preposterous (and equally transparent) fabrications of Alibi Ike are merely the explicit portrait of this sort of American man, a naïve dishonesty fused into Lardner's poetry. And like Lardner's truth, time itself, the outer-world and its formal chronology, must in a very similar manner be twisted and distorted into the pattern of the inner-world and its fantasies. Like their era, Lardner's people have no sense of the strange, of another past, and yet another future. They never hear the clock's ticking which alters our dear hopes and every second makes us new. As their period slipped away from them, the more frantically they insisted, like certain of our own industrialists, that everything must remain as it never quite was. And Lardner shows us, in 'The Golden Honeymoon,' the sterile old age which results from the narcissistic passion. All other human feelings fading, the hungry ego becomes more ravenous, even as the time which it despised reveals the individual's absurdity with the last proof of death.

As a Thomas Mann has recently been portraying, the basic human spirit is, in a sense, timeless, the fundamental urges of mankind behaving now as they behaved in our childhood, and regressing a step farther, somewhat as they behaved in the childhood of the race. Lardner, playing another phrase of this motif, tells us also how our more conscious motivation transforms all time into its own hollow nutshell. Lardner's U.S.A. egotism, though as a plain American Lardner would have scoffed at psychological science, is close to the Freudian 'id.' His view of human nature merely reveals this 'id' in action. And very weak too is the control which saves the unconscious from the follies of its own demands, for to Lardner the final characteristic of this egotism was that, conquering the intelligence of his characters, it led them to destruction.

Lardner reminds us that in their vanity his people have no capacity to learn, nor yet simply to survive. The errors they commit lead them not to knowledge but to catastrophe. They never see lying straight before them the chasms into which their assurance draws them. 'Things,' says the busher the day before he is fired, 'look pretty good for me, Al,' and General Keefe (or whatever higher officer he is by now) is so concerned with asserting his superiority in the war that he forgets he may be blown to pieces by it. Infatuated, Lardner's lovers are too complacent to read the letters which are informing them that their love no longer exists. The Edith Dole of 'There Are Smiles' believes she is far too adorable to perish in the automobile crash caused by her reckless driving. In her special case beauty will triumph over brakes, so she thinks. And the protagonists of Lardner's last book merely repeat the circle of complacency which doomed the heroes of Lardner's first book. This swollen, ever-present, devouring egotism makes Lardner's crooks gullible, and deprives his dupes of their pathos. If in his 'success' Lardner's American is mean, he is sure to fail in the end, and in his failure he is sure to be meaner.

Destruction itself may often be creative, and even that of stupidity may gain our sympathy. But here too Lardner, the image-breaker of the twenties, removed his era's last hope of dignity. In the range of his writing there are many catastrophes but very few tragedies; when he arouses our pity it is merely to intensify our aversion. Like Kafka in 'The Castle' continually promising us the glimpse of heaven we know will never come, Lardner, in the destruction of his characters, offers them the possibilities of human grandeur simply to show us how they ignore them. The last act of his people's life, their death, is only too often consistent with their previous activity. The aviator fiancé of Katie in 'Lady Perkins' has taken an involuntary nose dive while testing his new aeroplane. 'Him and his invention,' so Mr. tells us, 'was spilled all over Long Island' —

> Wile I and Ella was getting ready for supper I made the remark that I s'posed we'd live in a vale of tears for the next few days. 'No,' said Ella, 'Sis is taking it pretty calm. She's sensible. She says if that could have happened, why the invention couldn't of been no good after all. And the Williamses probably wouldn't of give him a plugged dime for it.'

And the great tragic invention of Lardner's era and ours — the war — becomes, as it is revealed through the Lardnerian patriots of 'Treat 'Em Rough' (heroic doughboys less fearful of the Huns than of their roommates), another gross and calculating antic. The only member of his family to die in the war, the 'Mr.' of 'Quick Returns' informs us, was his wife's profiteering stepfather, who died of grief because the war ended. 'I immediately had a black bandage sewed around my left funnybone, but when they read us the will I felt all right again and tore it off.' But perhaps to Lardner's American his wife's stepfather is 'fair game,' for it is true that 'Mr.' has no special reverence for marriage relations. 'Accordin' to some authorities,' he advises us,

> a person should ought to look up your oppenent's family tree and find out what all her relatives died of. But the way I got it figured out, if you're sure they did die, the rest of it don't make no difference.

Does 'Mrs.,' the American wife and daughter, have more appropriate feelings on the demise of her near ones? She does, to be sure, hang around her stepfather's sickroom day after day — 'in the hopes he would tell her how much he was going to leave...' And the Mabelle Gillespie of 'Some Like Them Cold' feels similarly about her father's passing. 'Poor old dad, he died of cancer three years ago, but left enough insurance so that mother and we girls were well provided for.' To the final disintegration, death, Lardner accords no greater dignity. If to Lardner the American life of the twenties was a bonanza quest, the American deathbed was the jackpot.

From birth to this death indeed Lardner's critique of the basic beliefs of '29 is thorough. A Mark Twain shared some of the illusions of his period, a Thackeray too many. In the company of the great, even such satirists as these felt the need to identify themselves with their society — or at least sometimes barely to cover their aversion. But Lardner, though he wrote much that was evasive, basically accepted none of the social myths which formed his time. Passing from one to another of the larger American credos of the twenties, he destroys the smaller ones, too, in transit. 'We passed through the green fields of old Virginia,' says Lardner's Mr. U.S.A., 'though it was too dark to tell if they was green or what color.' Under the heat of Lardner's increasing anger, the green fields of the post-war age grew parched, and in the dark despair of Lardner's final disillusionment, it became impossible, also, to tell what color they once had been. The citizens who were entertained by the various portions of Lardner's work might have been appalled at its complete significance. And Lardner himself, as we are to see, noticing these American phenomena so acutely, also saw them as disparate. In the total view of a writer's work, the whole may be greater than the parts, and that of which he is but imperfectly aware may dominate his conscious articulation. It was thus, bit by bit, that our Ring Lardner surrounded the American life of '29 with a barrier of suspicion, enmity, and at last, hatred.

3. O KEEP YOUR MOUTH SHUT.   So Lardner described the Jazz Age of American finance wisely, and too well The values of his era, its myths and beliefs, he now had demonstrated, a most weary theme without variation, all were empty. What was left? If the merit of Lardner's U.S.A. critique was that it seemed as indigenous as the McCormick reaper, his solution of the basic problems of '29 was also as much a part of

our world as the Dust Bowl. For he had none. He refutes the
national faiths. But he has no purpose in his anger, he has no
positive to his hatred, and he has no destination beyond destruction.

Under high pressure the Success Myth of the twenties
pumped ambition into the American ego, driving out the other
normal desires, inflating it beyond normal dimensions until it
burst, as Lardner saw. The American individualistic cultural
pattern, growing fiercer toward its close, selecting the competitive and aggressive elements of the human temperament,
forced the ego from a natural survival factor almost into a catastrophic force. But of this Lardner had apparently little comprehension. Savage history, reflecting the unimportance of the
balancing mind, working through the emotion's extremes,
brought about this merely preliminary democratic reaction to
the caste system of our ancient and medieval society. Is this the
fate of Tom Paine, Jefferson, and Lincoln? Is this the final
camping ground of our American covered wagon hitched to
the stars? No man must hold himself a slave, yet neither should
all conceive themselves as Napoleonic. History itself will in
time outbreed the outrageous individualism of Lardner's age —
though must we again suffer new varieties of totalitarian slavery
merely to achieve such moderation? What appeared to Lardner
as eternal was to a large degree sociological, and so transient
that before he died, it had; although its dying convulsions
would find echo in our own era also.

Lardner's business men, doughboys, athletes all reveal the
intellectual emptiness behind his portraits. Generating such
wonderful criticisms, his imagination had no base to operate
from. And in Lardner's lovers, a crucial test for any writer,
the case becomes clear. Brilliantly Lardner describes the disorganized postscript of American passion in his day. Beside
Lardner's Mr. U.S.A. the pathological Swann of Proust is a
wholesome cavalier. Perhaps the typical climax of Lardnerian
courtship occurs in 'The Young Immigrunts.' The 'fare bride
and the Lordly glum,' so 'little Bill the immigrunt' informs us,

are sitting together on the steamship carrying them to Niagara
Falls. 'Some night,' says the Lordly glum to his beloved, 'are
you warm enough?'

> I am perfectly comfertible replid the fare bride tho her looks
> belid her words what time do we arrive in Buffalo.
> 9 o'clock said the lordly glum are you warm enough.
> I am perfectly comfertible replid the fare bride what time do
> we arrive in Buffalo.
> 9 o'clock said the lordly glum I am afrade it is too cold for you
> out here.
> Well maybe it is replid the fare bride and without further adieu
> they went in the spacius parlers.

And for Lardner this is genial. The rest of his lovers are less
communicative and less agreeable. This indeed is the apotheosis of Lardnerian love. Such stammering baseless bliss is
hardly achieved by the protagonists of 'Some Like Them Cold'
or 'The Facts'; collapsing in 'The Water Cure' through Lardner's premise that lovers will not be lovers long if they are
forced to listen to each other; or culminating in the marital
treachery of 'The Love Nest.' Elliott's 'Roomy,' soliloquizing
as to whether he should help the mad hick marry his girl, sums
up Lardner's view of the 'hymeneal twain':

> If she's all right she'll take acid in a month — and it'll be my fault;
> but if she's really stuck on him they must be something wrong
> with her too, so what's the diff'rence?

In Lardner's version of the Hollywood romance, boy meets girl,
boy loses girl, or boy gets girl. 'So what's the diff'rence?' Vanity, not affection, is the mirror of love, and in it his personages
see only those sweet curves which enhance their ego and return
to their gaze their own beloved lineaments. 'Oh, you Violet!'
cries the infatuated busher. 'Oh, you Gertrude, Daisy, Florrie,
Jessie!' The name of his sweetheart and the personality it expresses are irrelevant, for he is in fact forever crying: 'Oh, you
Keefe!' Sick with self-love he can have little knowledge of any

thing or anyone beyond himself, and of himself he has no
knowledge. Love is blind. It is also a blind alley. So to the
adolescent heroine of 'I Can't Breathe' all her swains are
equally adorable, she loves them all, she gets engaged to all, she
is willing to marry them all. To her the matrimonial pledge is
as sacred as a European peace pact. These Lardnerian lovers
come. They see themselves. And they are conquered.

Keefe and all his subsequent Lardnerian compatriots atone,
however, for their deadly sin of narcissism. At their best their
spouses are hardly admirable. It is written into his contract,
Gleason tells us in 'Al,' that he 'is not to talk to no women,' and
similarly the 'Mr.' of 'Gullible' demands who passed the law
that women can't converse with each other? Are wives people
too? In 'Say It with Oil' Lardner admits they are.

> Wives is people that always wants to go home when you don't
> and vice versa.
>
> Wives is people that ain't never satisfied as they are always too
> fat or too thin. Of all the wives I ever talked to I never run acrost
> one yet that was just right.
>
> Wives is people that ask you what time the 12:55 train gets to
> New York. 'At 1:37' you tell them. 'How do you know?' they
> ask.
>
> They are people that never have nothing that is fit to wear.
>
> They are people that think when the telephone bell rings it is
> against the law to not answer it.
>
> They are people whose watch is always ¼ of a hr. off either one
> way or the other. But they wouldn't have no idear what time it
> was any way as this daylight savings gets them all balled up.

They are people like Lardner's Kate who 'can't stand the heat.
Or the cold. Or the medium. When it ain't none of these,'
Kate wishes the weather 'would do one thing another.'

And at their worst these Violets, Gertrudes, Maybelles become wolves, to prey in the darkness of the male self-adulation
upon the defenseless domains of the ego-bound spirit. Florrie,
the modern Beatrice leading Dante Keefe eternally downward

through the never-ending circles of extravagance into the Inferno, strips her consort of money if nothing else. For although the Lardnerian ladies ravish their lovers financially, they are not in themselves ravishing. You could not look at Bess, so Mr. reports in 'Gullible,' 'without a slight relapse.'

> She had two complexions — A.M. and P.M. The P.M. wasn't so bad, but she could of put the other in her vanity box for a mirror. Her nose curved away from the batsman and wasn't no wider than Julienne potato, and yet it had to draw in to get between her eyes. Her teeth was real pretty and she always kept her lips ajar.

Thus Lardner ends by depriving his heroines of their sex. They are not deceitful trollops; they are frigid usurers. A good business woman, Richardson's Pamela sold her virtue to the highest bidder. But this chastity, in Richardson's view the chief commodity of his heroines, the Lardnerian ladies have lost, or rather, perhaps, there is no consumer demand for it. Lardner's women are a curious mixture of gullibility, avarice, and sentiment, a mixture often more terrifying than curious, but which neither possesses nor gives rise to sensuous desire. They recall Samuel Butler's prophecy that the future wives of the race may give birth to pocketbooks to buy their children with. For them the dollar has replaced desire. Lardner's America of '29 is not so much fast or dissolute like that of O'Hara's 'Appointment in Samarra,' or Dos Passos's 'The Big Money.' It is rather profoundly sterile, sexless in the mere fantasies of its inhabitants, childless in wish, and very often in the fact. From a Samuel Richardson to Lardner this is one channel of the middle-class concept of love, and with the advent of Lardner's ladies we may no longer even say that in its sexual ethics this middle-class ethics has been attempting to sell off the human spirit. For while Bess and Florrie and Jessie and Kate of 'The Big Town' are always scheming, like Pamela, to trap and marry the rich lord, in their turn the Lardnerian nobility, unlike Richardson's, are always frauds. If the chief commodity of Lardner's heroines has run out, the bidders are also bankrupt.

Yet the author who thus annihilates passion hardly knows it. Lardner beautifully describes the neurotic individualism of his lovers, their commercialism, their egotism, and their sterility. But the specialized world which these lovers so sexlessly inhabit, if it has phenomena which no one noticed better than Lardner, has for him no pervasive laws. He is apparently unaware that what is implicit in his observation must imply something. He reports almost everything. He infers almost nothing. As to the economic conditions which define his lovers, as to the cultural myths which they embodied, as to the larger historical evolution to which they belonged and which they themselves were forming, Lardner is ignorant. While Freud in Austria was completing his researches, while a D. H. Lawrence in England was explaining, if sometimes perversely, many of these same attributes of modern love, in the United States, and in the very midst of the post-war sexual eruption, Lardner seeks no causes for his facts, or any possibilities for another future different from this dreadful present. What he thus very acutely saw was no subject for reflection. Blind to the central significance of what he wrote on sex, Lardner was evasive in the mere use of an honest terminology. And so with love, so with all of Lardner's world. If few other contemporary writers, in short, have so piercingly described the fabric of our life in the boom era, few others, also, have been apparently so unaware of the consequences of their own work. Hostile to almost every detail of the society around him, Lardner questions none of its basic concepts. He obliterates the story on the U.S.A. prosperity chronicle, and clings to the manuscript. He is like a man who removes each rung of a ladder and goes on climbing it.

In this, Lardner belongs, of course, to the American utilitarian view. It was inevitable that a busher culture, intent on taming a continent, should have as its ethic a single question: 'Does It Work?' On the depredations and chicanery which mark so much of our history from 1860, on the industrial ravaging of our older Rockefellers, Goulds, and Commodore Vanderbins, America stamped its approval. O.K. 'If they can get away with it, more power to them.' What they got away with was God's business, and they were not unwilling to bribe Him too, with their Gothic churches and Chinese missionary societies. Always concentrating on the thing in action, our modern Lardner merely represents the negative pole of this utilitarianism. To Lardner nothing worked — and there was the end of it. Pragmatism is, to be sure, a valuable spiritual weapon when it is used by thinkers who are more than pragmatic, who employ it not to solve issues, so to speak, but to avoid solving them. It is a weapon of delay, a useful evasion, a fact-finding mechanism. But the purely pragmatic is never in the long run practical, and Lardner, the functioning utilitarian, never reached the level of philosophical or indeed of conscious pragmatism. Was the social arrangement of his time producing, in fact, the greatest unhappiness of the greatest number? Lardner's answer carried American despair to a new peak, but it did not advance the cause of American rationalism.

In part Lardner's earlier works, 'Al,' 'Gullible's Travels,' 'Own Your Own Home,' and the continuations of the Keefe saga, 'Treat 'Em Rough' and 'The Real Dope,' are acute studies of our national *mores*, in part they are highly entertaining, but they reward us only in these parts. That they are not complete in their own terms, that coming out of a great imagination, they are not great and never led to anything more solid, is due in large measure to this basic block in Lardner's thinking. Culturally the causes of his failure are not very difficult to trace. Lardner was small-town America. The mature writer disapproved of his society's values, but the boy from Niles, Michigan, had learned no others. Lardner could see through the national traits which made a Coolidge petty, misquoting what a Franklin had never practiced. He could understand the actual functioning of such preaching — the degeneration of a tradition which ran from Luther to Jay Gould to a Harry Sinclair — as it occurred under the aegis of another provincial Zeus, Warren Harding. Yet Lardner could not look back to the America of

Paine, Jefferson, and Lincoln. He could not envision an America neither commercial nor corrupt.

Lardner was puritan America. Taking down the little moralists, the McDonalds who are so redundant with virtue in 'The Facts,' those who neither smoked nor drank nor gambled, Lardner himself remained among those who in their literature evade all the conventionally 'sinful' and basic aspects of human experience. And even the last remnants of our puritan sensuousness, its hidden salaciousness, the passions it emphasized if only by denial, Lardner reduces to his 'genteel spoonin.' As he himself dedicated it, always half-knowing and yet unable to gain a full comprehension, his example of a story with 'sex appeal' is 'The Golden Honeymoon.' And in this chronicle of U.S.A.'s aged 'Mr.,' elaborating in his senility the traits which hardly graced his maturity, the sexual impulses are conspicuously absent. In youth and age, indeed, how thin are Lardner's amorous desires as compared with his naked and ferocious power urges! Lardner's people have all the brute desires without the animal pleasures.

Yet even if he had believed that sex had now become a method of advancement rather than of procreation, he could hardly have said this in the pages of the *Saturday Evening Post.* The big thinkers usually defy the laws they fondly promulgate. But whatever chances Lardner may have had of escaping his inheritance were lessened by the third link of his triple bondage. During the formative, and even the final years of his career he wrote for the same middle-class audience he satirized. For them he had contempt, but they had money. Lardner may have drawn some sources of his power from his popularity; it is just as certain that through it he blocked himself. There was no outlet from his busher pragmatism and his puritanism in the hearts of Mr. and Mrs. America. Ironically they devoured his stories; ironically they devoured him too. When Lardner at last (still evasively, uneasily) broke away from literary gentility in the shiny freedom of *The New Yorker*, he merely revealed his origins, and his long captivity.

This triple bondage resulted in Lardner's fatal flaw. The scale of his thinking was too small. Lardner's Busher Keefe sailing o'er the Pacific Ocean to Japan (or so the Busher tells us), by route of 'swittserland, a hole lot of ilands, Rome and Paris and Africa and them other countrys,' is perhaps less informed than his creator as to geographical precision. But he is no less so as to any sort of historical perspective. For the answer to Lardner's U.S.A. critique lay in the patterns of society, the record of civilization, and beyond these the history of man's descent. What Lardner saw as rigid in humanity can be moulded. If we may never quite become angels, we needn't forever remain such brutes. In the pages of Lardner there is little glimpse of our evolutionary struggle, as indeed in the close view of humanity there seems to be no struggle. Like water, the civilizational conflict runs more beneath the ground than above it; and like boiling springs the veins of our progress come to sight in specified and perhaps too distant regions of history. For all its material success, its visions of scientific progress, no such region was '29 —

   (Mah-Jong, Oil scandals and dreadful B.O., Halitosis, Pyorrhea, and Peaches Browning. 'Grace, how about a highball?')

— and Lardner, seeing the present so acutely, saw it also as absolute. Lardner's provincial Elliott, his beautiful, reckless Edith Dole, Lardner's Nurse Lyons who, in the series of incredible romances which transform her 'Zone of Quiet' into an antiseptic torture chamber, ruins herself as well as her patients — these personages, so Lardner reminds us, will accept no advice. In this world we may help no one. 'Healer, cure thyself.' For Lardner was as helpless on the deeper meanings of life as his people about their immediate needs. If he was different from his characters in the smaller ways, and for that distinction he despised them, he was after all too close to them in the essentials, and that similarity crushed him.

   Since he had no historical perspective, he might have fallen back on that of his culture, but, world of breath-taking physical transformations, his America itself had little spiritual stability. It was barely a half-century since the land of Lincoln had become that of Morgan — a Herculean effort, which indeed led to Lardner's Augean Stable. Too fast, too new, and the American spirit could not cope with such tremendous change, nor gain any sense of continuity, nor, in the last analysis, of its own integrity. Who would bother to reflect on virtue when he might be ransoming the railways of a continent? The writers who turned away in disgust, a Bronson Alcott, Thoreau, Margaret Fuller, all the varied Brook Farmers and Transcendentalists, these were lost too: naked souls fleeing the Calvinist fire, who had their moment before they faced the bottomless pools of finance capitalism. In his lack of fruition Lardner thus belongs to another indigenous tradition — the American artistic inconsonance which has paralleled our materialistic conquests. An abundance of talent. A cultural aridity. An inadequate or malformed growth. Twain, Howells, Henry Adams. Dreiser, evidencing the rawness of his society with the crudeness of his own equipment. Even Thomas Wolfe, who was to survive his own ordeal, as we shall see, is held back and twisted by the superstitions of his society. And our Lardner, with gifts not remote from those of Swift, producing indeed a 'Gullible's Travels' — parody not merely of a great title but of his own great potentialities.

Yet what else, being Lardner, could he have done? 'I don't understand it,' says Fred Gross about his nightmare home, 'but I quit trying to understand about this here house.' So Lardner might have said about his own understanding of the civilizational structure of his age. Lardner had genius without its training. He could not understand the degree to which the economic framework and the social myths of '29 were to blame for the world he saw around him. His inheritance and environment had given him no means either to solve or to stand the facts of the life he presented. He saw no way to help his characters; he could only despise them. He could find no way to help himself. He began to despise himself.

Incarnate Success Story of '29, who wants knowledge, writing what he saw and landing in the big money, who thinks of sorrow? Life was a merry-go-round in the age of first mortgages and our Lardner drew a gold-plated ring. He did what the times demanded. On the rim of the U.S.A. land-boom he established his Long Island estate. 'The Mange' he called it, with enough perception. If everything around him had its price, the choice was of markets, not meanings. Lardner put himself on sale too. 'It seems to me,' says Caddy Dick, discussing a similar issue with his pal Joe, 'like $8000 . . . is a pretty fair reward compared with what some of these people sells their souls for, and I would like to tell them about it ——'

> Well said Joe go ahead and tell them but maybe they will tell you something right back.
>
> What will they tell me?
>
> Well said Joe they might tell you this, that when Mr. Thomas asks you how many shots he has had and you say 4 when you know he has had 5, why you are selling your soul for a $1.00 tip. And when you move Mrs. Doanes ball out of the rut and give it a good lie, what are you selling your soul for? Just a smile.
>
> O keep your mouth shut I said to him.
>
> I am going to said Joe and would advice you to do the same.

That there was a distinction between selling one's soul for a dollar tip and selling one's soul for a smile does not apparently occur to Lardner. The only answer to the confusion of his values was 'to keep his mouth shut.' Yet silence is no substitute for the writer: expression, indeed, is his catharsis.

4. LIKE SOMETHING WAS GOING TO HAPPEN BUT IT DON'T.   Perhaps, as he wrote to Congreve, genius must be born and never can be taught, but Dryden does not mention the case of genius which was stillborn because it was untaught. Yet, if it is melancholy to think what Lardner might

have done, it is pleasant to see what he managed to do. Was his
last book, 'Lose With a Smile,' merely a repetitive and feebler
account of a diluted Busher Keefe? Turning in this blind circle
back to his origins, Lardner could still summon his force and
dispose of a thousand saccharine mammy ballads. 'Onely this
song,' says Danny who aspires to be a 'grooner' like Rudy
Vallee, 'is to pop':

> My dad I love him
> My mom she loves him
> My sister Edna she loves him my dad
> He is a wonder
> Will live to be a hundred
> And never made a blunder my dad
> When I was a lad
> If I act it bad mom would scold me
> Then I would go to him
> And on his lower limbs he would hold me
> Theys no one greater
> Than my old pater
> He is my alma mater my pop.

'Alma mater and pater are Greek,' Danny adds, and 'means the
same thing.' What if Danny, his conceit overcoming his sense
precisely as Keefe's, goes the way we know he will, to the minor
leagues, Lardner's twentieth-century Limbo for his lost American souls? The original busher lacked Danny the grooner's
exit lines.

> Good night Rudy, aint it just a pity
> Good night Rudy sent to Jersey City
> After that old 15th of june
> Morn night and noon
> Weel miss your croon but may be
> You will lern a little sence and reason
> and be with us once again next season.
> Dont steal bases thats occupied
> Rudy Doody good night.

'Rudy Doody' Danny was dumb, but the smart were not exempt from Lardner's wit. The sophisticated lyricist also could be guilty of a *faux pas* in the writing of 'Night and Day':

> Night and day under the hide of me
> There's an Oh, such a hungry yearning burning inside of me.

Lardner, trying a few variations, makes the faux pas a fatality.

> Night and day under the rind of me
> There's an Oh, such a zeal for spooning ru'ning the mind of me.

and:

> Night and day under the fleece of me
> There's an Oh, such a flaming furneth burneth the grease of me.

and:

> Night and day under the bark of me
> There's an Oh, such a mob of microbes making a park of me.

and:

> Night and day under my cuticle
> There's a love all for you so true it never would do to kill.

and:

> Night and day under my dermis, dear
> There's a spot just as hot as coffee kept in a thermos, dear

and:

> Night and day under my tegument
> There's a voice telling me I'm he, the good little egg you meant.

In light verse Lardner could make Cole Porter look solemn; Lardner's surrealist plays transport us to the outskirts of a parchesi board; and in prose he could catch inimitably the sharpness of childhood mingled with its misapprehensions. 'We will stop at Ypsilanti,' remarks the father of 'The Young Immigrunts' in his unusual calm tones, 'that is where they have the state normal school.' The young Bill reflects:

> I was glad to hear this and hoped we would get there before dark as I had always wanted to come in contack with normal

peaple and see what they are like and just at dusk we entered a large size town and drove past a large size football field.

Heavens said my mother this must be a abnormal school to have such a large football field.

My father wore a qeer look.

This is not Ypsilanti this is Ann Arbor he crid.

But I thorght you said we would go south of Ann Arbor and direct to Ypsilanti said my mother with a smirk.

I did say that but I thorght I would surprise you by comeing into Ann Arbor replid my father with a corse jesture.

And the conclusion of this historic Lardnerian pilgrimage, if not exactly serene, is less dreadful than that of most of Lardner's vacations:

True to our promise we were at the station in Grenitch when the costly train puled in . . .

Did you have a hard trip my father arsked to our nurse shyly.

Why no she replid with a slite stager.

She did too said my mother they all acted like little devils. Did you get Davids milk she said turning on my father.

Why no does he like milk my father replid with a gastly smirk.

We got lost mudder I said brokenly.

We did not screened my father and accidently cracked me on the shins with a stray foot.

This little Bill the 'Immigrunt' is one of the few Lardnerian infants not wholly consumed by 'collect' and ignored by his parents. He is indeed one of the few Lardnerian infants. Yet if Lardner saw his America as sterile, homeless, childless, he had no desire, like the Mr. of 'Gullible,' of interfering with anybody's 'hymenial intentions.' Lardner promulgates indeed his ten rules on 'how to be a happy marriage in order to prevent our young singletons from remaining celebrates.' Firstly, so Lardner decrees, 'the two members of the marital twain ought to be of opp. sex if possible. . . . The bride should ought to have at lease as much money as the groom and a salary of her own. . . . The ideal marred life is for the 2 belligerents to live in the same town so as when they feel like a brawl they won't be no

toll charges. . . . Both partys should try (like the fare bride and
lordly glum) to talk about subjects that the other is interested in,
though in most familys its too cold to set up late. . . .' Marred
life is a job 'just the same as like a telegraph operator or a em-
balmer,' so 'try and forget once in a wile that you are marred
and go out somewheres together for a good time.'

Thus Lardner encourages the young celebrates 'so that they
should ought to assume the connubial yokel.' If he flayed the
'opposing gender, the squalling sex,' in his portrait of Florrie
and those who followed in her footsteps of avarice, if the distraught and drunken Harry Burton of 'Dinner' records their
fluttering chatter in seven incomparable pages of acid recalling
Swift's treatise on polite conversation, women after all are home
makers, and home, Lardner admits

> . . . is where you can take off your shoes. Its where you can
> have more soup. Its where you don't half to say nothing when
> they's nothing to say. . . . Its where you don't half to listen. Its
> where they don't smear everything with cheese dressing.

Home after all is less exhausting than the smart vacation resorts
that Lardner took off in 'Gullible' and elaborated into the fine
descriptions of 'Lady Perkins,' following the account of those
husbands who go down to Business, but 'who don't never go to
work.' In a phrase Lardner illuminates the entire social structure of the twenties. Here he repays us for the sometimes tedious chronicle of Ella and her Mr. in the wilds of the metropolis, just as his marvellous description of Ralston's play redeems
the dragging close of 'The Big Town.' And is Ralston's flop
very different from the successful Follies, with its hit song (inter-
preted by Lardner) on hangnails —

> But my most exclusive token
> Is a little hangnail broken
> Off the girl from Gussie's School for Manicures?

Here Lardner's imagination, freeing itself from the spite which
made him the moralist of 'Haircut,' 'Champion,' or 'The Maysville Minstrel,' making the obvious flagrant for a manifestly

stupid audience, flourished. As it did again in 'What of It?' when he proposes to Segregate the Fats. 'That is, they would be towns in every state set aside for the exclusive use of fat folks only, where it would be vs. the law for a skinny person to set their ft.' The doors, sidewalks, streets, beds, chairs, etc. 'of fat towns will be widened, while in skinny towns the same articles could be shrank to fit the leans.' Coping with the magnitude of the flesh, Lardner reveals magnificently the magnitude of his own fancy; and again in the 'sears and yellow' he managed, with a certain release of his previous repressions, to view even the symptoms of thirty-five with equanimity:

> Like for inst. a few wks back I was up in Boston where I got a young and beautiful sister in law. When it came time to part from she and her husband she kissed me 6 times which was suppose to be once for me and once apiece for the Mrs. and 4 kiddies. Well I thought it was pretty nice and got kind of excited about it till I looked at her husband to see how he took it. He took it without batting an eye. To him it was like as if she was kissing an old cab horse on a bet for the benefit of the Red Cross. And when I had left and they was alone together, instead of lepping at her throat with a terrible curse he probably says 'Janey, you're a good game gal,' and she gave him a kiss that meant something.

Too late, 'reaching his dottage, losing his foliage, his plummage on the egg, no longer a larva and leave bad enough alone for his slogum,' Lardner saw the allure of the love he had scorned and feared, and in this last moment of renunciation he attained perhaps the sort of spiritual grandeur he himself had removed from the American scene.

In his light moments Lardner was thus our greatest comic personality, in his serious work an incomparable artist, and for his new American literature Lardner fashioned a new American language. After him refined English can never be quite so respectable. Lardner the puritan scoffed at one immaculate conception: he deflowered the virgin word. As a Joyce is elaborating a new vocabulary from the top of our knowledge up, onward, beyond the esoteric, Lardner made one from the bottom, from the talk of the people, from the genuine base, and not the theoretical one, of our society. Here at least he cut through the binding of his birth and time. Those who hesitate to group together the scholar and the untutored sports reporter might look again at Lardner's true-meaning words, his ladies shaking like an 'aspirin leaf,' his pointed language to compare with the 'woebecanned and the funferall, the agonbite of inwit, the all zed and done' of the poetic and pedantic Irishman. But 'good riddance is rubbish,' as the busher says, and to his creator there was in the end also no good or final riddance of his thwarted destiny. What Lardner did was marvelous, but after all he could not do enough. The dynamite of his talent gave forth only fireworks. He could not see a way to change his time, and the myth-breaker of '29 came to his last point when he ceased to believe in himself.

For at the last, of course, we live mainly through our pleasure in living. In a period of such crisis as Lardner's was for him, and ours again is for us, when we may no longer follow the prevailing beliefs of our time and are yet unable to formulate satisfactory new ones, we must fall back upon this standard minimum requirement of our individual existence — this personal faith in our own separate lives, this obtuse but vital conceit, the blind belief in our own progress even while the larger social sphere around us cracks and crumbles. This is indeed the last and only genuine base of men's actions everywhere, writers no more than grocers, plumbers, undertakers; those who are ignorant, untrained, those who may be aware and yet unable to decide; those who if they have chosen their faith may yet be unable to cast their activity into one or another of the larger social credos. At the last the larger world does not count. We at the last may not count. 'I must count.'

Absurd, selfish, even ruinous, this personal faith is, however, the expression of the great myth which transcends the particular and temporal ones, the wish of the race to endure. In time economic, political systems, religious and nationalistic frameworks, small and large chauvinisms of all natures die too. Collective man continues merely because the individual members, in confidence or in despair or obliviously, go on living — continue believing, that is to say, in the noteworthy significance of their own individual action, whether they happen to be, in our current nomenclature, Fascist or Socialist or Capitalist or nothing at all, whether they are full of pomp or stricken and in exile. Reduced to ghettos, defiled in concentration camps, oppressed in slums, homeless, without work or stature in the world, each particular individual counts still. While Rome burns we fiddle — and indeed we should fiddle.

But to Lardner the minimum and basic belief in his own significance became impossible. Increasingly inimical to the Success Myth and the conceit it engendered in the individual, he grew too suspicious of its manifestations, including those in himself, and finally including those which it was necessary for him to live by. If as in Lardner's American, our vanity, replacing our intelligence, may lead us to catastrophe, an excess of intelligence even more surely will bring us to ruin. 'I count.' Who can say such a thing soberly and believe it? The rational estimation of the conditions of our existence, our origins, duration, and probable destination, would lead us to negation. The full and frank use of our intellect would probably discourage us from any further use of it. It is only because we assume these limitations of our fate so fully as in effect to ignore them that we live at all and make whatever advances we do. By this blind and vital conceit we exist, and do our work of importance in the belief that we can achieve the impossible: if the belief is strong enough, it is not impossible that we may do so. The egotism that Lardner revealed and abhorred in his characters was, in this sense, more correct than his own intelligence which now, in himself, broke down his necessary faith in his own life as he had previously destroyed the meaning of American life around him.

For was he not precisely that to which he had denied all merit? In a variety of stories he had showed the compromises, the evasions, the pretensions of the popular artist. Throughout his work he had condemned the entire pattern of the American Success Story — the egotism, the commercialism, the false ambition, the lack of balance, generosity, humanity, the sacrifice of all personal values for a 'reward' which itself only emphasized the sterile traits necessary for its fruitless culmination. Certainly Lardner had shown the theatrical magnate 'Conrad Green' and his cinema twin of 'The Love Nest'; the big-time boxers in 'Champion' and 'Frameup'; the hit songwriters in 'Nora'; the prosperous business men in 'Mr. Frisbie,' 'Conference,' and 'Ex Parte'; the highpolloi in 'Liberty Hall,' the bridge élite in 'Contract,' the big-league ballplayers in 'Horseshoes,' and a hundred other tales. These were the successes of '29, and who would emulate them, or wish to? But what of the successful story-writer? Lardner was also occupying the throne he was disestablishing. He himself was the image he was breaking.

This psychological paradox explains in part the pattern of Lardner's hatred shown throughout his work: the hatred which Clifton Fadiman first fully comprehended. Striking at these 'successes' with a series of blows that only a fine imagination could conceive, Lardner makes them at the same time so insensitive that they cannot be hurt. In a sort of compulsive design Lardner creates indestructible characters whom he vainly attempts to destroy. Devising new tortures for his people, he reveals their new defenses. Here is a ceaseless masochism which illuminates the painfully divided personality of an author continually tearing down what he is in the process of building up, who, in short, is unable to accept what he has made of himself. Hatred can be for the writer a cogent and emancipating weapon. To Lardner it was enslaving. In it he found no catharsis, merely the endless mirrors of his confusion. Subject and object in one, it seems, he saw in his work continual new methods of torment: as if the artist used his art form to scourge himself.

This is, of course, a highly complex issue, about which in the end we can have no certainty. There must be taken into account the purely psychological elements of Lardner's despair. What were the hidden conflicts which led into this deep and dark bitterness? There are also the facts of his mature life, his human relations, the financial difficulties, the physical sickness of the last years. The relationship of the inherited to the environmental, the physical to the psychic, the economic and the sociological to the temperamental — these delicate, haunting, and interwoven patterns form the biographer's despair. It is safe only to say that if we follow any one strand of this interacting pattern, we shall lead ourselves to absurdity. What we are showing here is rather the impact of the sociological pressures of Lardner's time upon his temperament; and we read the social history of his disintegration. (His portrait, again, of his age is surely colored by his own distemper.) Yet seeing Lardner thus in the context of his time, the issues we have traced are still the dominant ones. Nor did they only affect Lardner: they find echoes in the writers to follow him, and in the American writers who led up to him. Comparing, indeed, Lardner's history with the impact of Mark Twain's age, as Van Wyck Brooks has described it, upon the earlier humorist, we find many resemblances. Both Twain and Lardner were highly gifted, both immensely popular, both accepted the credo of American materialistic success which in their own spirits they could barely tolerate. Both accepted the restraints and inhibitions of that credo. And both, without historical perspective or sociological resources, ended their lives in hatred and black despair. The eventual 'philosophy' which Mark Twain evolved was a memento of his society's prejudices and ignorances. And as for Lardner, there evolved no philosophy.

How else shall we explain the frustration which forms the dominant pattern of Lardner's humor? In its prevailing form, he continually builds up to optimistic climaxes, which hardly ever occur, and if they do are hardly welcome. Lardner's Mr. and Mrs. U.S.A. are forever starting out on glorious vacations, which fizzle out, interminably, dreadfully. 'A trail of vengeance,' Lardner remarks about 'Horseshoes,' 'ruthless and sin-

ister, is uncovered to its hidden source by a flat-footed detective.'
If the Lardnerian hero does not exist, and even his villains
hardly survive, Lardner's boredom with his characters conquering his anger at them, this flat-footed detective becomes the true
Lardnerian protagonist. As Lardner's unpleasant Boswell, the
'Miss Sarah E. Spooldripper' who introduces his last volumes,
informs us, Lardner was a great radio enthusiast, designing his
own set:

> At first he was unable to get any station at all, and this condi-
> tion held good up to the day of his death. But he was always try-
> ing to tune in on Glens Falls, N.Y., and it was only in last illness
> that he found out there was no broadcasting station at that place.

American life became for Lardner Glens Falls, New York, and
Glens Falls was silent, and then he realized there was nothing
there. The double or even the triple anticlimax became for
Lardner superior to the single: frustration the more frustrated.
In all his humor there was never any broadcasting station at
that place — and perhaps we may add, in all his life. Saturday
nights, the Mr. of the 'Big Town' remarks about his expensive
hotel life, 'everybody puts on their evening clothes, like something was going to happen. But it don't.' This is the verdict of
Lardner on his time, and not his alone, as we shall see; this is the
verdict of Lardner on himself.

To attempt to escape from this psychological impasse, moreover, would be simply to display the obverse of the egotistic success pattern that Lardner was at once attacking and personify-
ing. Was it not typical of the American champion, that master
of one field, he believed himself master of all, the bombastic
American ego aspiring to outdistance Marlowe's Elizabethan
conqueror? Every writer, like every business man, boxer, and
caddy, thought himself the discovery of the age, and was it he,
Ring Lardner, who actually, in fact, was? Remembering military 'stragetist' Keefe, the 'grooner' Danny, the inordinate opinion of comedian Ralston as to his own serious dramaturgy, remembering that in the entire range of his Americans, there was

apparently none who did not feel himself competent to be immortal, Lardner renounced his serious intentions. It's a wise Jester who does not play Hamlet.

He was a popular entertainer with no pretensions. Lardner insisted on this throughout his work, flatly, and then brutally. Here, he would not be guilty of false practice any longer; through himself he obliterated the Success Story of his era. Could he, unlike his Ralstons and Harry Harts, and the Maysville Minstrels of every sort, have been great? He crushed his ambition in the self-abuse, the cheap humor, the lame and heavy clowning which runs through his autobiographical material and prefatory notes. In the record of letters is there another volume as fine as 'How to Write Short Stories' which is so profoundly minimized by its author? 'Frameup' is an example 'of what can be done with a stub pen.' 'Champion' is an example of the mystery story. 'The mystery is how it came to get printed.' The true title of 'What of It?' Lardner suggests, should have been 'Hash,' as though there is much to choose between in these double phrases of self-denial. 'Zone of Quiet' was written outdoors during the equinoctial gales. 'Nearly every other sheet of copy was blown away or destroyed by stray dogs.' But the dogs were hardly stray, and it's a sorry Hamlet that plays the Jester. Uneasy, apologetic, Lardner propitiates the reader, while he negates himself. If it was typical of his American monomaniac that he would never accept his own limitations, it was characteristic of Lardner that he refused to grasp the extent of his own potentialities.

In these prefaces and self-commentary, moreover, comes the worst of Lardner's humor, his cheap irrelevancies which often culminate in blank unintelligibility, his sadism (to be precise, this is the essence of his humor, which was disguised and made civilized in Lardner's text, and here is made quite clear). The forewords of his later volumes become cheaper, crueler; by 1926 the sadism assumes its genuine face of masochism; images of death and destruction come in more heavily, and very shortly cease to be mere images. In Lardner's 'autobiography,' 'The

Story of a Wonderman' (notice how the title itself illuminate
our thesis), this disintegrative process reaches its climax. De-
coyed into his publisher's office, as Lardner explains the origin
of his autobiography, he was 'bashed in the stomach by some
blunt instrument':

> When I regained consciousness I was laying on my back in the
> gun room while the head of a midiron had been shoved into my
> mouth with the heel resting vs. the roof of same and the toe on
> my tongue, and a Mr. Perkins the manager had began to pull my
> teeth with some blunt instrument.

Even the instruments of Lardner's self-torture, we see, are
blunt; and when this had got past 'the amusing stage,' Lardner
tells his publisher he will write his autobiography provided the
work is not published prior to his death. ' "That suits us," said
the boss, "if you'll promise to die by the Fourth of July." ' Surrounding Lardner, the spectators take up this refrain:

> If you'll promise to die
> By the fourth of July.

In his own recording, at least, Lardner shortly thereafter does
die, and 'Miss Sarah E. Spooldripper,' the grotesque apparition
of Lardner's prefaces, describes his final agonies in 'The Love
Nest.' Miss Spooldripper hopes, she says, to dispel the general
illusion that Lardner was just

> a tiresome old man induced by financial calamity and a fond-
> ness for narcotics to harp constantly on the futility of life on a
> branch line of the Long Island Railroad.

And thus revealing the general illusion of himself that pre-
vailed in Lardner's own mind, Miss Spooldripper proceeds to
picture some 'irresistible traits of The Master.' Lardner always
bolted his food, she says. 'He was afraid the rats would get it.'
Every so often Lardner and his friends would become maudlin,
'or, better still, inaudible.' (A strange confession for a great
artist to make, whose catharsis lies in expression!) The chief
interest of Lardner's life, Miss Spooldripper continues, was

'the wolf.' (And strange companions for this popular artist of the twenties, given every gift of a society unsurpassed in material splendor.) Lardner, having unfortunately contracted a cold, so Miss Spooldripper concludes her account of our most talented author in the twenties, is dying of conchoid, 'a disease which is superinduced by a rush of seashells to the auricle or outer ear.'

> Present during the last hours were only myself and the wolf, Junior (Lardner's name for the wife in these episodes), having chosen this time to get a shampoo and a wave in preparation for the series of dinner dances that were bound to follow.

Under such auspices and surrounded by such companions, Lardner, so he wishes us to believe, and like John Donne having carried his bitterness beyond the grave, passes to his eternal reward.

'The Master,' Miss Spooldripper records, 'is gone, and who will succeed him? Perhaps some writer still unborn. Perhaps one who will never be born. That is what I hope.' Stripping his dignity from his own death, as he had from that of his era, Lardner may indeed have wished that he had never been born. Without perspective on the social values of '29, holding the pain of genius without its freedom, he fiercely played the Jester. But his endless hatred found its catharsis when at last he disestablished his own throne with such poor comedy. In his thoughts of serious literary achievement, so he warned himself in these prefaces to his work, he was merely following the American national fantasy of '29 — this egotistical nightmare nourished by the Success Myth, moving through which every other boxer, business man, artist also thought himself unique, always dressing up 'like something was going to happen —'

> (Mah-Jong, oil scandals, dreadful B.O., Halitosis, Pyorrhea, and Peaches Browning. 'Grace, I'd like another highball.')

'But it don't.' And who would wish to emulate the Successes of the twenties? Was it he, Ring Lardner, the truly unique one? Echoing Hemingway's Nada (Hail nothing, full of nothing,

nothing is with thee), Lardner heaped abuse on his own claims
to greatness, smothered them with lame comedy, obliterating
the age in himself, until Miss Sarah E. Spooldripper, this vir-
ginal, sterile Hyde to Lardner's Jekyll, buried them and him
too. For after Miss Spooldripper's advent, Lardner in effect
wrote no more fine tales. Yet the joke, said Lardner, turning in
upon himself once more and for the last time, refusing to tolerate even this distorted fragment of his genius, was on Miss
Spooldripper. 'For she is gone too':

> Two months ago she was found dead in the garage, her body cov-
> ered by wolf bites left there by her former ward who had probably
> forgotten where he had left them.

Except that to Ring Lardner, we must understand, something
did happen after all.

Chapter Two

Ernest Hemingway : YOU COULD ALWAYS COME BACK

◇

1. THERE AND BACK   2. WOODS OF MICHIGAN TO CAPORETTO

3. THE MATADOR AND THE KUDU   4. NO MAN ALONE

5. RETURN OF THE NATIVES

Chapter Two

Ernest Hemingway : YOU COULD ALWAYS
COME BACK

1. THERE AND BACK.   'You could always come back,'
said the Hemingway who stood in exile among the green hills of
Africa, about the American culture he had renounced. And it
is with a writer who left us and came back that we must deal.
With Ring Lardner we saw the history of an artist so much a
part of his society that he could imagine no other; and who ends
by condemning that society so completely that he must also
question his own work and life. In Hemingway we have the
artist who starts with Lardner's conclusion. Here we take up
our history at the point which formed the tragic termination
of '29's favorite child. For the basis of Hemingway's early writing is a total renunciation of all social frameworks; the separation of the writer from the common activity of his time; the acceptance of a profound isolation as the basis for the writer's
achievement.

This voyage of Hemingway to the extremes of solitude and
back has its drama. In many ways it is a spiritual act as courageous and bold as any of his famous, violent episodes. It has
its enigmas. Beneath the 'discipline' of Hemingway's style, the
strictly modulated feelings, the flat tones which were to impress
themselves upon a section of American prose, there lies a temperament that is fresh and new in literature. Hemingway's
character is deep and complex, ruled over by a sort of rigidity,
an iron restraint which, however, allows the spirit's true visions

to slip through from moment to moment, to tear themselves out from under his discipline, to emerge and create the wonderful tension of his best work. His temperament has its weakness also, its temptations, forebodings, and fears. Does it seem strange to talk of Hemingway in these terms? This writer who is to travel alone into the shadows of death, the author who has given us so many immortal studies of strength, the story-teller specializing in toughness, the advocate of the boxer, the matador, the revolutionary, and the killer? The artist who has above all proclaimed courage as his supreme value in life, the daring hunter of big game who, with his writer-protagonist of 'The Snows of Kilimanjaro,' may equally declare he has 'sold vitality, in one form or another, all his life'? To these dilemmas do our hidden forces bring us.

Like Lardner, Hemingway is another western American boy, a doctor's son, born in Illinois in 1898. His youth was spent in the Michigan woods whose quality he catches so nicely in his early tales of our last stretch of frontier. In Hemingway's first book, 'In Our Time,' we meet the young Nick, his family, the hunting and fishing trips in these Michigan forests, the encounters with Indians, Nick's introduction to reading, drinking, first friendships and early love — a wonderfully idyllic youth that Hemingway does not forget. He went to a Michigan high school, no further formal education; like Lardner, too, he became the journalist of a small-town newspaper. During the First World War Hemingway enlisted with the Italians; saw, recorded, and was wounded. The impact of this experience coming directly upon his adolescence was to condition a part of his writing; there are other factors, however, operating beneath this. There was a sharp break now with his environment. Europe in 1921, and we see the middle-western boy surrounded by Parisian bohemians, among them those who believed the salvation of literature lay in the lack of punctuation, Gertrude Stein, Ezra Pound, Ford Madox Ford, and William Bird who published the work of the young Hemingway, sometimes rejected by others as merely 'sketches.' These were exciting times in Paris, Ford tells us. 'Young America from the limitless prairies leapt, released, on Paris. They stampeded with the madness of colts when you let down the slip-rails between dried pasture and green.' We are to suppose that the dried pasture was the United States of the twenties; there was certainly enough stampeding. Among the new aesthetes Hemingway would advance, with 'rather the aspect of an Eton-Oxford, husky-ish young captain of a midland regiment of His Britannic Majesty ... balancing on the point of his toes, feinting at my head with hands as large as hams, and relating sinister stories of Paris landlords.' Fiestas and Spanish bullfights, the trailing of the kudu in Africa, and there came the long decade of Hemingway's rebellion, isolation, and search for the meanings of death. In his writing now there was the abrupt transition from the 'Nada,' echoing his despair, to the Florida of Lardnerian yachtsmen still grimly bent on pleasure. Hemingway was home again. Home; and then he was in the midst of the Spanish Civil War; the isolated chronicler of man's fatal impulses transformed into the Cassandra of social crisis.

Living this life with its twisting turns and sudden reverses, and apparently so remote from our own manners and shores, Hemingway must be seen as a typical figure. The underlying causes of his art are, I believe, particularly American. In his evolution Hemingway is to anticipate the new literature of the nineteen-thirties, the transition from Lardner's dead end to new faiths — however extreme, erratic, or, as with Hemingway himself, imperfectly realized, faiths which were nevertheless to form the dominant literary tradition of America in social change. But Hemingway is more than typical. Our written patterns do not altogether define him. There is a sort of magic touch with him, an inherited depth and reaching awareness in the midst of his obvious and sometimes exasperating limitations. Magic is a delicate adjective nowadays, an embarrassing admission for the literary analyst to propound. And yet at the end of Hemingway as at the start, we can do little better than admit it: a confession, an evasion perhaps, and with these we have a sense of

gratitude that in the age of formulas we are still allowed to feel
some mysteries of creation.

2. WOODS OF MICHIGAN TO CAPORETTO.   It has
been the common view to attribute the solitary position which
is at the bottom of Hemingway's work to the post-war reaction,
and to class him with other social rebels as the English D. H.
Lawrence, the French Jean Giono, or the German Rainer
Maria Rilke, those who during or after the World War moved
away from a society whose international murder they could no
longer tolerate. We cannot deny the importance of the war in
Hemingway. With his first collection of stories, 'In Our Time,'
published in 1925, Hemingway himself established such a pattern. In the series of alternating episodes which comprise the
volume we see first the adventures of a sensitive American adolescent; one without, however, the typical traits of most literary
adolescents. It is almost impossible to convey the admirable
quality of these early Hemingway stories, seeming so light in
their fiber and yet so rich in feeling, the tone which marks 'The
End of Something' or 'The Doctor and the Doctor's Wife.'
And in a lighter vein we have such sections as the incomparable,
if inebriated, 'Three Day Blow':

'What are you reading?'
' "Richard Feverel." '
'It's all right . . . It ain't a bad book, Wemedge.'
'What else have you got I haven't read?' Nick asked.
'Did you read the "Forest Lovers"?'
'Yup. That's the one where they go to bed every night with
the naked sword between them.'
'That's a good book, Wemedge.'
'It's a swell book. What I couldn't ever understand was what
good the sword would do. It would have to stay edge up all the
time because if it went over flat you could roll over it and it
wouldn't make any trouble.'
'It's a symbol,' Bill said.
'Sure,' said Nick, 'but it isn't practical.'

In these plain tones, of course, is heralded the new style, the new manner, the new philosophy which, along with Lardner, would influence a generation. This is literary revolution as well as literary criticism.

The contrast with the alternate half of 'In Our Time' is startling, and intended so. The juxtaposition with these early, lyrical sketches already represents the full reaction of Hemingway as the war novelist. Quite abruptly as the volume indicates, the war scenes placed directly against the Michigan woods, Nick is plunged into horror. Here in this new world of battle, suffering, and death, every accent is tortured. Pain no longer emphasizes the peace of living; now indeed there is no peace to balance or even to intrude upon the province of pain, as if it were immutable, immemorial. The entire structure of this new world, the anatomy of war, all its tissues are saturated with suffering:

> They shot the six cabinet ministers at half-past six in the morning against the wall of a hospital. There were pools of water in the courtyard.... One of the ministers was sick with typhoid. Two soldiers carried him downstairs and out into the rain. They tried to hold him up against the wall but he sat down in a puddle of water. The other five stood very quietly against the wall. Finally the officer told the soldiers it was no good trying to make him stand up. When they fired the first volley he was sitting down in the water with his head on his knees.

No protest could be much more effective, no rhetoric more eloquent, I suppose, than this impartial, expressionless recording of 'facts' in wartime. It is only, indeed, by noticing that these facts recur endlessly, that the monotone of terror never changes, that we may fully realize the intention of Hemingway's objective, almost statistical diagram of things as they are.

The quality of Hemingway's war reaction becomes, however, somewhat curious. Its emphasis comes to rest not on intelligence, or action to avert such scenes or to eliminate their future possibility; nor on any moral intention to renounce such horror as incompatible with all human effort. There is rather a sort

of inevitable acceptance of it. The recording of war scenes, so
intense, is also, as it were, motionless. The maimed, bleeding,
sick human beings; the army mules, their forelegs broken, who
must drown slowly in water hardly deep enough for drowning;
the water too with its 'nice things' floating around in it; these
humans and animals and the scene of warfare itself are shown as
if frozen, as though the writer were doing a 'still' of them which
has no continuation, and does not even culminate in death but
remains fixed in its endless dying. The scenes of horror are indel-
ible. If there is a protest in their recording, it is a protest which
itself must continue endlessly. Both the sickness in the world
outside the writer, and the sickness within him as he observes
the world, will continue in their rigid, static relationship, in this
equation of pain which has no equivalent.

Thus, while the early Nick was in the midst of his life, however casual it may have been, the later Nick, in the midst of
extreme tension, has withdrawn. While the young Nick was
functioning, if only to read and drink and hunt, the older Nick
is watching. (It is a terrible sort of watching, to be sure, insistent, an observation which is almost compulsive in its fixed
stare.) We may see this more clearly if we recall the larger body
of war literature in which Hemingway belongs, the work of
Arnold Zweig or Erich Remarque, for example, H. G. Wells, or
Henri Barbusse, or Jules Romains. If these writers do not often
compare with Hemingway in their statement of the war's shock,
their accent lies more fruitfully on human effort rather than
Hemingway's rigid embracing of disaster; on the human will if
it is only to question the inevitability of Hemingway's scene.
And in the weaker sections of Hemingway's new craft we may
see more clearly what in its perfection we suspect. In his over-
emphasis, sometimes flippant or ostentatiously virile, or with a
sort of disdainful bravado, Hemingway shows us his defenses.
'It was a pleasant business. My word yes a most pleasant business.' This is just a little too jolly, and in these phrases we may
often see Hemingway's post-war attitude in the process of con-
struction. Such an attitude, of course — at its best, this intense

but immobile observation, and often descending into a callous acceptance of a mannered boredom — is understandable both in its moral and psychological aspects. The latter runs into the 'weariness' of the post-war generation; a weariness resulting from the extremes of the war experience itself; in the face of which the psyche must retreat to protect itself, and after which the routine existence of civilized society — a life operating under the usual conventions and restrictions — could make little impression. The activities of peace, all the complex relationships and tensions of normal life were no longer vital. And in moral terms, the artist, having assumed Hemingway's rôle of the spectator, disclaims his responsibility for the war world of horror and agony which he, certainly, had never made.

A variety of later stories — 'The Revolutionist,' 'In Another Country,' 'A Simple Enquiry,' 'Now I Lay Me,' 'A Way You'll Never Be' — affirm the various phases of Hemingway's thesis: the suffering of the war, the resistances and defenses of his people, their ways of ignoring the scene around them which apparently they cannot control. Perhaps no other contemporary writer, in fact, has brought us so many vivid studies of the war's impact on the defenseless human temperament; the almost unbearable episode which closes 'A Natural History of the Dead' is typical of these. In 'Soldier's Home,' one of the earliest of his stories and still perhaps the best of them, we have the story of Krebs, who went to the war from a Methodist College in Kansas, and returns after the war to his home town. The town, the family and friends of Krebs, even his father's car are still the same. 'Nothing was changed in the town except that the young girls had grown up.' But Krebs was changed. He no longer had the desire to become part of the town's life. Even the attractive young girls who appealed to him now lived 'in such a complicated world of already defined alliances . . . that Krebs did not feel the energy or the courage to break into it.' From a distance, from his front porch as they walked on the other side of the street, Krebs liked to watch the young girls in their round

Dutch collars and silk stockings, but when he was next to them
'their appeal to him was not very strong':

> He did not like them when he saw them in the Greek's ice cream
> parlor. He did not want them themselves really. They were too
> complicated. . . . He did not want to get into the intrigue and the
> politics. He did not want to have to do any more courting. He
> did not want to tell any more lies. It wan't worth it. . . . He did
> not want any consequences. He did not want any consequences
> ever again. He wanted to live along without consequences.

Nowhere more clearly than in the story of Krebs has Hemingway given us his underlying attitude — this living along without consequences, the emotional withdrawal from experience
and moral renunciation of life's responsibilities; this looking at
things henceforth from a variety of porches rather than partici-
pating in all the streets of life. And 'A Farewell to Arms,' four
years after Krebs, gives the unified history of the events which
led up to such a conclusion.

Returning to read the famous novel after all the prefaces by
Parisian bohemians like Ford Madox Ford, and the excitement
of the American popular reception, is, I believe, still a fine
experience. For the book is without doubt as fresh today as in
1929, as gay and moving. Against the gaiety, the warmth of 'A
Farewell to Arms,' Hemingway portrays, of course, the cumulative degeneration of the human temperament under the conditions of war. The novel is a series of human defeats within one
continuous and terrible sequence: the rains, the cholera, the
soldiers who mutilate themselves rather than go on fighting, the
growing weariness of the Italian army which led up to Caporetto, the degeneration of Rinaldi himself who is symptomatic of
the novel's pattern, and at its start is so quick and alive. Con-
trasted against this in turn, in the love of Lieutenant Henry and
Catherine Barkley we have another antithesis of increasing joy.
The love and the despair are constantly related, intensely inter-
twined, and in the end almost gain the feeling of life and death
themselves: the death preying upon the living organism of the
lovers' hope, eating into the flesh and destroying the form from

page to page. Yet each change of form, each advance of destruction makes the life of the novel more vital, the life we know must yield, but in the manner of its yielding asserting itself beyond its destruction.

'A Farewell to Arms' in this sense lies quite outside of the pattern of Hemingway's development which we have been showing. For the feeling of tragedy in the novel comes precisely from the struggle to participate in life despite all the odds, from the efforts of the lovers to fulfill themselves in a sterile world, from the exact impact of the human will which Hemingway has negated. Yet even here we must notice that Lieutenant Henry turns his back upon our society after Caporetto. Following his personal objectives he abandons his friends, his responsibilities as an officer, the entire complex of organized social life represented by the army and the war. This farewell to arms is accomplished without request or permission. Lieutenant Henry, in fact, deserts, and his action is prophetic of his author's own future movement. 'You and me,' says Nick to the Rinaldi of 'In Our Time,' 'we've made a separate peace.' And Hemingway's separate peace was to embrace the woods of Michigan as well as Caporetto, the activities of normal times as well as war, and even at last the ordinary purposes of the individual's life within his society, as well as the collective purposes of society as a whole.

Hemingway's withdrawal from experience and denial of human responsibility, in short, are to run their course in his work from Nick and Krebs of 'In Our Time' for some ten years until 'The Green Hills of Africa' in 1935. The implications of this appear throughout his stories for the decade. His work has little significance, indeed, without the framework of revolt and isolation which gives it unity. That it has sometimes been misinterpreted in this respect, his novels seen from an immediate or fragmentary view, is due primarily, I believe, to the fact that Hemingway gives so little articulation to his dominant attitude. It is rather by piecing together his fragments of editorial expression that we may approach anything like a logical statement of his position. It was only in 'The Green Hills of Africa' that he him-self gave a fuller view of the matter:

> If you serve time for society, democracy, and the other things quite young, and declining any further enlistment make yourself responsible only to yourself, you exchange the pleasant, comfort-ing stench of comrades for something you can never feel in any other way than by yourself. That something I cannot yet define completely but the feeling comes ... when, on the sea, you are alone with it and know that this Gulf Stream you are living with, knowing, learning about, and loving, has moved, as it moves, since before man, and that it has gone by the shoreline of that long, beautiful, unhappy island since before Columbus sighted it and that the things you find out about it, and those that have always lived in it are permanent and of value because that stream will flow, as it has flowed, after the Indians, after the Spaniards, after the British, after the Americans and after all the Cubans and all the systems of governments, the richness, the poverty, the martyrdom, the sacrifice and the venality and the cruelty are all gone as the high-piled scow of garbage, bright-colored, white-flecked, ill-smelling, now tilted on its side, spills off its load into the blue water, turning it a pale green to a depth of four or five fath-oms as the load spreads across the surface, the sinkable part going down and the flotsam of palm fronds, corks, bottles, and used electric light globes, seasoned with an occasional condom or a deep floating corset, the torn leaves of a student's exercise book, a well-inflated dog, the occasional rat, the no-longer-distinguished cat; all this well shepherded by the boats of the garbage pickers who pluck their prizes with long poles, as interested, as intelli-gent, and as accurate as historians; they have the viewpoint; the stream, with no visible flow, takes five loads of this a day when things are going well in La Habana and in ten miles along the coast it is as clear and blue and unimpressed as it was ever before the tug hauled out the scow; and the palm fronds of our victories, the worn light bulbs of our discoveries and the empty condoms of our great loves float with no significance against one single, lasting thing — the stream.

We notice, moreover, that if this view of Hemingway's position is more complete than any other statement of his, it is still in

effect one sentence. Such a sentence to be sure! So complex
and modulated, and representing so much of the bewilderment
and despair of the post-war decade: consigning us, and all our
works, our victories, discoveries, and great loves, to oblivion in
these haunting and elegiac cadences; and holding in its rhythms
again so much of the passive, the drifting, and solitary individual on the unfathomable waters of existence. And as Hemingway with such a statement left behind him the European framework of society, this the final fruit of Lieutenant Henry's desertion at Caporetto, he also abandons his own American culture.
Again we generally perceive this as a fact rather than a mani-
festo, marked not by Hemingway's references to America but
rather his lack of references. We shall notice a little later the
factors leading to this decision; here we see only the statement
which Hemingway gives us on his decision:

> It is easier to keep well in a good country by taking simple pre-
> cautions than to pretend that a country which is finished is still
> good. . . . Our people went to America because that was the place
> to go then. It had been a good country and we had made a
> bloody mess of it and I would go, now, somewhere else as we had
> always had the right to go somewhere else and as we had always
> gone. You could always come back. Let the others come to
> America who did not know that they had come too late. Our
> people had seen it at its best and fought for it when it was well
> worth fighting for. Now I would go somewhere else. We always
> went in the old days and there were still good places to go.

As Hemingway had previously condemned all our work to
the depths of the Gulf Stream, blue and unimpressed, now he
has added our continent itself. What a tremendous renunciation of human effort this is, which can sweep away a continent,
as rich, as young, as powerful as ever! What a supreme and
final contempt for the common existence of humanity, our customs, songs, and land! And so renouncing the smells of peace
as well as the 'comforting stench' of comrades in war, the land
of his birth as well as that of his adoption, our native earth in

addition to our social patterns, Hemingway is to follow alone the narrow and tortuous path of the rebel.

Such, then, is the reaction of our American writer, in the interpretation of Hemingway's art which sees him primarily as the product of the post-war disillusionment. It is our belief, however, that to remain content with the interpretation of Hemingway as the war novelist is somewhat limited. We intend to show that in terms of his own personality Hemingway's rebellion against society is more complex than this, deeper, and antecedent to the war itself; and that the sociological factors conditioning this rebellion are also more profound. To accomplish this we must follow him along the path of his exile for the middle period of his writing. We must consider him, as Hemingway himself might insist that every human being be considered, without benefit of society, a single individual on a spiritual expedition, indeed, to avoid all societies. It is, to be sure, a long and perhaps dangerous search for the critic, as for the author whom we follow; a solitary excursion of the psyche into the last enigmas and shadows of life. Yet to avoid it is to lessen the meaning of Hemingway. What are the truer causes, what are the consequences of Hemingway's safari into the haunted and isolated regions of the spirit's darkness?

3. THE MATADOR AND THE KUDU.   'The day of death,' we are told in the wisdom of the Preacher, 'is better than the day of one's birth'; and perhaps no American writer has come to explore the ultimate truth of Ecclesiastes more deeply than Hemingway. It is indeed this 'day of death' which was to preoccupy him steadily from now on, and was to fill the bulk of his mature work; a day of doubt and torment which was to last a decade.

In the transition from the Hemingway who is defined by the boundaries of the European war to the new Hemingway who

has renounced the boundaries of society, we may notice, first of
all, what our more strictly Marxian critics have rather conven-
iently ignored: how often the 'sociological' patterns of Hemingway seem to reflect a particular temperamental stress. The
actual passages we use so convincingly to establish the disillusionment of Hemingway themselves indicate a sense of futility
which is earlier and stronger than the war. In the midst of
Hemingway's war action, we may feel the elements of an internal struggle more crucial perhaps than that which Hemingway
is describing:

> It was a frightfully hot day. We'd jammed an absolutely per-
> fect barricade across the bridge. It was simply priceless. A big
> old wrought-iron grating from the front of a house. Too heavy to
> lift and you could shoot through it and they would have to climb
> over it. It was absolutely topping. They tried to get over it, and
> we potted them from forty yards. They rushed it, and officers
> came out alone and worked on it. It was an absolutely perfect
> obstacle.

But this 'absolutely perfect obstacle' is to appear and reappear
so often in Hemingway's work, sometimes changing its shape
but never its meaning until we are tempted to speculate whether
life itself is for the writer Hemingway simply a larger sort of
absolutely perfect obstacle. We cannot dismiss it as a symbol of
merely external action. The battles of the war, themselves the
expression of the larger strain of the era of modern industrialism, were also for Hemingway the convenient framework for
the manifestations of a spirit itself in the throes of conflict.

Again the post-war reaction of resignation and of renunciation that Hemingway expressed in the story of Krebs, and
which, as we saw, became his own dominant attitude, corre-
sponds to an inner reality. We may hazard the speculation that
the secret of 'The Sun Also Rises' lies here — in the exact and
rare meeting of the writer's individual temperament with the
ostensible demands of his subject. For if 'A Farewell to Arms'
is Hemingway's master work of the war itself, 'The Sun Also
Rises' is that of the epoch which followed. What portrait of the

'lost generation' is more convincing, eloquent, accurate, full of
sympathy which does not soften its perceptions? In 'Antic Hay'
or 'Point Counter Point' Aldous Huxley has the intelligence
of Hemingway but hardly the feeling. The 'Rainbow' volumes of D. H. Lawrence, whose post-war studies approximate
Hemingway's, lacks the incisiveness of 'The Sun Also Rises,' the
clear purpose and the craft which fulfills it. Has it been questioned, as Thomas Wolfe was to question and turn the phrase
in a new direction, whether there ever was in fact a lost generation? After 'The Sun Also Rises' there had to be one. All of us
have known our own Lady Bretts and Jakes, these gifted and
despairing souls, revealing their disillusion in a variety of nuances in the vain hope that perhaps they also were out of Hemingway. Vainly we say, for it was only in a novel that a lost
generation could feel its plight with such intensity and live it
out with magnificence. Yet paradoxically the novel was so real
that it took us another generation to discover that being lost
was a delicate art in itself; and our own Lady Brett Ashleys, so
beguiling in literature, were apt to be boring in life.

For in this union of Hemingway's temperament with the post-
war attitude, it is the writer's beliefs which very subtly control
his people's; which dominate his setting and, using it as the perfect projection of his feeling, carry it beyond his private convictions into the realm of universal connotations. Why must
these modern lovers continually nourish the passion that is
denied them? Rather like reversing the ancient fable of Pyg-
malion, Brett is the perfect woman who has turned to marble,
for Jake at least; but why must Jake continue moulding this
marble; as all the personages of the novel constantly emphasize
the methods of their own destruction? The lightest conversation in 'The Sun Also Rises' seems quite inevitably to turn the
screw upon the wounded spirits of this group of pleasure-seekers.
And we see finally how the entire action of the novel — this tor-
turing and self-torture — takes place in Parisian cafés, along
the fishing streams of the Basque country, and, as its climax, in
the orgiastic rejoicing of a southern fiesta — in a setting, that

is to say, of almost absolute pleasure. Yet, if this is the life of joy, it seems we might do better through deliberately seeking pain.

We see, in fact, that the lost generation is, in the end, much more than lost. Just as none of us could live up to the disillusionment of Hemingway's people, none of us, or few, could be so overwhelmingly ineffectual. Hemingway's post-war generation is frustrate with an intensity and cunning of purpose, with a natural and unconscious knowledge of the best methods to defeat itself, with an almost diabolical sense of frustration. If these people are meant to be representative, they must derive not merely from a disorganized society but from, so to speak, an entire genealogy of frustrated ancestors, from a race of the disillusioned. What we have in 'The Sun Also Rises,' as a matter of fact, rather than an 'objective' history of the lost generation, is the functioning of an immensely delicate imagination guiding these people so skillfully that they seem to be genuine, independent personalities — an imagination tormented as well as intricate which in the actions of its characters is revealing the depths and the shades of its own anguish. 'The Sun Also Rises' is a complete and beautiful treatise on this sort of anguish, physical and spiritual, profound and light, intentional and accidental, delivered upon others and self-determined. Toward this every episode, almost every line in the novel contributes its exact weight, the most careless gesture or phrase of Hemingway's characters seeming to provide the one stroke in the pattern hitherto missing. That is what the novel is, really, and as we know, reality is neither quite so accurate nor artistic. There is, indeed, only one thing the matter with 'The Sun Also Rises.' It is not like life.

That it was like Hemingway, however, the years following it were to show. After this novel, Hemingway's theme becomes more sharply defined. The sequels to 'The Sun Also Rises' and to all of Hemingway's war novels reveal even more clearly that, in the precarious interaction of the temperamental and the environmental which we are tracing, the balance seems to lie with

the factors of Hemingway's personality. For now it is the nineteen-thirties. Now the war and the post-war have both slipped
away to give us that moment of peace in our time, the illusion
of permanence in which so many tragic historical errors were
committed simply because the wish of men was for permanence, thus refusing to see, what was clearly shown, that under
these conditions there could be no peace. And what is our
writer saying?   'Death in the Afternoon' (1932), 'The Green
Hills of Africa' (1935), and the bulk of Hemingway's mature
stories are to tell us, and their answer is, I think, unmistakable.
The war affected Hemingway, surely, yet many other temperaments were affected and recovered. With him the impression
was so deep, so natural and final as to make it seem that the war
experience released his energies rather than inhibited them.
We may almost say, to paraphrase Voltaire, that if there had
been no war, it would have been necessary for Hemingway to
invent one.

Of these works, 'Death in the Afternoon' is often described as
the most absurd, perhaps, of Hemingway's works. What is this
major writer doing, with his consuming passion for bullfighting
to which he seems to subordinate everything else in his life?
We must agree with many of the objections raised by the critics. Here certainly are the imperfect attributes of Hemingway,
the braggadocio, the rather sophomoric, sophisticated smartness which marked his earlier work. There are the mannerisms
into which Hemingway sometimes falls. Yet these are the reflection of something more central, the marks of an uneasy
spirit. Hemingway protests rather too constantly (as he was to
do again in 'The Green Hills of Africa') the significance of his
achievement, and his own pleasure, and the ignorance of those
who would doubt his importance and pleasure. And there is a
misplaced irritation which runs through the book, of which we
never seem to find the true object; all the unhappy evidences of
a morality which is disputing, by all sorts of indirection, its own
moral values. The tone of 'Death in the Afternoon' is hence
often wrong, denying and accusing, wrangling and quibbling;

yet again often rich and amusing, and including some of Hemingway's sharpest studies of the human constitution.

But what sort of constitution? In these transparently bad moments, and in his superbly good ones, what after all is the enemy Hemingway is attacking, the friend he embraces? It is the conception of the matador, we may say, that has caught Hemingway's admiration: the dignity, courage, discipline, and honor, all these traits which are embraced in the Spanish 'pundonor.' 'Bullfighting is the only art in which the artist is in danger of death and in which the degree of brilliance in the performance is left to the fighter's honor.' This dignity and courage, however, the sense of man's virtue, comes out infrequently and against large odds: the fickle crowd, the sacrifice of the horses with their horrid disembowelings, the diseases, too, and sorts of death which overtake the matadors, the commercialism of the sport as a whole, the easy tricks and the commercialism of the matadors themselves. And the sense of man's virtue, rare, composed of such dubious components, lasts for only a moment: the moment when the matador and the bull are both ready for the kill; not when victory is easy; but when it is one strength against another, one skill, one will meeting its counterpart in the brief seconds of the last act of the bullfight.

In the final moment of decisiveness, then, which evidences the grand style of man, the bull is equally important; in a sense, more so. As the matador gains his dignity by facing death, and in the end, in one form or another, sooner or later, almost inevitably succumbing to it, the bull, even more surely, has less chance to escape it, and so gains a greater sense of crisis and tragedy. He is the victim, the sacrifice, the sufferer. He dies the death, not remotely or by chance, but through purpose here and now. Thus the actors of 'Death in the Afternoon' are double. The matador and the bull are united in the moment of fusion; they become one; the one who suffers and the one who makes suffer, to use Edmund Wilson's discerning phrase; the active and the passive elements in Hemingway's fundamental thesis; the matador who gains his power by killing and the bull through being killed. And beneath the formalized murder which joins these curious lovers lies the true protagonist of the book, death itself — 'death uniting the two figures in the emotional, aesthetic, and artistic climax of the fight.' As 'The Sun Also Rises,' despite the narrative, was in fact a single treatise on the destructive instincts of the human temperament, 'Death in the Afternoon,' while it is ostensibly a text on bullfighting, is another such treatise on these destructive instincts carried to their ultimate conclusion. For the 'death' which Hemingway is here describing with such skill and brilliance is not merely the good death, but very often the evil death; not the physical, but the spiritual death; and not, of course, the final and big death alone, but all the little deaths we die from moment to moment — those of cowardice and frustration, of hatred, of guilt and expiation; of all our obscure longings for defeat and destruction which, like an immense and submerged antiphony answering and often guiding all our life instincts, run through the human temperament. In the pretty play of the matador and the bull which forms the core of 'Death in the Afternoon,' Hemingway, in short, has gathered together an elaborate and meticulous compendium, perhaps uniquely in the Anglo-Saxon literary tradition, of dissolution.

But while in his earlier work Hemingway's meaning came out clearly, here there are evasions. Hemingway is uncertain both about his audience's reaction and his own. What he could admit about our destructive impulses in their lesser form, he cannot altogether admit about their extension. It is the uneasiness as to his own purpose which brings forth the justifications, the complaints, evasions, denials which give 'Death in the Afternoon' its broken form:

> Killing cleanly [Hemingway says] and in a way which gives you aesthetic pleasure and pride has always been one of the greatest enjoyments of a part of the human race.

But Hemingway never quite reaches into the profound causes which make this killing the 'greatest enjoyment' for a very large part of the human race. And we must notice how many of the descriptions in the book are in reality not those of 'clean' killing with the attendant emotions of 'pleasure' and 'pride' and 'enjoyment.' Perhaps rather the opposite, and perhaps the majority of Hemingway's descriptions. 'Death in the Afternoon' is indeed, if you like, a text of unclean killings, of the horrors and diseases and various uglinesses of death, such as that of Gitanillo and other matadors and animals. The entire structure of the bullfight, with its 'classical form,' its strict requirements which Hemingway constantly stresses, in this sense is a sort of moral justification for Hemingway's concern with death, a concern which often breaks through his defensive structures and shows the very meaning to which he denies validity. The fact that Hemingway must so often stress the 'rules' of bullfighting — his contempt for the man or beast who breaks them, sometimes in what seem to the uninitiated very sensible ways — indicates his fear of the opposing forces within him. He must again defend his study of death in terms of Spanish ethics as opposed to Anglo-Saxon:

> Because they [the Spaniards] have pride they do not mind killing; feeling that they are worthy to give this gift. As they have common sense they are interested in death and do not spend their lives avoiding the thought of it and hoping that it does not exist only to discover it when they come to die.

What a curious statement, like so many others found here, formed of confusion and perception! What is the 'pride' which grants death, the death which is a 'gift' (as indeed it will come to be in the deep feeling of Hemingway)? It is certainly not wise to avoid the thought of death in our life. Neither is it wise to avoid the thought of living in the midst of death. And that 'Death in the Afternoon' does this in effect, that Hemingway's concern with death is a little more than the Spaniard's 'interest' in it, is obvious by now. The Spaniards, Hemingway adds, are not preoccupied by death. 'It has no fascination for them.' Can the writer say as much for himself? It was only a little later that Hemingway's protagonist in 'The Snows of Kilimanjaro' was to admit that with him death had been an obsession.

Then why must Hemingway deny his fundamental concern with the darker elements of the human temperament — with this pain and torment and suffering, with these destructive impulses common to us all, and commonly vented from moment to moment upon ourselves and our environment, unpleasant perhaps but powerful? If it is only in our modern era we have come to a more systematized knowledge of these forces, we have not come to this knowledge by falsifying our intention, or again by minimizing the forces. Yet, despite the uncertain self-realization of his theme, Hemingway's conflicts conditioning the volume, 'Death in the Afternoon,' is nevertheless a central book in Hemingway's development. For here at last he has accepted his true métier. During the period of his war writings there was around Hemingway the pressure of his immediate environment, forcing suffering and destruction upon him, and, so to speak, legitimizing it. 'The only place where you could see life and death, i.e., violent death,' Hemingway says, 'now that the wars were over, was in the bull ring.' We have seen that in effect Hemingway's 'life' is merely the brief prelude to his death. And now that the wars were over, seeking this death of his own wish, affirming it from his own convictions, he makes it truly his own. If death no longer generally exists, he must seek it out; battles being over, the bull ring must do, or the jungles of Africa, the matador or the kudu.

That he does seek it, and finds it, all of Hemingway's mature work bears witness. 'The Green Hills of Africa' in 1935 contains again the same central trinity of the hunter, the hunted, and death as the only resolution of the hunt. And despite the flat, invariable thesis of his own, Hemingway's, happiness which accompanies the record of his hunting of the kudu, we have such passages as this:

> Highly humorous was the hyena obscenely loping, full belly dragging at daylight on the plain, who, shot from the stern, skittered on into speed to tumble end over end. Mirth provoking

was the hyena that stopped out of range by an alkali lake to look back and, hit in the chest, went over on his back, his four feet and his full belly in the air. Nothing could be more jolly than the hyena coming suddenly wedge-headed and stinking out of high grass by a *donga*, hit at ten yards, who raced his tail in three narrowing, scampering circles until he died.

It was funny to M'Cola to see a hyena shot at close range. There was that comic slap of the bullet and the hyena's agitated surprise to find death inside of him. It was funnier to see a hyena shot at a great distance, in the heat shimmer of the plain, to see him go over backwards, to see him start that frantic circle, to see that electric speed that meant that he was racing the little nickelled death inside him. But the great joke of all, the thing M'Cola waved his hands across his face about, and turned away and shook his head and laughed, ashamed even of the hyena; the pinnacle of hyenic humor, was the hyena, the classic hyena, that hit too far back while running, would circle madly, snapping and tearing at himself until he pulled his own intestines out, and then stood there, jerking them out and eating them with relish.

'*Fisi*,' M'Cola would say and shake his head in delighted sorrow at there being such an awful beast. Fisi, the hyena, hermaphroditic, self-eating devourer of the dead, trailer of calving cows, ham-stringer, potential biter-off of your face at night while you slept, sad yowler, camp-follower, stinking, foul, with jaws that crack the bones the lion leaves, belly dragging, loping away on the brown plain, looking back, mongrel dog-smart in the face; whack from the little Mannlicher and then the horrid circle starting. '*Fisi*,' M'Cola laughed, ashamed of him, shaking his bald black head. '*Fisi*. Eats himself. *Fisi*.'

A magnificent passage again, of which we may say, as with all the best of Hemingway, that any amount of rationalization, both self-deception and the projection of this outward, while hardly deceiving himself to assuage his readers, is worth its price. And we notice how this 'comic' hyena seems to compress into one the trinity of death which Hemingway has been describing, this view of man's hidden motivation which in the Spanish arena had elements of dignity, at least, and here seems more dubious. The hyena is the killer and the one killed. He is the hunter, now become a scavenger, who is being hunted. And caught, traveling in his 'frantic circles' (rather like our own), he snaps unaware at his own vitality. Impelled by the 'little nick-elled death' within him (which, I suppose, we also carry in one form or another), he performs his ironic rôle, eating himself out in the fond illusion he is nourishing himself. We often hardly do better.

The hyena is typical of many other such dark and brilliant passages which form the center of Hemingway's work over this period. The choice is neither limited nor the passages acci-dental. Of Hemingway's stories, almost all the later ones con-firm this; certainly the last four contained in 'The Fifth Column and the First Forty-Nine Stories.' If it is profitable to isolate the best of these, we may mention 'The Short Happy Life of Francis Macomber' or 'The Capital of the World.' And if it is possible to surpass them, we may mention 'The Snows of Kili-manjaro.' Perhaps indeed no story written by an American has a more profound and pervasive sense of dissolution than this. And here, more directly than before, Hemingway gives us — in an incomparable burst of disturbed emotion — the human guilt, the frustrations, the acts of destruction, the series of little deaths we cause or are stricken by, the losses we suffer by chance and by design before the final one, which are the truer elements of the pattern of destructive behavior he has been recording. For thus, always seeking the patterns of death in life, Heming-way has very seldom given us their full nature. His basic theme reaches us only in fragments. His truths do emerge in his work. But they break through it. They are hardly ever directly faced and dealt with. The human emotions which in Heming-way center around his search for death have their logic as well as their phenomena. Though we do not yet know all about them, or even perhaps very much about them, we know more — and almost every major writer dealing with them has known more — than Hemingway tells us. A play like Eugene O'Neill's 'Days Without End' is artistically uneven, yet it does make a full effort to understand the destructive impulses of its protagonist who is not unlike one of Hemingway's figures. Except in 'The Snows of Kilimanjaro,' there is hardly with Hemingway such a sustained and whole attempt to reach into the annihilation which he has embraced as his own.

Our long and uneasy development from inanimate to organic matter, the evolution of the race, the history of man under civilizational restraints, the study of human maladjustment, all teach us differently. The death instincts at the center of Hemingway's creation are not at all so broken and causeless as he would seem to have them. Though we seek to destroy perhaps more often than we should like to believe, we do not seek to destroy without reason: some very good reasons. If Hemingway's element of destruction, very much like his 'little nickelled death,' resides in all of us also, making us, like the animal, both hunters and hunted, unlike the animal we have, at any rate, a fuller consciousness of the forces which urge us into our devouring and self-devouring actions. If modern man is still unfortunately governed by these deep, fatal, irrational feelings, his little triumph is that now at least he recognizes himself. Yet Hemingway's people, so concerned with suffering as in 'In Our Time,' so engaged in torment as in 'The Sun Also Rises,' and finally so obsessed with death in 'The Green Hills of Africa' and 'Death in the Afternoon' — these people and Hemingway himself give us no adequate motivation for their dominant concern. So real, so full of life, however destructive, so convincing in all their outward movement, they are yet like puppets in their true internal action: drawn upon the strings of forces which neither they nor their author seem to understand. With Hemingway, the destructive impulses are unchanging and causeless. Pretending to such power, such omnipotence, they are also impotent to understand themselves.

In his descriptions of these dark and submerged factors of the human temperament, Hemingway is easily comparable with the major writers before him who have also dealt with them — the Shakespeare of 'King Lear' or 'Timon of Athens,' or the Ibsen of the later plays, a Kafka, Proust, James Joyce, and particularly perhaps the Russian Dostoevsky. But we see that Hemingway describes these depths of our motivation in a reportorial sense. He is without the comprehension of the Europeans, without their fuller freedom of search and speculation. And if among these other writers he seems closest to the Russian, playing upon the same themes of guilt, expiation, and death, Hemingway is also a peculiarly Nordic Dostoevsky. For his writing is almost compulsive as well as reportorial. The absence of freedom and knowledge of his theme is less significant, I believe, than his wish to remain in ignorance; his writing, as it often seems, as if against his own will. Much of Hemingway's work seems emblematic of a conflict between his desires and rejections. A portion of the writer is unable or unwilling to deal with the other parts of his temperament. So we have the series of rationalizations, the protestations, the apologies and evasions which we have already noticed. Much of Hemingway's best achievement also, the dramatic tension marking his work, springs from his personal conflicts: this temperament so deep and so complex, tortured and inhibited, ruled over by a sort of iron discipline. And yet its true visions slip through from moment to moment, breaking through its restraints to emerge ambiguously, equivocally, themselves in torment. With other writers the word is a catharsis. With Hemingway it seems rather a weapon of coercion. In his work the reason, or the conscious and moral standards, fight against these visions of catastrophe rather than work with them; or retreat from them; or again in a sort of burst of frenzied effort attempt to destroy them. The boy in 'God Rest You Merry Gentlemen,' who mutilates himself rather than continue to endure his sexual desires, is symptomatic of the many other Hemingway protagonists who eliminate their problems rather than solve them.

And once we have reached the disturbed source of Hemingway's creation, we see the significance of his two dominant artistic effects. There is first the emphasis on action, virile and violent, which runs through his work. Yet the quality of this vitality is enigmatic also. It is an action so utterly self-engrossed, so heedless of consequences, as to suggest that it is a confession rather than an affirmation. In our lives such bold action is necessary at particular junctures. In Hemingway's work these junctures occur from moment to moment. The Robert Cohn of 'The Sun Also Rises' who answers all criticism with an uppercut is another typical Hemingway protagonist, and in Cohn this virility is not a rational value but rather the expression of an emotional weakness. Hemingway's courage is often that of desperation rather than reflection. It is really as if he were attempting something like the ancient ordeal by fire which sought to establish innocence through its immunity to flame. And thus, in the pattern of Hemingway's creative process, his constant emphasis on virile action accomplishes its double function. It at once reassures the writer as to his apparent fear of thinking through the basic problems of his work, and at the same time obviously removes the opportunity to think. It was Henri Bergson who advised his pupils to think like men of action and act like men of thought. With Hemingway the axiom has been somewhat simplified. His people act as if thought were unthinkable.

And we notice how the other dominant mood of Hemingway fits into the pattern, the scenes of blank despair running parallel to those of concentrated action. Throughout Hemingway's work how many protagonists there are like the punch-drunk 'Battler,' the condemned victim of 'The Killers,' the veterans of 'To Have and Have Not' — those whom 'circumstances' place beyond the possibilities of thinking! Reflection and now even action are impossible for them. They await their fate with a magnificent but impotent resignation. We remember the Billy Campbell of 'A Pursuit Race' who, at last abandoning the effort to keep up with life, has shot himself full of dope and retired to his bed. 'They got a cure for that,' says his manager. 'No,' William Campbell says. 'They haven't got a cure for anything.' The Hemingway figure, his moment of blind and frenzied struggle against the forces of life having

dropped away, places himself in the true and final position of
drugging himself against the knowledge of these forces. Hemingway's emphasis on action is itself, of course, a sort of drug;
here the pattern emerges without evasion. How full, indeed, of
opiates is Hemingway's work; this emphasis which is summarized so eloquently in Frazer's monologue in 'The Gambler,
the Nun, and the Radio.' Usually Frazer avoided thinking,
Hemingway tells us, 'except when he was writing.' But now he
meditates on the remark of the Mexican Marxist: 'Religion is
the opium of the people . . .'

> Yes, and music is the opium of the people. Old mount-to-the-
> head hadn't thought of that. And now economics is the opium of
> the people; along with patriotism the opium of the people in
> Italy and Germany. What about sexual intercourse; was that
> an opium of the people? Of some of the people. Of some of the
> best of the people. But drink was a sovereign opium of the
> people, oh, an excellent opium. Although some prefer the radio,
> another opium of the people, a cheap one he had just been using.
> Along with these went gambling, an opium of the people if there
> ever was one, one of the oldest. Ambition was another . . . along
> with a belief in any new form of government. . . . But what was
> the real one? What was the real, the actual opium of the people?
> He knew it very well. It was gone just a little way around the
> corner in that well-lighted part of his mind that was there after
> two or more drinks in the evening; that he knew was there (it was
> not really there of course). What was it? He knew very well.
> What was it? Of course; bread was the opium of the people.
> Would he remember that and would it make sense in the day-
> light? Bread is the opium of the people.

The true meaning of Hemingway's dominant artistic mood
becomes clear. The emphasis on frenzied action which characterizes his work is merely the masculine counterpart of the
passive emphasis on opiates, until all forms of life are seen as
themselves drugs to soothe us rather than any sort of stimulant
toward knowledge, or intelligent behavior. Whatever we may
try to do, or be, is in the end an action to avoid the fact. And
this passage anticipates too the final 'solution' of Hemingway's

conflicts, caught as he is between the major working of his temperament toward the destructive instincts of man and the restraints of his spirit which apparently prevent him from following through this effort to any full conclusion. In 'A Clean, Well-Lighted Place' Hemingway reaches this solution in another of these magnificent, despairing passages. It is late in the café where the story takes place. The old man who is drunk wants to stay on. The young waiter is impatient, but the other waiter agrees with the old man. 'I too,' the other waiter says, 'am of those who like to stay late at the café. . . . With all those who do not want to go to bed. With all those who need a light for the night.' And each night, the older waiter continues, he is reluctant to close the café because there may be someone who needs it —

> 'Hombre, there are bodegas open all night long.'
>
> 'You do not understand. This is a clean and pleasant café. It is well lighted. The light is very good, and also, now, there are shadows of the leaves.'
>
> 'Good night,' said the younger waiter.

'Good night,' the older waiter says, and he, like the Frazer of the previous story, continues the discussion in his own mind:

> 'It is the light of course but it is necessary that the place be clean and pleasant. You do not want music. Certainly you do not want music. Nor can you stand before a bar with dignity although that is all that is provided for these hours. What did he fear? It was not fear or dread. It was a nothing that he knew too well. It was all a nothing and a man was nothing too. It was only that and light was all it needed and a certain cleanness and order. Some lived in it and never felt it but he knew it all was nada y pues nada y nada y pues nada. Our nada who art in nada, nada be thy name thy kingdom nada thy will be nada in nada as it is in nada. Give us this nada our daily nada and nada us our nada we nada our nadas and nada us not into nada but deliver us from nada; pues nada. Hail nothing full of nothing, nothing is with thee. He smiled and stood before a bar with a shining steam pressure coffee machine.'
>
> 'What's yours?' asked the barman.
>
> 'Nada.'

But the 'nada' is not in itself a clear or positive solution. It has been the considered verdict of many other writers, starting with Ecclesiastes, whom in so many respects our Hemingway resembles, that life is vain. Yet it has never been with the others so causelessly, so completely vain, a nothingness so blind and so blank: a despair without past or future, both so artistically incomparable and intellectually incomprehensible. We have noticed the apparent increase of Hemingway's conflict as in his work he came steadily closer to the central meaning of it. We must conclude that he was unable to follow through his direction. For the true illumination of the destructive impulses in life, he has substituted the emphasis on meaningless action, the reliance on the drugged consciousness to avoid thought, and now the final nada — the emptiness which covers the frustration of the writer who is unable to cope with his true material. This is the opiate of the spirit which, unable to reach solutions for its own turmoil, projects itself outward to declare that the world itself offers nothing to be solved. This is the nada which denies meaning because it has been unable to discover it: the nada which is a final spiritual death of the writer who for so long has been searching for the secrets of death.

For with Hemingway's nada we come to the conclusion of his safari into the wilderness of our life alone. Beyond war and peace, the collective organisms of security, beyond continents and customs, our discoveries, songs, laws, and loves, here is the solution offered us by our author in his pursuit of meaning, and like Ring Lardner so richly endowed with life's favors. 'Hail nothing, full of nothing, nothing is with thee.' And in his next novel, 'To Have and Have Not,' in 1937, Hemingway carries the lesson of 'A Clean, Well-Lighted Place' to its own end. Here in turn is a nothingness gone brutal, callous. 'To Have and Have Not' offers a portrait of suffering in which the writer has given up his attempt to understand suffering. The book is a sort of apotheosis of stale horror, a Walpurgis-night of delirious and sadistic orgies within a strictly ignoble framework. It might be difficult to reconcile this destruction, both so extravagant and trivial, with the careful and deep work of Hemingway at his best, if we did not realize that 'To Have and Have Not' is in this respect the last point of Hemingway's long isolation and rebellion. It is a release of the blocked and despairing temperament; but a release that is a surrender. The literary mind no longer wishes to understand or control itself. The all-consuming sense of nothingness has at last struck at the temperament which has been so beautifully projecting it. And in this way the lessening of Hemingway's craft which marks 'To Have and Have Not' seems to add to the total disillusionment of the novel. It is almost as if the final remaining stability of the writer, his art, so brilliant, so magnificent, always so much the product of an iron will, as if his art itself had now crumbled before the advancing corrosion of his thesis. And why should it not? Surely the nada which applied to all life must also apply to the art which records life?

Yet we notice that after these many years of solitary struggle, 'To Have and Have Not' is placed within the setting of the modern United States. 'You could always come back,' the African Hemingway said of the America he was deserting, and now he has. The biographer of the matador, the artist of Parisian cafés, the hunter of kudus, has returned from foreign boulevards and savage hills. With his return to the boundaries of states and societies, to all the social complexity he had renounced, we realize that 'To Have and Have Not' represents a crisis novel for Hemingway. Like the 'Mice and Men' of John Steinbeck, as we shall see a little later, this novel of negation is both a death and a resurrection.

4. NO MAN ALONE.   Hemingway's temperament is thus curiously contradictory; yet when we look for its causes we find they are more than temperamental. The interpretation of him as the war novelist seems inadequate to explain the deep ten-

sions of his art. And in the midst of our preoccupation with him as a unique personality, we may not ignore the sociological pressures antecedent to the war which helped to form this personality. We must remember that Hemingway is one of the few writers of the depths — of the buried forces of guilt, destruction, and death, our primitive impulses, the inversions and psychic aberrations, which we have been treating — to emerge from the American tradition: from our modern industrial ethics which, as we saw with Ring Lardner and will see again with Thomas Wolfe, reinforced the harsh mould of our puritan, pioneer, and provincial patterns.

In our past and present literature, indeed, we can think of few Americans to compare with Hemingway in his intention and achievement. Through our eagerness to compensate for the lack of these deeper values in our heritage we have, I believe, rather overinterpreted Herman Melville. Edgar Allan Poe, concerned with many of Hemingway's themes, and so becoming the model of the French Symbolists while relatively ignored in America, was often condemned to a false release of his talent. Hawthorne is in many ways perhaps the closest of these to Hemingway — with his 'cloudy veil' which stretched 'over the abyss of my nature.' And Hawthorne, arousing our intense interest with his studies of guilt and expiation, does not strike at our feelings, as Hemingway surely does. It is interesting to notice that these three who most closely perhaps approach Hemingway's métier are working somewhat apart from the strict American pioneer culture and before the deep impression of contemporary industrial society.

That both of these cultural pressures left their mark on the early Hemingway, 'The Torrents of Spring,' his second work, provides us with sufficient proof. Usually ignored, certainly the weakest of his books, 'The Torrents of Spring' is nevertheless one of the most illuminating in respect to Hemingway's creative motivation, for it provides us with an unequivocal judgment on the America of Hemingway's youth. Often uncertain in its satiric touch, the novel is a sort of mélange of Hemingway's

early aversions, pertinent and irrelevant, deep or trivial. The
somewhat infantile, the smart, the snobbish elements which dis-
turb Hemingway's work are shown here. What concerns us
primarily, however, is the novel's portrait of the American ethics.
Scripps O'Neil, the hero, travels amongst the paraphernalia of
the industrial age. He meditates profoundly, though with no
appreciable effect, upon the locomotive, the barber shop, the telegraph office, the dynamo. In his youth he remembers being
entranced by a fascinating electric sign in three colors: 'Let
Hartman Feather Your Nest.' Feathering his nest to Scripps is
making money. 'Ah yes, there was big money to be made in the
furniture business if you knew how to go about it. He, Scripps,
knew all the wrinkles of that game.' As with Ring Lardner, the
Success Myth of the twenties has transformed our national spirit
into this sterile refrain. 'Ah, these drummers,' Scripps thinks,
meeting a salesman who to him is the essence of our culture —

> Going up and down over the face of this great America of ours.
> These drummers kept their eyes open. They were no fools.
> 'Listen,' the drummer said. He pushed his derby hat off his
> brow and leaning forward, spat into the tall brass cuspidor that
> stood beside his stool. 'I want to tell you about a pretty beautiful
> thing that happened to me once in Bay City.'

Ironic echo of the American fate which Thomas Wolfe was to
redeem from this context and return to us! And again Scripps,
or Hemingway, meditates on the great sweep of America:

> Near there Gary, Indiana, where were the great steel mills.
> Near there Hammond, Indiana. Near there Michigan City,
> Indiana. Further beyond, there would be Indianapolis, Indiana,
> where Booth Tarkington lived. He had the wrong dope, that
> fellow. Further down there would be Cincinnati, Ohio.... Ah!
> there was grand sweep to this America of ours.

But this 'grand sweep' of our land, we know very well, is in the
end limited to steel mills, flashing electric signs, the furniture
business, drummers, Indiana metropolises, and Booth Tarkington. Scripps works in the 'Peerless Pounder Pump' factory.

He dines at Brown's Beanery, 'Best by Test.' After 'an endless succession of days of dull piston-collaring,' he meets a strange waitress; together they pursue the life of the mind, and fall in love. But there are no decent human relationships possible in this social context, according to the young Hemingway. Though Scripps finds his best friends among the Indians, even these primitives, we realize, have been affected by the blight of the machine age. If Hemingway has often returned to his Michigan scene with tenderness, that of 'The Torrents of Spring' has been corrupted by the factory. The American earth itself — the primal forest, the virgin land whose quality Hemingway catches so beautifully in his Michigan stories, the fishing streams and woodland haunts, the scenes of his young hunting and reading and drinking and early loves — has yielded its nourishment to feed the new mechanical colossus whose body tends the conveyor belt and whose spirit is absorbed in the fabrication of such dazzling electric advertisements. Perhaps it was not 'the passing of a great race' which Hemingway tells us is mourned by 'The Torrents of Spring.' But it was certainly for Hemingway the passing of the American land he had so early loved and which, now under the imprint of industrial society, he was here renouncing.

This background, so closely affecting his youth as Hemingway shows it, was obviously no support for the work he was intent upon. The American physical effort, so Hemingway felt here, was too much like Scripps O'Neil's 'endless succession of days of dull piston-collaring.' The America of spiritual effort was too much like Brown's Beanery, the 'best by test' perhaps, but hardly sufficient for the artist of the depths. The American background denied Hemingway by and large the values which he needed for his exploration of the deeper instincts of man. When we notice in Hemingway's work the persistent impulses toward Catholicism, these impulses denied, tormented and recurrent, the issue becomes clearer. For the ethics of Catholicism include the elements of human nature which are omitted by Hemingway's own American environment. Thus

Hemingway is in a state of creative ambivalence. He is the writer concerned with the shadows and enigmas of man's life, arising from the American tradition outlined in 'The Torrents of Spring' — tougher, harder, practical, more elementary in its values, less observant of the areas of human motivation with which Hemingway is concerned, perhaps more 'sensible' and certainly less truthful. He is the writer close to the final mysteries of life who comes out of the society which has exploited the Indian and exalted the Engine.

That Hemingway was himself aware of this in his later work as well as in 'The Torrents of Spring' we recall from his statement that the Spaniards 'are interested in death and do not spend their lives avoiding the thought of it and hoping it does not exist.' Unlike the Americans. Yet we remember also the uneasy and evasive tone of this realization: Hemingway's inability to state the full nature of his own concerns. His American background, not only unequal to his demands as a writer, was often indeed in direct opposition to it. It not only withheld from him the freedom of thought, the knowledge, the spiritual values which he needed for his central purpose. It increased, I believe, the actual conflict we have noticed in his work. The repressions which seem to block Hemingway from the full comprehension of his material have, of course, a particularly 'American' ring to them. They too echo a society which, with its emphasis on work and material achievement, had little time for these disturbing factors of our behavior. American society has uneasily pushed Hemingway's problems away from its own consciousness in the hope, perhaps, often like that of Hemingway himself, that by ignoring them we may solve them. (Even now, I dare say, we may consider the dominant concerns of Hemingway's work as rather more 'Russian' than American.) That Hemingway must break away from his native tradition was inevitable. But then it had already conditioned him more perhaps than he realized; and that working in exile as he did, he could only reach his ultimate purpose in fragmentary, if sometimes quite superb forms, seems almost as inevitable.

The conviction of 'The Torrents of Spring,' moreover — that the meanings of life with which Hemingway was dealing lie outside of the American framework — persists through his work. In 'A Very Short Story,' which was the early outline for 'A Farewell to Arms,' the original hero comes to an ignominious end in the United States:

> A short time after he contracted gonorrhea from a salesgirl in a loop department store while riding in a taxicab through Lincoln Park.

This, we see, is the American equivalent for the love of Lieutenant Henry and Catherine Barkley, so warm and rich and touching on a foreign shore! Or if Hemingway will grant us the echoes of genuine tragedy in 'One Reader Writes,' it is a tragedy that is incoherent and unaware. 'Maybe he can tell me what's right to do,' the heroine thinks, after writing to a newspaper columnist about her husband's syphilis:

> Maybe he can tell me. In the picture in the paper he looks like he'd know. He looks smart, all right. . . . He ought to know. I want to do whatever is right. It's such a long time though. It's a long time. And it's been a long time. My Christ, it's been a long time.

It was a long time, too, between 'The Torrents of Spring' and 'To Have and Have Not' where Hemingway returns to the American scene — the decade of rebellion and exile which we have been tracing. Yet in his second novel on the United States, the quality of Hemingway's American reaction remains essentially the same. Here indeed he renders his harshest judgment on the past patterns of our society, summarized perhaps in his statement on American love as the focus for our human relationships. 'Love is the greatest thing, isn't it?' says Richard Gordon's wife in the novel:

> Slop. Love is just another dirty lie. Love is ergoapiol pills to make me come around because you were afraid to have a baby. Love is quinine and quinine and quinine until I'm deaf with it. Love is that dirty aborting horror that you took me to. Love is my

insides all messed up. It's half catheters and half whirling douches. I know about love. Love always hangs up behind the bathroom door. It smells like lysol. To hell with love.

The happiest of Hemingway's human relationships has no happy end, we know, the most intense as well as the most transient of them resulting alike in the inevitable nada. Yet it is doubtful whether anywhere else in his work Hemingway's conception of a human passion is quite as frightful as this, so mechanical and sterile, detached from all human feeling. The 'rummies' and 'vets' who fill the pages of 'To Have and Have Not' are another illustration of the American tragedy which is perhaps best described in the legalistic phrase as 'incompetent, irrelevant, and immaterial.' But the sharpest example of its essentially broken nature comes with the Mrs. Tracy of the novel. Her husband brought home to her dead, she screams, 'Albert! Albert! Oh, my God, where's Albert?' In her despair and agitation she falls off the dock into the water, loses her dental plate, emerges to wail: 'Basards! Bishes!... Alber. Whersh Alber?'

It seems evident that in Hemingway's search for the dark and tragic abysses of the human spirit, there was no place for his work in America. And the only positive Hemingway could find to place against the power of the destructive instincts, the sense of man's dignity which was realized in the Spanish matador, also did not reside in America's commercial order. With Hemingway as with Lardner, the American meaning is blurred, bathos too often supplanting sorrow. 'I losht my plate,' says Mrs. Tracy in the midst of her tragedy. What single image could better convey Hemingway's judgment than this, itself so Lardnerian in tone? And for Hemingway it is our national dental plate, as it were, which has been swept away by the flowing and unperturbed waters of the Gulf Stream. In this respect the American nada is emptier than any other. Whatever has been in it of man's struggle, his courage, dignity, and grand style, transient at best and inevitably doomed, is here rendered indistinct by the prevailing pattern of our society.

Here in America the rare and few accents of humanity's divine articulation have been reduced to a sort of grotesque mumbling.

The similarity of Hemingway's verdict with Lardner's, extending even into the quality of their imagery, is of course marked. Is it curious that these two of the distinguished talents of '29, and in some ways two such distinct talents, should come to an identical agreement on their time? It is illuminating. And with other corroborations, both in these writers and their successors, it is almost conclusive. For it is essentially the ethics of the twenties which Hemingway is dealing with in 'To Have and Have Not.' This is still the Florida of Lardnerian millionaires, playboys, and yachtsmen, so grimly intent on entertainment. In this framework Hemingway places his protagonist Harry Morgan. Morgan fights to make a living for himself and his family against the encroaching forces of the depression. Single-handed he plays against the odds, living out in his own struggle the individualistic code of the '29 era. But his career is an ever-sharpening disintegration. Morgan's jobs grow more dangerous; he himself grows more reckless; his final defeat is implicit, although the manner of it may still shock us. The individualistic motivation fails him. And in a scene which is saturated with the orgiastic destruction marking the novel, Morgan pronounces his final words on his own struggle. Shot in a fight with Cuban revolutionaries, he has been rescued by a Coast Guard cutter. The men standing around him are trying to learn the facts of the shooting. 'A man,' Morgan says —

'Sure,' said the captain. 'Go on.'

'A man,' said Harry Morgan, very slowly. 'Ain't got no hasn't got any can't really isn't any way out.' . . .

'Go on, Harry,' said the captain. 'Tell us who did it. How did it happen, boy?' . . .

'Who did it, Harry?' the mate asked.

Harry looked at him.

'Don't fool yourself,' he said. The captain and the mate both bent over him. Now it was coming. 'Like trying to pass cars on the top of hills. On that road in Cuba. On any road. Any-

where. Just like that. I mean how things are. The way that
they been going. For a while yes sure all right. Maybe with
luck. A man.' He stopped. The captain shook his head at the
mate again. Harry Morgan looked at him flatly. The captain
wet Harry's lips again. They made a bloody mark on the towel.

'A man,' Harry Morgan said, looking at them both. 'One man
alone ain't got. No man alone now.' He stopped. 'No matter
how a man alone ain't got no bloody . . . chance.'

He shut his eyes. It had taken him a long time to get it out
and it had taken him all of his life to learn it.

With these words, of course, Hemingway might have been
passing judgment on the egotistic morality of '29 which Harry
Morgan embodied; on all the Lardnerian unique individuals.
The last quarter of the novel, indeed, dealing with the Lardnerian aristocrats of the prosperity decade, is a superb satirical
elegy on the passing of the age: Wallace Johnston, a yachtsman
who had originally defrauded Harry Morgan, '38 years old,
M.A. Harvard, composer, money from silk mills, unmarried,
interdit de séjour in Paris, well known from Algiers to Biskra.'
His guest, Henry Carpenter, '36, M.A. Harvard, money now
two hundred a month in trust fund from his mother, formerly
four hundred and fifty a month,' who 'with his rather special
pleasures' is now postponing 'his inevitable suicide by a matter
of weeks if not of months.' The sixty-year-old grain merchant
who lies awake, on his handsome, black, barkentine-rigged
threemaster, worrying about the report from the Internal Rev-
enue Bureau which is pronouncing the end of his sensational
success as a speculator. — These and others of the American
industrial élite are showing the ravages worked on their lives by
the new age of crisis. And their decline is marked in a memorable epitaph for '29:

> Some made the long drop from the apartment or the office win-
> dow; some took it quietly in two-car garages with the motor run-
> ning; some used the native tradition of the Colt or Smith and
> Wesson; those well-constructed implements that end insomnia,
> terminate remorse, cure cancer, avoid bankruptcy, and blast an

exit from intolerable positions by the pressure of a finger; those
admirable American instruments so easily carried, so sure of
effect, so well designed to end the American dream when it becomes a nightmare, their only drawback the mess they leave for
relatives to clean up.

Thus the final word on the unique and miraculous age of material power which Lardner and his fellows had thought so
absolute and eternal. Lardner's nightmare had preceded that
of his time by only a few short years.

'To Have and Have Not,' then, records the disintegration of
Lardner's age of individualism. But for Hemingway the novel
is critical in a double sense. Simultaneously, as the first of his
new works dealing with modern social problems, it records
Hemingway's farewell to the solitary course he himself has been
pursuing. 'No matter how a man alone ain't got no bloody
chance.' With these words also Hemingway might have been
judging his own decade of isolation. In this respect 'To Have
and Have Not' is the projection into artistic form of Hemingway's personal struggle, and the decision of the writer to move
henceforth in new directions. Equally with his protagonist
Harry Morgan, Hemingway might say it has taken him a long
time to deliver such a verdict upon his own life, upon his own
single-handed revolt against country and culture and the continents of man's work. Like Morgan, Hemingway has also been
'the man alone.' And now, seeing the error of his isolation, he
may almost say in turn that, if his judgment was long in coming,
'it had taken him all his life to learn it.'

With the return of the expatriate artist and the rebellious
individualist to the land of his birth and the patterns of society,
we may ask ourselves how much of the frustration which
marked the end of Hemingway's isolation was emphasized by
the solitary nature of his search. In themselves, as we know, all
such explorations as Hemingway's of the destructive impulses
of human nature are very delicate. Our normal ignorance of
these forces and our normal desire to remain in ignorance are
perhaps dictated in part by Nature's long-tried wisdom. For

most of us it is safer here as elsewhere to know too little rather than too much. And when such explorations are conducted, as by Hemingway, with no balancing forces of culture and country, it is little wonder the stress upon the artist becomes acute, the despair more pronounced, the sense of human weakness in the face of such enigmas greater. We may wonder how much of the futility, the lack of meaning in life which Hemingway summarized so eloquently in his nada, was not merely the product of his own inability to reach these meanings, but also of his sense that there was no purpose in reaching them? How much of the emptiness he saw before him in man's life was in fact the emptiness he felt behind him in his own life?

There are, moreover, other even more curious connections between the writer and the society he had repudiated. It is somewhat ironic to realize that in his total rejection of it Hemingway seems often to embody the fundamental motivation of post-war America. What is Hemingway's complete individualism as an artist but the extension of that which marked Lardner's commercial egotist? The 'I' which for so many years was the single star to guide Hemingway over foreign boulevards and African jungles is not, after all, very different from the self-absorption of the typical man of America's boom era. The artistic métier was simply replacing the economic. In the method of his renunciation Hemingway bears the sign of the society he is renouncing. Disowning his social and his human obligations in favor of 'art,' Hemingway was in the end very close to the business man of the twenties who spoke in similar terms of his own commercial achievement. There is a distinction, obviously, between Hemingway's genuine devotion to his craft and that of Lardner's commercial superman to himself. Yet this qualifies rather than alters the essential similarity of their patterns. The illimitable desert of pure individualism is the same wherever its boundaries may lie. Even the artist may not pursue the rich fruits of his unique temperament too far. In the midst of the 'I' there must still be the 'we.' He, like the rest of humanity, must lose his soul to save it.

And that in his method of opposition to his age often Hemingway proves himself typical of it is, I think, clear. The rejection of the American twenties need not imply, as it did with Hemingway, the rejection of America. The rebellion against one society does not necessarily imply a rebellion against all society. In Hemingway's apparent ignorance of this, his feeling so much like Lardner's that such a transient age as '29 was permanent, in the extremes of his reaction into almost total isolation, Hemingway is characteristic. And in the failure of his total individualism, however spiritual its objectives, we may see the final comment on the Lardnerian epoch. What could certainly never 'work' in the sphere of material achievement (we use the terms of American pragmatism by intention) could not work either in the realm of the spirit. This is the last and most profound death of '29: the true end of the age's egotism.

And so our rebellious, anti-social, and uniquely aesthetic individual, the artist Hemingway, must be viewed as something of a sociological phenomenon even at the moment of his total escape from society. It is usually so. The more desperately we shake off the chains of our humanity, the more they cling to us. No one is of no value to society however much he may try to be. Attempt as we may to cut through it, the circle of our human heritage moves around us. The omniscient Lord of the mediaevalists, scrutinizing every little blade of grass as well as monarchs of the realm, was merely the materialization of man's growing perception of the indivisibility of man. Yet if Hemingway reached the end of '29 in his own flight from it, he came back to record the age's death and his new birth. In 'To Have and Have Not' the rebel returned to all the human works he had condemned. And from now on Hemingway will deal with the crucial aspects of the contemporary world he has so often, and often so brilliantly, negated. His next novel and the play which formed its prologue show a major reorientation of his values. As the outlines of the prosperity decade gave place to those of exile, these in turn have brought us to a new social framework. So in his own career Hemingway will illustrate the

transition of the American writer in the depression of the nineteen-thirties, the turning from Ring Lardner's dead-end toward
new beliefs.

5. RETURN OF THE NATIVES.   It is within the entire
pattern of Hemingway's renunciation, exile, and return that his
latest and most popular novel, 'For Whom the Bell Tolls,' must
be appraised. Its limitations come directly out of the series of
crises and transitions which have marked Hemingway to this
point, his career embracing so much spiritual ·turbulence and
seeming to include in it the decisions of an entire generation.

For when we compare 'For Whom the Bell Tolls' with comparable works of its own genre, the revolutionary novels of
André Malraux, for example, or the anti-Fascist work of
Ignazio Silone, the difference in quality becomes apparent.
'For Whom the Bell Tolls' hardly reaches into the depths and
nuances of its theme. The protagonist of the novel, Robert
Jordan, is fighting for 'the dignity of man,' for the Spanish Loy-
alists against the oppressive forces of native and foreign Fascism. But beyond the broad outlines of the Spanish Civil War,
we are given relatively little of the impact of the struggle in
either sociological or personal terms. Malraux's 'Man's Fate,'
Silone's 'Bread and Wine,' or lately Arthur Koestler's 'Darkness at Noon' — these works are filled with penetrating insights
on the patterns of social crisis, the gains and losses worked by
such crisis upon the human temperament, the problems of human behavior today when individuals and societies are making
inestimable decisions as to the future. Silone's 'School for Dictators,' again, reveals the background of specialized thinking
which both the Frenchman and the Italian have poured into
their human narrative. By contrast, the new concern of Hemingway with this material often seems romantic or immature
for the writer of a major work of art. How could this not be

true, after Hemingway's long isolation from precisely this sort
of material? He has shown us his contempt for the 'politics' or
the 'economics' or the great sociological movements which form
the background for his new novel. Everything we might say on
this issue, in fact, is admitted by the protagonist of 'For Whom
the Bells Tolls.' The Spanish Civil War is his education, Robert
Jordan continually emphasizes. 'It is part of one's education. It will be quite an education when it's finished. You
learn in this war if you listen. You most certainly did.' In
terms of Hemingway's own development we may surmise that
the Spanish War was also a central part of his own education, or
re-education, as a member of society. As the returning individualist, the knowledge which Hemingway gained often seems
too new, too complex and foreign for him to integrate fully into
the artistic structure of 'For Whom the Bell Tolls.' And the
strain of his transition from the rebellious individualist seems
to interfere with Hemingway's artistic achievement. Robert
Jordan is not only an untutored apprentice, he is more or less
undistinguished. Maria is on the whole more theatrical than
substantial. She is a sort of compendium of the virtues of the
modern proletarian mistress. She emerges to the heights of romance from the depths of the class-struggle. Yet despite the
horrors heaped upon her and the fortitude with which she bears
them, she is in the end hardly as appealing as some of Hemingway's more typical, vain, trivial, and quite useless leisure-class
ladies.

The merit of 'For Whom the Bell Tolls' often resides, in fact,
in the material which Hemingway has previously dealt with.
The Spanish peasants and anarchists, the bullfighters and bandits — these lesser personages hold us where the major figures
fail. So too in the novel there are the familiar forces of Hemingway's despair, of the destruction which for so many years has
preoccupied him. If he is now fighting for the good life, Jordan
is nevertheless surrounded by the omens of death which marked
the doomed protagonist of 'The Snows of Kilimanjaro.' The
pillaging of the Fascist town is more coldly brutal perhaps than

any previous episode in Hemingway's work. The dynamiting of the bridge, which forms the plot of 'For Whom the Bell Tolls,' is hardly a creative act to begin with. And progressively more frustrating, it becomes an act of complex destruction worthy of the best Hemingway of the past. As Hemingway used the framework of the First World War to project his own emotional tensions, here again he often finds the destruction and death marking the Spanish War appropriate for his present concern with these negative forces of our temperament. And certainly in the ethics and practices of civil war he finds many suitable outlets.

Yet in the past, if Hemingway's expression of these elements was sometimes limited, its purpose was clear. Here it is ambiguous. At the center of 'For Whom the Bell Tolls' there is a basic confusion of Hemingway's intention. The novel attempts to be a constructive statement on human life. Yet Hemingway's underlying sense of destruction often contradicts this. As the story progresses, in fact, the older Hemingway accents of futility seem to increase. The 'yes' of Robert Jordan is progressively minimized by the submerged nada of his creator. Hemingway is thus still apparently caught between his previous and future purposes. Intellectually, his affirmation of man and his life have become clear, but his emotions have not altogether accepted the mind's dictate. The patterns of negative belief which Hemingway has built up over his long period of isolation are not so easy to modify: the nada has left its imprint upon Hemingway's new positives. The conversion of our writer in crisis is, after all, not quite so simple. We can hardly remake the temperament of a lifetime by a single affirmation, however insistent, or loud. As we see in Hemingway's novel, the buried feelings may yet use, despite all our good intentions, our new intellectual transformation for their older purpose. This then is the last and most crucial dilemma for Hemingway's future, and that of some of his followers in the new period. Here is the last price that the prosperity era of American post-war society has demanded of its high talent — this luxury time, so

splendid in materialistic vanity, so unique and changeless in its
own eyes, priceless, and demanding such a high price of its
artists; casting the blight of its gilded glory over its writers even
in the midst of the new age of chaos which rang out its dazzling
and empty splendor. 'You could always come back,' but you
also paid for the trip.

Yet, stating this of Hemingway — and this is, I believe, the
crux of his future work — and of 'For Whom the Bell Tolls,' we
do not intend to minimize the book, its effect on its society, or,
with these limitations, its importance in the growth of Hemingway himself. If the novel remains inchoate in its comprehension of the central social issues of our time, and sometimes inarticulate in its expression of them, it represents nevertheless a
transitional step beyond that of 'To Have and Have Not' and
the embryonic 'Fifth Column.' And this third step on the path
of Hemingway's return to humanity expresses the possibilities
inherent in Hemingway. If the study of the individualist Pablo
remains perhaps the most effective single portrait in the novel,
it is nevertheless a study of Pablo's conflict between self and
society: a new theme for Hemingway, a rich theme for the
artist who in his former period hardly considered such a thesis
worthy of attention. With Pablo's statement after his desertion
from his fellow Spaniards ('Having done such a thing there is a
loneliness that cannot be borne') we perceive that Hemingway,
the advocate of Lieutenant Henry's desertion at Caporetto
with no such conflict, has come near to the source of much of
his own previous feeling of corrosive solitude. In General Golz,
again, Hemingway has achieved the outlines of a genuine
tragic protagonist — Golz who ends the novel still 'believing
in how things could be, even if they never were,' and who
replies, on being told the Spanish offensive is futile: 'Bon. Nous
ferons notre petit possible.'

These are close to the potentialities of Hemingway's reorientation of values. We are not asking that he become a rotarian
optimist or a party propagandist. Yet the true sense of man's
depths and his tragedy, first denied to Hemingway by the social

patterns of '29 and then in turn thwarted by his isolation, the tragedy of Ecclesiastes which at his best Hemingway so magnificently approaches, is possible only within the framework of man's effort. The supreme renunciation of The Preacher himself came, not from any withdrawal from experience, but from the middle of it. It was the verdict on man's struggle, not on its absence. And that this sense of high tragedy has been conspicuously missing from much modern art may lie precisely in the fact that Hemingway, like other moderns, could not find the materials for genuine tragedy in the '29 era, nor ultimately in isolation. With his return now to the common fate and the common lot Hemingway is thus enriching the potentialities of his work.

And if as yet much of this transformation of Hemingway manifests itself in merely intellectual affirmations, what surprising affirmations they are! It is Anselmo — the sweet man of peace in the midst of the war's horrors, the soldier who wishes to convert all and shoot none, Anselmo who is perhaps the purest example of the basic tenderness of Hemingway, so often twisted and warped into bitterness and here freed — who most sharply contrasts the old and the new Hemingway as he rebukes the guerrilla leader, Pablo:

> Now we come for something of consummate importance and thee, with thy dwelling place to be undisturbed, puts thy fox-hole before the interests of humanity.

A strange statement indeed for our own writer individualist, our hunter in the lonesome hills, the despairing spectator of man's fruitless struggle; the tormented follower of fiestas who eschewed the sweat of comrades on the battlefield for his African solitude; who consigned our works and loves and willing achievement to waters of oblivion for the residence in his own fox-hole of abstract art. The interests of humanity! A curious conclusion to be born from the passing of '29's industrial fiesta, its own savage jungles of commercial ethics and floridian paradises: the interests of humanity rising from the death of an age where interest meant only dividends, and humanity was the material for exploitation.

Whatever the imperfections of 'For Whom the Bell Tolls,' it must be seen as the decisive step in Hemingway's circuit of escape from the trap of the American twenties. Doing this, Hemingway has illustrated the direction of our writers in the thirties from Ring Lardner's impasse to new beliefs which are themselves based on the elements of social conflict whose culmination Hemingway has recorded in terms of the Spanish scene — beliefs, however erratic or extreme, or, as with Hemingway, imperfectly fulfilled, which are to be the dominant tradition of the new age of American expression in crisis. And it is no coincidence that with Hemingway the first step of his transformation took place in 'To Have and Have Not' which simultaneously recorded the end of the prosperity era. The death of '29 accomplished what apparently its life could not. To Hemingway and his successors whom we are now about to discuss, the American depression, changing the face of our culture within a decade, came as a sort of salvation. Making the writers of the thirties aware of the transience of our materialistic power which they had felt so inimical to creative values, the crisis gave them new directions. Like Hemingway they were willing to return to a society in chaos where, in one form or another, they had fled from its aspect of permanence. For chaos implied transition. And the transition held in it the hope, at least, of a new system of social values less rigid and less empty than those of the twenties. The cultural optimism of '29 produced the nothingness of Lardner and the early Hemingway. The crisis of the thirties brought in the new faith of the later Hemingway, Wolfe, Dos Passos, Steinbeck, a rising cycle of belief in our future, a restatement of the vision of Jefferson and Lincoln rather than that of Jay Gould and Henry Ford. The dissolution of our material splendor cut away, for the first time in a century quite so sharply, the spiritual blight which the advent of the industrial order laid, in 1860, upon these earlier meanings of American society. Filled as it was with social distress, the new era was to be one of spiritual affirmatives.

The depression of the nineteen-thirties was thus a sort of shock to our writers, rather like the insulin treatment in modern therapy, which brought them back from the shadows of apathy to American life at best, and active hostility at worst. This much of the expression of the thirties Hemingway anticipates in his own withdrawal and return to our common life, though the pattern will vary with our other literary figures, and with John Dos Passos and William Faulkner we have both an apparent exception to the rule and a real one. But we cannot deny that if the return to social sanity through shock is better than no return, it is in the end a method of desperation rather than a counsel of perfection. Our Americans are also to show its effect in their work of the decade, as Hemingway has already. The crisis of the new age has caught him well along in his career. Can he discover, who has discovered so much and left much unsaid, the genuine method of unifying his work and his times, the fusion of the 'I' and the 'we' which will further illuminate the tragic impulses he has made his own? We recall the phrase which summarized Hemingway's solitary position: 'a way you'll never be.' With such native capacities, the inheritance of wisdom and eloquence, the sense of bottomless intuitions we often have with Hemingway, the prophetic texture which marks his talent, will Hemingway now find a way to be? For what a marvelous teacher Hemingway is, with all the restrictions of temperament and environment which so far define his work! What could he not show us of living as well as dying, of the positives in our being as well as our destroying forces, of 'grace under pressure' and the grace we need with no pressures, of ordinary life-giving actions along with those superb last gestures of doomed exiles!

[handwritten marginalia:]
negative individualism → faith in the future

cultural optimism → "nada"
crisis → new faith

Chapter Three

John Dos Passos : CONVERSION OF A HERO

◇

1. THE RATIONAL MAN   2. THE FAILURE OF NERVE

3. AMERICAN RETURN   4. THE RADICAL HISTORIAN

5. OUR STORYBOOK DEMOCRACY

Chapter Three

John Dos Passos : CONVERSION OF A HERO

---

1. THE RATIONAL MAN.   'You were a fool, if you imagined yourself a rational man, to pray to God,' J. B. Priestley
has remarked, summarizing the movement of modern thought,
'then afterwards it turned out you were a fool even to imagine
yourself a rational man.' We have noticed with Hemingway
the buried depths, the dark and destructive intuitions of the
race within the artist. In contrast, John Dos Passos is the archetype of the rational writer within our tradition, the conscious,
moral, progressive writer, the embodiment, not of the destructive rebel, but of all our communal and civilizational aspirations.

The two Americans standing so at opposite poles of the
artist's function, it is interesting that both should start their
work at almost the same psychological, and precisely the same
geographical point. Both the early Dos Passos and Hemingway are motivated by the post-war disenchantment. There is,
as we shall see, the same central evocation of a detached and
remote hero drifting on the tides of social renunciation. Both
writers, retreating from the ethics of twentieth-century American society, found in Republican Spain the sense of pleasure,
vitality, of dignity in human life which their own land could
not apparently offer them. Spain, Hemingway's Spain of
fiestas and fishing streams, of pitchers of beer and, at night,
dancing to the pipes, of anarchists and ice-cold horchata, be-

came also the center of Dos Passos's early affections. But how soon the Spain of Dos Passos becomes distinct from Hemingway's Spain. While 'Death in the Afternoon,' in 1932, is talking of the matador, the 'Rosinante' of 1922 is already discussing the masses. From 'Rosinante' on the paths would separate — Hemingway throughout the major part of his career working deeper into the despairing and destructive emotions of the isolated individual, while Dos Passos turns outward to deal with the structure of society, the patterns of our communal life, the technics and ideals of social progress. Our study of Dos Passos then is the conversion of his early hero, the change of the writer's values, the education of Dos Passos as the radical critic of American culture — an education which will end by becoming profound and brilliant, distinct among the records of the contemporary novel. And if Hemingway, with his own conversion in the nineteen-thirties, illustrates the general movement of the American writer from exile and individualism to his place in our society, Dos Passos, a decade before, was in this as in so much else the true innovator and experimentalist.

The personal facts of Dos Passos's life can be summarized briefly. He was born in Chicago in 1896 — the Chicago with which the 'U.S.A.' trilogy opens, the symbol of the new American industrialism which lies at the center of Dos Passos's work. His mother came from a Maryland family, his father, a lawyer, Dos Passos tells us, 'was the son of a Portuguese immigrant.' The phrase is to be important in the development of the novelist, as now in his youth he travels to Mexico, England, Belgium, as he travels indeed through Harvard (there is little sense of belonging to the American college in the accounts Dos Passos gives us) and to the Spain where his education began. The record of war service, volunteer ambulance corps, Red Cross in Italy, the Medical Corps of the American army, is typical of his generation, as are perhaps the books which spring immediately from that experience. And the rest of this life to date — the European travels and American exploration, the Provincetown home, painting, translating, sailing, the 'regular and industrious working' — seems calm enough, producing as it does the novels of Dos Passos, so filled with stridence and turbulence, with cultural crisis and catastrophe: the novels which above any others have caught the stress of a tremendous young technology that is bursting apart the social structure of monopolistic capitalism; a social structure itself hardly past its gauche and violent adolescence; and now antiquated; no longer adequate to contain the American industrial genius.

But these autobiographical 'facts' of Dos Passos's history are hardly as important as others we shall deal with in the social education of the novelist we are now about to start: the evolution of our conscious, moral artist. And if with Hemingway we have stressed the power of the depths within us, let us now freely acknowledge that of the heights. Our age, discovering, has indeed glorified the unconscious, the twisted turnings, the aberrations and perversions of the buried psyche. Now in the work of Dos Passos we reaffirm the value of rational man. If we are cast in the mould of the diseased angel, we are angel as well as diseased; and the achieving ape has nevertheless achieved.

Yet, like the civilizing struggle itself against the brute instincts which drag us back, how difficult, particularly today, this rational view of life may be for the artist! And for the artist like Dos Passos, in particular, who expounds his view despite his own internal contradictions. His early hero undergoes a conversion. But we shall see in the history of Dos Passos how still the exile mocks the citizen, the social rebel thwarts the reformer, and how always seeking social positives Dos Passos is at his most eloquent as the artist of dissolution also. This seeker after Utopia is himself to be consumed by the fires of the Inferno. The Diogenes in modern dress among our novelists, looking for an honest society, examining the good of man over two decades of painful search, Dos Passos is not to be unaware of evil, and indeed of the merely contemptible traits of men.

2. THE FAILURE OF NERVE.   'Like the red flame of
the sunset ... the old exaltation, the old flame that would
consume to ashes all the lies in the world ... stirs and broods
in the womb of his grey lassitude.' Dos Passos is describing the
central figure of his first novel, the Martin Howe of 'One
Man's Initiation,' in 1920. On the next page of the novel we
hear the conversation of Martin's comrades in the American
army:

> 'See that guy ... he lost five hundred dollars at craps last
> night.'
> 'Some stakes.'

These tones, of course, sound more familiar. They are the
forerunners of many such discussions in the work of the later
Dos Passos, the harkenings of his American critique. And so
in the opening section of 'One Man's Initiation' the two worlds
of the novelist are sketched in — the inner spirit of Martin
Howe, aloof, sensitive, unhappy; and the outer scene of Dos
Passos's social realism, the society of gamblers, the big money,
the American stakes which are to form the major preoccupation of the mature novelist.

The relationship between these two worlds, however, is a
strange one. As the novel proceeds, we realize that Martin's
indignation is not primarily directed against the adjoining
scene of gambling which epitomizes the ordinary army life,
nor even, indeed, against the evils of the First World War
which the novel itself accentuates. Martin is not so much re-
belling against the war as by his temperament he seems in-
sulated from it. He seems hardly to participate in those basic
human activities for which even a young poet, we should
imagine, should feel some common desire. There is little effort on Martin's part, indeed, just to ignore the world around
him. He is exempt from its demands; his natural rôle is that of
passive remoteness. The center of his thoughts is the Gothic
abbey, near his hospital post in France, where Martin spends
his days meditating over a better past of culture and classics.

It is to the mediaeval past that Martin looks for his salvation, or to the sky itself perhaps:

> Might it not really be, he kept on asking himself, that the sky was a beneficent goddess who would stoop gently out of the infinite spaces and lift him to her breast, where he could lie amid the amber-fringed ruffles of cloud and look curiously down at the spinning ball of the earth?

And when Martin does reflect about the war, it is to remind us how pointless, absurd, vicious it is:

> God! if there were somewhere nowadays where you could flee from all this stupidity, from all this cant of governments, and this hideous reiteration of hatred, this strangling hatred!

What a curious origin this is, to be sure, for the social critique of Dos Passos, the radical novelist who will devote a major part of his work to the detailed scrutiny of precisely this 'cant of governments' from which his first hero seeks to flee!   And what a curious hero — the Martin Howe who muses about his own disappointments in the midst of the catastrophic destruction of the First World War. This stirring and brooding young man seeking refuge in his amber-fringed clouds, so engaged in the throes of incipience, hardly so much frustrated (since his desires have no focus) as agitated. Martin Howe, nevertheless, is to be typical, as Malcolm Cowley indicates in 'After the Genteel Tradition,' of a whole range of early Dos Passos protagonists.

The central thesis of 'Three Soldiers,' a year later in 1921, is still that of 'One Man's Initiation' — the impact of the war upon the sensibilities of the artistic individual; and John Andrews, the musician of the novel, is a more concrete elaboration of Martin Howe. It is just the sense of elaboration, however, which marks 'Three Soldiers' as an advance over Dos Passos's first novel, and particularly in the portrait of army life toward which Martin Howe is so disdainful. In the opening pages of the novel, when John Andrews is having his physical examination, we hear the voice of an army private monotonously typing out the case history of a discharged soldier:

> No... record of sexual dep... O hell, this eraser's no good!...
> pravity or alcoholism; spent... normal... youth on farm...

While Andrews is being prodded and poked, the recruiting sergeant is shouting at him, the voice at the typewriter continues:

> Scores ten years... in test **B**... Sen... exal ment... m-e-n-t-a-l-i-t-y that of a child of eight. Seems unable... to either... Goddam this man's writin'... Forgets to obey orders... Responds to no form of per... suasion. M-e-m-o-r-y, nil.

The cumulative effect of these moronic manifestations, the effort of the typist to spell them out, the ignominious position of Andrews, the stupidity of the sergeant, the total veneer almost of comedy given to the chronicle of low-grade man, mark one of the earliest memorable scenes of Dos Passos. 'Three Soldiers' brings us a new novelist who will use all the weapons of the mind in his portrayal of the social scene: these privates who spell out and live out their desolate histories in such halting accents, the ministers and 'Y' men, the relievers and radicals, the Southerners in the novel who are still waging their private war against their negro comrades, the officers, undertakers, taxi-drivers, and Harvard aesthetes who comprise the military organization in the A.E.F. — or perhaps rather the military disorganization. The panorama of army life in 'Three Soldiers' shows a fine range and vitality for a young novelist, as later the scenes of Parisian society often compel our admiration. And here too is the developing mixed tone of Dos Passos, the start of that juxtaposition of the ridiculous and the disastrous which will distinguish the social studies of the mature novelist. As a study of the World War itself, however, we must notice that if many of the military abuses which Dos Passos indicates are quite true, the point of view behind the novel is still primarily that of the special individual. Dos Passos has already broadened the base of his social critique by including the pathetic Italian boy Fuselli and the Southerner Chrisfield along with John Andrews as the central figures of the novel. But it is evident that while the writer's talent has gone into the social panorama, the ordinary types and facts of army life, all his sympathies still remain with the disdainful and superior musician.

If John Andrews, however, is still cast in the mould of Martin Howe, he has apparently reached a superior point of self-realization:

> He was sick of revolt, of thought, of carrying his individuality like a banner above the turmoil. This was much better, to let every-thing go, to stamp out his maddening desire for music, to humble himself into the mud of common slavery.

If the alternative to individualism seems hardly very glamor-ous, the Dos Passos hero has become more aware of his own traits. And with his wound and subsequent illness in 'Three Soldiers,' Andrews reaches a new decision. He will no longer be timid, fearful of consequences, he tells us, he will hence-forth 'live recklessly.' His effort toward a new life, moreover, is coupled with a new aspiration toward social progress:

> What right had a man to exist who was too cowardly to stand up for what he thought and felt . . . for everything that made him an individual apart from his fellows?

But we realize that Andrews still sees social progress in terms of rebels, anarchistic individuals, martyrs 'apart from their fellows.' How this new life of his seems always to swing back to its original premises! For a long while Andrews's determina-tion to be recklessly himself finds its culmination in the reading of Flaubert's 'Tentation de Saint Antoine.' It is difficult, in fact, for him to escape from the patterns of his past: the traits of isolation and retreat, of losing himself in dreams, in reading and reveries, rather than making companions, friends, or love relationships. Throughout 'Three Soldiers' Andrews is still characterized by his vague aspirations, and the inability to fulfill them. (His affairs with Jeanne and Geneviève Rod are surely artificial, and reveal the confusion of Andrews more than his passion.) So again we have Dos Passos's early concept of a hero, nerveless, passive, remote, so poetic, in his being; reminding us a little of his more famous prototype — the 'ultra-poetical, super-aesthetical out-of-the-way young man' whom Gilbert made into Bunthorne.

In 'A Pushcart at the Curb,' moreover, in 1922, this hero receives further illumination. How full, indeed, of classical and literary allusions is the early verse of Dos Passos — of mediaeval doges and marmosets, of Cybeles and Pans, Roman poets and Greek bronzes, of embarkments after Watteau and lines to Debussy, of literary ladies from Ishtar to Juliet! And how, despite these, the sense of solitude nevertheless marks this verse, human relationships turned into scholarly visions and literary feelings doing service for the natural emotions the poet is seeking. The note of the solitary grows more emphatic as the book progresses, and is emphasized by what appears to be a greater awareness of the poet as to his own temperament; by his regret for his own nature; an increasing self-disdain that is not far removed from distaste:

> Through all these years...
>> I have bruised my fingers on the windowbars
>> so many lives cemented and made strong

> While the bars stand strong, outside
>> the great procession of men's lives go past.
>> Their shadows squirm distorted on my wall.

And in 'Rosinante to the Road Again,' the first of Dos Passos's travel accounts, this process of self-realization grows stronger with the novelist. For here most sharply is the contrast of the two worlds of Dos Passos which have been paralleling each other, and in a sense struggling with each other, over these early years from 1917 to 1922.

There is again the interior world of the introspective solitary, the classical impulses and literary associations, the stiff, shy, aloof young men of these early novels. 'Telemachus,' the semi-fictional and semi-autobiographical narrator of the Spanish travels, by his name is the embodiment of this pattern, and by his behavior the illustration. It is the 'Lyaeus' of the book, his friend who seeks the real adventures in gaiety or vulgarity, human relationships, in love or purely carnal encounters. Telemachus steps aside, gazes enviously at Lyaeus, 'too free and easy' perhaps, but the object of admiration as well as disapprobation. How forced the traveler is through the personal sections of 'Rosinante,' the young Telemachus, so restrained, so awkward in his own attempts at adventures, searching for a reality he may receive only by hearsay, eager for life and yet seemingly always cheated in his quest for it! Yet we notice that Dos Passos himself, growing more aware, is correspondingly more satiric about the traits which mark his hero. What was solemnly recorded about Martin Howe is here narrated half in mockery. The youth Telemachus may be on a search 'for a father' as he tells us in true classical form. But he is undoubtedly on the road toward a modification of his own literary form. For now the early Dos Passos hero, breaking through his embryonic shell of refinement, is about to emerge as a new and very different figure.

Much of this change is foreshadowed in the alternate half of 'Rosinante,' the essays in which Dos Passos talks directly about Spanish society, as against the adolescent wanderings and chatterings of his Telemachus. There is a great difference between these admirable essays, so straight and thoughtful, and the confused sensibilities of the early Dos Passos hero. 'Is there much poverty in these parts?' the young Telemachus 'stiffly' asks a Spaniard, 'wanting to show that he too had the social consciousness.' But the Dos Passos who talks of Cordova, of Blasco Ibañez, of Antonio Machado's 'verse of places' (recalling the street scenes of 'A Pushcart at the Curb'), and of Miguel de Unamuno as a radical poet — this Dos Passos is neither stiff nor wanting to show us anything but the facts of Spanish society as he feels them. And he feels them very intensely. It is this Spain, we realize, which has first caught and

then released Dos Passos's major intelligence and emotion.
It is Spain, moreover, which now seems to give Dos Passos the
initial impetus toward the rôle he will assume in American
letters, as we see in his study of Pío Baroja, the novelist of revolution. Baroja's heroes, Dos Passos tells us, are no longer the
jolly knaves of the seventeenth and eighteenth centuries.
Rather —

> they are men who have not had the willpower to continue in the
> fight for bread, they are men whose nerve has failed, who live
> furtively on the outskirts, snatching a little joy here and there,
> drugging their hunger with gorgeous mirages.

We notice how concerned Dos Passos is here with this modern
'failure of nerve' (there are full expositions of its nature and
causes), and how it seems also precisely to describe the young
men whom Dos Passos has been portraying — the Martin Howe
who waits for a goddess to transpose him to the clouds; the
Fuselli who watches his mistress from outside the window while
other men engage her company; the Andrews who buries himself in the gorgeously modulated sentences of Flaubert, 'as if
the book were a drug in which he could drink deep forgetful-
ness of himself'; the Telemachus of 'Rosinante' itself who regards with such envy the sexual adventures of Lyaeus — all
these pale, good young men who seem also to be marked by
the failure of nerve.

But Baroja's protagonists, of course, are not aesthetes.
Baroja, Dos Passos tells us, subscribes to a sort of philosophical
anarchism; he sees his own rôle as the destructive critic of existing society:

> He says . . . that the only part a man of the middle classes can play
> in the reorganization of society is destructive. He has not under-
> gone the discipline which can only come from common slavery in
> the industrial machine, necessary for a builder. His slavery has
> been an isolated slavery which has unfitted him forever from be-
> coming truly part of a community. He can use the vast power
> of knowledge which training has given him only in one way. His

great mission is to put the acid test to existing institutions, and to strip the veils off them.

'To put the acid test to existing institutions and to strip the veils off them.' How familiar this sounds, in one phrase almost the precise analysis of Dos Passos's mature achievement; as if in 1922 the U.S.A. trilogy had already been written, and not the very different meditations we have been discussing; or as if the writer were describing, rather than Baroja, his sense of his own future function. And how clean the phrase comes through here, without the rather sententious disenchantment of the early Dos Passos heroes, often too contemptuous of their own existing institutions to notice the veils.

'Rosinante to the Road Again' is, then, the key work of Dos Passos's first period. Here he has sketched in a world of thought and action very prophetic of his future. He has fixed his road — surely an abrupt turning from the classical wanderings of Telemachus and Lyaeus, these odd associates in 'Rosinante' of the revolutionary Baroja. And viewed now in retrospect and as a group, what atrocious young men these early heroes of Dos Passos are — have we ever seen their like? I am afraid we must answer yes: in the bulk of the post-war literature of the nineteen-twenties. We recall the central figures of Aldous Huxley's early novels, equally literary and ineffectual, the Gumbril of 'Antic Hay' who changes his appearance in the vain hope of changing his temperament, the hesitating young Denis of 'Chrome Yellow' who waits for the course of the entire novel to deliver an apt quotation, to have it, on the last page of the book, fall on deaf ears. And our own American literature was perhaps even more specifically marked by these drooping aesthetes. A similar 'failure of nerve' is very likely the real complex underlying the typical protagonists of the Jazz Age, the heroes of Scott Fitzgerald, though they are more commonly identified with the orgies of a flaming youth which, rolling its stockings and its cigarettes, burning brightly at both ends, made inroads upon its own constitution while making advances upon its sexual partners. Yet it is obvious that beneath the

extravagant antics of these palpitating adolescents lies a fundamental weakness: a lack of any real purpose in life, and of the
energy not merely to fulfill such a purpose but to conceive one.
As a reaction to the First World War, we have already noticed
some causes of this attitude in Hemingway. And in many respects we feel the similarity of the early Dos Passos with the
central evocation of Hemingway. How marked the emphasis
of drifting in both these authors — whether on the unfathomable tides of the Gulf Stream or amidst amber-fringed clouds
— and how much stronger it is, in fact, with the early heroes
of Dos Passos! I believe it was Wyndham Lewis who remarked
that the Hemingway hero is a man to whom things happen.
But the early Dos Passos hero is in effect a man to whom very
little can happen.

For Dos Passos in his first period represents perhaps the last
point in the modern failure of nerve, since any further development from this aesthetic inertia would lead to sheer torpor.
And we must now confess our own belief, in respect to both
Hemingway and Dos Passos, that this movement is not purely
a post-war reaction. We must see it also as the final stage of
that separation of the American artist from his society which
 began with the industrial domination of the American Republic in 1860 and which culminated in the American nineteen-
twenties. But now with Dos Passos the society against which the
artistic revolt is directed has receded so far beyond the horizon
of the individual's interest that an effort of the will is no longer
needed to dispose of it. The early Dos Passos hero no longer
rebels against his society so much as he ignores it. The revolt
of the individual against the communal forms of his time has
become a movement of indifference. What a paradox the work
of Dos Passos in the American twenties thus presents us: these
innocuous rebels defining their futility in the midst of a supremely energetic and ambitious American materialism!
Surrounded by the Lardnerian luxury and gross cultural optimism, the American writer feels never more sharply the sense
of his own exile and lack of function. And this sense of exile

will now pursue Dos Passos, even as all his sad young men —
these pallid spectators, and nerveless modern adolescents, these
voyeurs rather than entrepreneurs — undergo their transformation. For whatever the abruptness of the change in Dos
Passos's 'Rosinante,' whatever heritage of mixed feelings not
easily to be resolved the Dos Passos hero will carry with him,
he will now travel along a new route — one that carries him
from the temptations of Saint Anthony to the barricades of
Detroit.

3. AMERICAN RETURN.   'Streets of Night' in 1923,
dealing with Boston and Harvard society, is the first Dos Passos
novel to be laid in the American setting. (Perhaps we should
remember that the previous Dos Passos heroes have been
Americans, in the manner of the literary times in Europe.)
'Streets of Night' has been generally considered a weak novel,
and its central figures still cast in the adolescent mould we have
been examining, this is perhaps a fair estimate. Yet if the
Fanshaw Macdougan of the story is again an irresolute aesthete,
the treatment of him has become definitely satirical. As the
novel progresses, Fanshaw becomes so elegant, poetic, sexless,
and superior in the best middle-western version of the Oxford
classics that we become aware just how sharply Dos Passos is
showing up the inadequacies of his former hero. Confessing
himself a disciple of Pater, Fanshaw is really a parody of Pater's
disciples from the mid-American belt. The portrait of him in
'Streets of Night' is done with great acumen, just as the Nanci-
bel Taylor of the novel is an interesting precursor of the Ellen
Thatcher of 'Manhattan Transfer.'

And at first glance the strains and conflicts of Dos Passos's
entire apprenticeship period from 'One Man's Initiation' in
1920 to 'The 42nd Parallel' in 1930, a long period of trial and
experimentation, of conscientious step-by-step evolution, would

seem to have found their fulfillment now. The 'Manhattan Transfer' of 1925 is rather like one of those fantastic 'sports' of Nature which ridicule the laborious, inching evolution which produces them. In 'Manhattan Transfer' we have a new novelist, a very different view of the world expressed in a fresh and often excellent craft. Here are the technical devices of which we have noticed the origins in 'Three Soldiers' and 'Streets of Night' and which are to impress us with their full brilliance in 'U.S.A.' The popular songs and slogans, the newspaper headlines, the speech of the people as against the rather proper Harvard English which the Dos Passos heroes have been using, the historical figures and events from King C. Gillette (no stropping no honing) to Woodrow Wilson — all the indices of the sociological climate of New York City in the twenties are fused into the panoramic view of the city culture. But it is exactly this view of the city which attracts us, of course, the energy, curiosity, and vitality of the novel. For we must admit the previous work of Dos Passos has hardly been marked with this, but rather, on the contrary, by a sort of distaste for ordinary experience, of which the views of the early Dos Passos hero were the explicit declaration, and which their inner motivation, filled with fantasies and gestures, reinforced.

But now transferring from classical fantasies to social realities, from the sensibilities of the individual to the wide cultural scene, Dos Passos has dropped his lassitude along with his literature. In 'Manhattan Transfer' he has caught the turmoil, the noise, absurdities, and cruelties — all the manifestations of sheer energy, extravagant and often irrelevant, but nevertheless energy as the prime trait of life — which mark urban society, and particularly urban society in America, the land of energy. Within the four hundred pages of 'Manhattan Transfer' Dos Passos has re-created (the writer who could hardly seem in the past to sustain the tenuous thread of one pale, tedious existence) a dozen metropolitan sagas full of fury and anguish, the distortions of being. Congo, Emile, and plump, coy Mme. Rigaud; the reckless drunkard Stan Emery, recalling the Dan

Cohan of 'Three Soldiers,' but more effectively done; the pure but lisping Cassie and her vulgar Morris who destroys their beautiful relationship ('I mean spiwitually'); the pounding, relentless despair of Bud Korpenning's search (anticipating the Joe Williams of '1919') for 'the center of things'; the degeneration of George Baldwin as he 'gets ahead' in the world; and that of Joe Harland, the bankrupt stock-market wizard as he slides down the other side of the social scale — these are a few of the stories through which Dos Passos has engaged our sympathies. And in the center of most of these lives, of course, the Ellen Thatcher of 'Manhattan Transfer,' Dos Passos has struck a new note. Fascinating but frigid, acting out her bright alluring part while she lives in childhood fantasies and in the memories of her dead lover, unable to yield her emotions, Ellen is the first full-length portrait of the thwarted women who are steadily to mark the novels of Dos Passos — who, succumbing to money, power, prestige, to art, to fads, to everything in short but their natural rôle as women, are fated to become hard careerists like the Eleanor Stoddard or shallow dilettantes like the Eveline Hutchins of 'U.S.A.' But Ellen Thatcher has nerve. Opposed to the powerless, drifting indolence of Dos Passos's males, she stands in contrast as the dominating, devouring modern heroine. If her goal is hardly worth it, her determination is admirable.

For a while at least. For the point of 'Manhattan Transfer' is that Ellen fails at the end, just as all these other lives end in disaster. It is almost as if a dead weight had fallen, at the close of the novel, over all the vitality which differentiates this work from Dos Passos's previous books, as if all the pulsing drives of these new Dos Passos people had been turned off, as if the initial energy of the writer himself, so new and refreshing, had run out — and returned, for lack of sustenance, into the previous patterns we have noticed. If 'Manhattan Transfer' is a good novel, it is also in the end a Dos Passos novel. And through Jimmy Herf himself, the central masculine figure of 'Manhattan Transfer,' again cast in the mould of a blushing, watching, innocent and unhappy aesthete, we realize that Dos Passos is still influenced by his earlier view of life. Herf does have a job, he does get married, he is concerned with social issues — we see in him the start of the integration of the solitary with his society. But at the end of the novel, his job pointless, his marriage a disaster, his attempts at social integration blocked, his will paralyzed, and his mind again turning into the confused fantasies so familiar to us — returning in short to the original mould of the isolated, nerveless individual — Herf wanders off, a ghost from the past. A ghost which will pursue Dos Passos. Conceived in the mediaeval abbey of Martin Howe, it will yet appear to haunt, a strange atavism of the spirit, the stock-yards of Chicago, the glass-brick factories of America, and the bottlenecks of twentieth-century finance capitalism.

The works of Dos Passos which appear now between 'Manhattan Transfer' and 'The 42nd Parallel' are relatively minor, although they are often revealing of his advance. 'Orient Express' in 1927, recording the post-war ferment in eastern Europe from 1921 to 1926, written in a much straighter style than the travel adventures in 'Rosinante,' is certainly a more mature record. In the appreciation of places and people for their own quality — Constantinople, Teheran, Prinkipo, on the stony desert of Damascus, surrounded by those Arabian brigands whom around this time T. E. Lawrence was to adopt as his intimates — 'Orient Express' is perhaps the gayest of Dos Passos's works, placed as it is amidst massacres, plagues, and revolutions. Among these, of course, it is the Russian society which we should expect to take up Dos Passos's major attention. As early as 'Rosinante,' treating the exploitation of the Spanish peasants, Dos Passos had noted that 'everywhere Russia was the flame.' And the 'U.S.A.' trilogy is to be strongly permeated with the sense of the Russian impact on twentieth-century society. Yet attending here the birth of the Great Red Mother (who with strange caresses was to take to her bosom so many western spirits of our time, to soothe, stimulate, and horrify them, to spin the most fantastic tale of our epoch from the bright days of Jack Reed to the deep night of Jan Valtin), our Dos Passos is curiously cautious. Watching in 'Orient Express' the earliest stirrings of the Utopian infant that was to become such an enigmatic giantess, our novelist is hesitant. 'Orient Express' records, not the conversion of Dos Passos to the Russian socialism with which his work is to become strongly colored, but indeed, as he faces the facts of Russian life in person, an increasing emphasis on the doubts which color his sympathies. At this point of his radical education, his revolt is rather against the entire framework of western materialism, and the property it glorifies. There is a 'wind out of Asia,' he says, which may destroy the Things that are our gods —

> the knickknacks and scraps of engraved paper and the bases and the curtain rods, the fussy junk, possession of which divides poor man from rich man, the shoddy manufactured goods that are all our civilization prizes. . . .

This wind, Dos Passos says, has swept Russia clean for the moment. But will the result be 'the same old piling up of miseries again, or a faith and a lot of words like Islam and Christianity?' The Russia of 'Orient Express' is too early, too new and strange for the Dos Passos who felt at home in Spain, and gave us there his straight convictions. And it is again here a Latin writer who seems to engage his sympathies most fully. The analysis of Blaise Cendrars is undoubtedly the most pointed and revealing section of 'Orient Express.' It is Cendrars rather than Russia who seems to condition Dos Passos's thinking most sharply, through whom Dos Passos sees the function of the artist in the world of the machine:

> That is why in this age of giant machines and scuttle-headed men it is a good thing to have a little music. We need sons of Homer going about the world beating into some sort of human rhythm the shrieking hullabaloo, making us less afraid.

And certainly his own work from now on is to deal with the 'gods of uranium and manganese,' the age of giant machines

and scuttle-headed men, and the effort of the artist to go about
in this world beating it into some sort of human rhythm.

'The Garbage Man,' published in 1926, though started as
early as 1923, is the first of Dos Passos's three plays which in
effect retrace the entire development of his views which we have
been discussing here. In his plays, as in his travel records, Dos
Passos confirms his growth in another technic, working and
reworking his themes, consolidating his views, as we've seen,
before new advances. The plays are indeed the laboratories
of Dos Passos's experimentation. Filled with hindsights and
prophecies, at once old, middle, and new Dos Passos, his heritage and his intentions poured into them, they are a sort of
kaleidoscopic record of his momentum. And thus compressing
in three acts, it almost seems, the content of ten years' trial,
they are often hardly as effective as they are interesting. The
Tom of 'The Garbage Man' is perhaps the extreme form of the
early Dos Passos hero. The most unhappy and uncertain of all
these unhappy and uncertain rebels, he aims the arrows of his
wrath successively at a variety of oppressive forces: (1) a hostile
spirit in life itself (which early and late Dos Passos, like Hardy,
seems to feel); (2) the respectable conventions of middle-class
American life, puritan and bourgeois; and (3) the ethics and
manners of the machine age. As the fusion of these three re-
bellions, of course, Tom is not a dramatic success. Our effort,
reading 'The Garbage Man,' is hardly so much to identify ourselves with the hero as to identify the objects of his anger. But
the second half of the play is a great gain in the sections of
pointed satire. The nightmarish Prosperity Parade, in the
manner of Jean Cocteau's 'Maries de la Tour Eiffel,' is witty
and impressive; the sequence of the three oppressive forces we
have listed is itself an indication of Dos Passos's growth. And,
in 'Airways, Inc.,' Dos Passos's second play in 1928, this
growth is made really effective. 'Airways' is the link between
the views of 'Manhattan Transfer' and those of 'The 42nd
Parallel.'

The social critique behind 'Manhattan Transfer' is also

triple in its view: the protest against western materialism in general, the post-war despair, and the early study of the American Success pattern. In 'Airways' the description of metropolitan society has been extended into that of our national cultural framework. The study of American Success is much more penetrating and incisive. And the generalized, romantic protest against materialism, the rule of 'Things' which we noticed in 'Orient Express' (this protest which has been the leit-motif of so many modern writers, and their pitfall, and from which now Dos Passos emerges), has become a realistic study of the American politico-economic society. The change of attitude in 'Airways' is often expressed very eloquently (again the people and action of the play are hardly as valid as this development behind the play), as when the father of the Turner family talks on the American values of '29:

> 'Everywhere they're building ramshackle houses for young folks ... Ozone Park, Crystal Meadow, Joyland. ... Quickbuilt demountable homes for young people. Maisonettes knocked together out of laths and plaster and enamel paint and kindlin' wood, and no place for an old man in them, no place for a tired man without a job.
>
> When they hustle for money to buy bonds to pay the interest on mortgages to grab stocks on a tip
>
> they think they'll buy acre lots of happiness where the fountain of youth was in Florida
>
> they think they'll buy a nickelplated future with monogram engraved to order like I did ...'

Many of these passages in 'Airways' hold us where the central action fails; thus intense and effective they reveal perhaps a new sort of American poetry, recalling the technic, though indeed not the themes of Whitman. And it is curious that as the poet of personal emotion and the superior individual, Dos Passos was so inadequate in his earlier work, while now as the harsh lyricist of the American industrial order he is often to be so eloquent.

For with the new style of 'Airways' we are reaching the

mature work of Dos Passos; we stand on the edge of the 'U.S.A.'
trilogy. The period of apprenticeship is over. The total conversion of the Dos Passos hero who moves so aloof and disembodied through the pages of the earlier novels is about to
take place. The Jimmie Herf who wanders off at the end of
'Manhattan Transfer,' declaring his intention to travel 'pretty
far,' has landed with 'Airways' in the midst of an airplane factory strike: the typical product of the American twentieth
century. Now everything is ready. The technics of Dos Passos
have been evolved from the songs and slang of 'Three Soldiers'
through the Boston panoramas of 'Streets of Night,' through
'Manhattan Transfer' to the prose-poems of 'Airways' which
are now to be divided and become, on the one hand the Biographies, and on the other the Camera Eyes of 'U.S.A.' We
have seen the evolution of Dos Passos's social views, now
sharpened, the satire more pointed, the bitterness reaching
down deeper. The last lines of 'Airways' are illuminating as to
the total change of the Dos Passos we have been following:

> Street where I've lived all these years shut up in a matchwood
> house full of bitterness.
> City where I've lived walled up in old dead fear.
> America, where I've scurried from store to subway to church
> to home, America that I've never known.
> World where I've lived without knowing.

We feel the resemblance between these lines and those of the
poetic solitary in 'A Pushcart at the Curb' — he who, 'caged
in the grey cell his fathers had built,' as he tells us, laments also
'the bitter blood of joyless generations.' But in what a different
context these similar images appear. The aesthete's cell is now
converted into the United States of social crisis. And now the
determination of the pale and brooding and classical young
poet is to know the truth of the America he has never known.

As with the Veblen whom Dos Passos accepts as his symbol,
it was to be a bitter truth, perhaps foreshadowed by the pamph-
let in 1927 on the Sacco-Vanzetti case, 'Facing the Chair.'
The significance of the Sacco-Vanzetti trial, the slow, stran-

gling death of the post-war liberal hopes which the Dedham jury brought about, cannot be underestimated in the radical education of Dos Passos. This was very likely the catalyst of his career. As Dos Passos's emotions go out to the Latin cultures, so the image of the Italian anarchists who were framed and crushed by the American industrial ethics is to remain with Dos Passos, underlying his entire social critique, giving rise almost ten years later to his most eloquent passages of protest:

> they have clubbed us off the streets   they are stronger   they are rich   they hire and fire the politicians the newspaper-editors the old judges the small men with reputations the collegepresidents the wardheelers (listen businessmen collegepresidents judges   America will not forget her betrayers) they hire the men with guns   the uniforms the policecars the patrol-wagons
>
> all right you have won   you will kill the brave men our friends tonight. . . .
>
> America our nation has been beaten by strangers who have turned our language inside out who have taken the clean words our fathers spoke and made them slimy and foul
>
> their hired men sit on the judge's bench they sit back with their feet on the tables under the dome of the State House they are ignorant of our beliefs they have the dollars the guns the armed forces the powerplants
>
> they have built the electricchair and hired the executioner to throw the switch
>
> all right we are two nations.

It is with the two American nations that the 'U.S.A.' trilogy deals.

4. THE RADICAL HISTORIAN.   As the early novels of Dos Passos recorded the adventures of his adolescence, 'The 42nd Parallel' is another journal of youth — the youth of the

American protagonists whom Dos Passos has selected to typify our society, the youth of the twentieth century in America, and that of American culture itself. But if Martin Howe, John Andrews, or the young poet of 'Rosinante' or 'A Pushcart at the Curb' were to step into the pages of the 'U.S.A.' trilogy, what a shock would be theirs — enough to shake all these disdainful and disembodied young men out of their classics!

It is the birth of the century, the Newsreel informs us, Nation Greets Century's Dawn:

> Noise Greets New Century
> *Labor Greets New Century*
> CHURCHES GREET NEW CENTURY

'The twentieth century will be American,' Senator Albert J. Beveridge is quoted as declaring. 'American thought will dominate it. American progress will give it color and direction. American deeds will make it illustrious.' And as his horse falls on General Miles, as the sanitary trustees turn the Chicago River into a drainage canal, and officials know nothing of vice, as the British are beaten at Mafeking, McKinley works in his office, the Gaiety Girls are mobbed in New Jersey, and as

> ... many a good man murdered in the Philippines
> Lies sleeping in some lonesome grave,

the trilogy opens.

Against the Newsreels (we notice in them the wonderful use Dos Passos makes of juxtaposition: political and industrial events, popular songs, crimes and fads, forming the headline record of the disjointed forces and varied strains which go into the surface portrait of our society: the economic facts, the romantic aspirations, and the normal human eccentricities) Dos Passos places his Biographies. What is the record of the American century, the American deeds and thought as revealed by our key figures? *Eugene Debs*, the lover of mankind

> (While there is a lower class I am of it, while there is a criminal class I am of it, while there is a soul in prison I am not free.)

is ground down by the oppressive forces of the First World War:

> Where were Gene Deb's brothers in nineteen eighteen when Woodrow Wilson had him locked up in Atlanta for speaking against war,
>
> where were the big men fond of whiskey and fond of each other, gentle rambling tellers of stories over bars in small towns in the Middle West,
>
> quiet men who wanted a house with a porch to putter around and a fat wife to cook for them, a few drinks and cigars, a garden to dig in, cronies to chew the rag with
>
> and wanted to work for it
>
> and others to work for it.
>
> Where were the locomotive firemen and engineers when they hustled him off to Atlanta Penitentiary?
>
> And they brought him back to die in Terre Haute....

Luther Burbank, who sowed the seed which cashed in on Mr. Darwin's Natural Selection

> on Spencer and Huxley
> with the Burbank Potato

was one of the grand old men of America until the churches

> and the congregations
> got wind that he was an infidel and believed
> in Darwin.

Big Bill Haywood was a working-class leader known from coast to coast —

> Now the wants of all the workers were his wants, he was the spokesman of the West, of the cowboys and the lumberjacks and the harvesthands and the miners.

— until the dream of empire swept over Wilsonian democracy, the A.E.F., the Morgan loans, Napoleon's tomb; it was 'worth money to make the eagle scream,' and

> they lynched the pacifists and the proGermans and the wobblies and the reds and bolsheviks

Another spokesman of the west, *Bryan*, the boy orator of the Platte, barnstormer, exhorter, evangelist, silver tongue of the plain people, whose

> voice charmed the mortgageridden farmers of the great plains, rang through the weatherboarded schoolhouses in the Missouri Valley, was sweet in the ears of the small storekeepers hungry for easy credit, melted men's innards like the song of a thrush or a mockin' in the grey quiet before sunup, or a sudden soar in winter wheat or a bugler playing taps and the flag flying. . . .

— Bryan, this silver tongue came to its end auctioning lots at Coral Gables. Thus the patterns of American society distort or prostitute America's talent, as we go through the list of Dos Passos's Biographies; through *Minor C. Keith*, the 'capitalista yanqui,' symbol of the great industrial fortunes whose making and spending form the sociological climate of 'The 42nd Parallel,' through *Steinmetz, Edison. La Follette*, the last of these key American figures, is in turn the symbol to Dos Passos of our political genius — but a genius based on illusion ('orator haranguing from the capital of a lost republic that had never existed') and even the illusion, finally, extinguished. 'With the death of the 65th Congress representative government died in this country, if it had ever been alive.'

With La Follette the point of view behind the Biographies of 'The 42nd Parallel' becomes clear — these portraits, often so brilliant if they are marked with the accents of despair, public poems in which Dos Passos gains a lyricism often lacking in his personal histories. And against the framework of the panoramic novel in 'The 42nd Parallel,' the Newsreels, the Biographies, the Camera Eye (which is the subjective, stream of consciousness history of an individual, usually considered to be the writer himself) — against this entire framework which attempts to evaluate the sociological climate of a culture more fully than in any previous novel, Dos Passos places the group of central fictional characters who are the typical products of the culture. The mark of a society lies after all in its human products rather than in its mechanical ones, or indeed rather than in the buildings and books and symphonies by which we judge it later, and which, difficult as they are to estimate, are less so than the humanity which gave rise to them. What is the evidence, then, of these typical people of the American century, moulded, so the novelist tells us, by these cultural forces, the storms of society which sweep across our land from the Rockies to the Atlantic seaboard along the forty-second parallel itself?

The Success Story of J. Ward Moorehouse is to be the central theme of the entire 'U.S.A.' trilogy. Around Ward's career as a publicity wizard, the histories of Eleanor Stoddard, Eveline Hutchins, Janey Williams, Dick Savage, and Barrow rotate in one fashion or another, and through these the other characters of the trilogy. But each of the novels has its special figure also, and Mac, the radical, whose life starts and ends within 'The 42nd Parallel,' is the typical life of the first volume. But such a life — a youth and apprenticeship filled with poverty, drinking, disease, deceit, and disaster, all the cheap horrors of the dispossessed. Very early in Mac's history we realize this is Horatio Alger in reverse; the chronicle of American Failure; the portrait of Tarkington's sixteen turned sour. And very early in Mac's narrative, the moral is sketched in. His early career as a book (pornography) salesman ended by a farmer's shotgun, Mac is joined by another young vagrant. The two boys eat their breakfast in a cheap restaurant filled with the smell of 'ham and coffee and roachpowder,' their talk in turn filled with Hearst, the 'interests,' 'The Appeal to Reason,' and the Revolution. 'Ever read Marx?' says Ike:

> 'No ... golly, I'd like to though.' 'Me neither, I read Bellamy's "Looking Backward," though; that's what made me a Socialist.' 'Tell me about it; I'd just started readin' it when I left home.' 'It's about a galoot that goes to sleep an' wakes up in the vear two thousand and the social revolution's all happened and everything's socialistic an' there's no jails or poverty and nobody works for themselves an' there's no way anybody can get to be a

rich bondholder or capitalist and life's pretty slick for the working class.' 'That's what I always thought . . . It's the workers who
create wealth and they ought to have it instead of a lot of drones.'
'If you could do away with the capitalist system and the big
trusts and Wall Street things 'ud be like that.'

'Gee.'

'All you'd need would be a general strike and have the workers
refuse to work for a boss any longer . . . God damn it, if people
only realized how friggin' easy it would be. The interests own
all the press and keep knowledge and education from the workin'-
men.'

Would the earlier Dos Passos adolescent — the Martin Howe
of 'One Man's Initiation' listening rather disdainfully to the
first European intimations of social conflict — recognize his
new brother Mac in these words? What a cleft, indeed, now lies
between the two worlds of Dos Passos. And how the earlier
Dos Passos hero would shrink from the coarse and worldly
Fenian McCreary of 'The 42nd Parallel' — this urchin so sick
and wise, so marked with the imprint of an exploiting society,
the new Marxist cherub in the nursery of the class-struggle.
(We also recall now, with nostalgia perhaps, the innocent inebriated chatter of Hemingway's adolescents.) But we must
admit that the American portrait of Mac has a labored, a
pedagogical tone to it. So too the other Novels of 'The 42nd
Parallel' are in general inferior to the Biographies, News, and
Camera Eyes. As Mac is here revealing, Dos Passos is gaining
his own radical education, and very often the other lives of the
novel (Moorehouse, Eleanor Stoddard, Janey Williams, Charley Anderson) seem to be portions of the novelist's thesis; the
expressions of Dos Passos's views rather than the products of
his art: documents more than destinies.

In '1919,' the second volume of the trilogy which appeared
in 1932, the technic becomes sharper and the point of view
more radical. In its entirety '1919' is an exciting novel, a better
novel than 'The 42nd Parallel,' as the third volume of the
trilogy, indeed, is to surpass the first two. Here the study of

American society is carried from the close of 'The 42nd Parallel' through the years of war tension and their climax with the 'Peace' of Versailles. Again the opening Newsreel sets the stage with some magnificence of satiric juxtaposition: the 'vast new No Man's Land of Europe reeking with murder and the lust of rapine, aflame with the fires of revolution' —

> Oh the oak and the ash and the weeping willow tree
> And green grows the grass in North Amerikee.

In the first Camera Eye, and perhaps the most effective of them so far, we get an intense evocation of personal death, of the death of acquaintances, of the generalized death of the war, centering around the 'She' (the mother) of the reveries:

> when the telegram came that she was dying the bellglass cracked in a screech of slate pencils   (have you ever never been able to sleep for a week in April?)   and He met me in the grey trainshed my eyes were stinging with vermillion bronze and chromegreen inks that oozed from the spinning April hills   His moustaches were white the tired droop of an old man's cheeks She's gone Jack grief isnt a uniform and the   in the parlor the waxen odor of lilies in the parlor   (He and I we must bury the uniform of grief)
>
> then the riversmell the shimmering Potomac reaches the little choppysilver waves at Indian Head   there were mockingbirds in the graveyard and the roadsides steamed with spring   April enough to shock the world

In the first Biography of Jack Reed, turned Communist by the war, catching typhus and dying in Moscow, we get the refrain of the war years:

> ... machinegun fire and arson
> starvation lice bedbugs cholera typhus

— this refrain, the central motif of '1919' which will sound with variations throughout the lives and events of the novel. And thus invoked with all the accents of death, the chronicle of the war years starts.

Set within the panoramic framework once more, Dos Passos

carries forward the lives of the central figures in 'The 42nd
Parallel.' Johnny Moorehouse has married and divorced
Anabelle Strang, one of the most dissolute and devasting of
Dos Passos's women. Their relationship initiates the financially
calculating but humanly innocent Johnny into the perversi-
ties of the female temperament; continues on a basis of mutual
contempt; leaves Johnny with a 'faint rancor of desire for
women,' and the declaration that he has no more time 'for that
stuff' when he joins the Bessemer Metallic Furnishings and
Products Company.

> His mind was full of augerbits, canthooks, mauls, sashweights,
> axes, hatchets, monkey-wrenches. . . . Shaving while his bath was
> running in the morning he would see long processions of andirons,
> grates, furnace fittings, pumps, sausagegrinders, drills, calipers,
> vises, casters, drawerpulls pass between his face and the mirror
> and wonder how they could be made more attractive to the retail
> trade. . . . Why should our cottarpins appeal more than any other
> cottarpins, he'd ask himself as he stepped on the streetcar.

The fine section on Johnny's distorted fancies in 'The 42nd
Parallel' (and the best section of the Novels) is almost the
only indication we ever get of his actual publicity talent.
Through learning golf, nevertheless, joining the right clubs,
manipulating the right people in his boyish blue-eyed way,
through his marriage to Gertrude Staple (and the Staple
fortune), Johnny gets ahead. The industrial violence of the
Homestead strike brings him the idea of educating the public
to the facts of Labor Relations (as viewed by the Steel Industry).
And with his growing financial and political contacts, his teas
'in the English style,' and the change of his name to J. Ward
Moorehouse, Johnny confirms his career as Public Relations
Counsel.

Here then is the American male. This, our author tells us,
is the dominant cultural pattern of our society. And following
the glittering star of Lardner's Success Myth, J. Ward carries
along with him the lesser satellites of the big money. Janey
Williams, now Ward's secretary, grows tighter, primmer,

dryer as she grows more respectable. Barrow, the 'liberal' adviser to Ward (and another fine portrait), becomes more unctuous in phrase as he becomes more treacherous in fact. Eleanor Stoddard herself, platonic mistress to Ward, her life-time spent in obliterating her memories of childhood, supple-menting Ward's English teas with her own bohemian gather-ings, and Ward's sexlessness with her own narcissism, Eleanor as the key feminine study of the trilogy becomes steadily more refined and bloodless. But in '1919' the view of this group of people, also embodying the basic American cultural pattern of getting ahead, has changed. Though their lives are carried forward, we no longer see them through their own eyes, but now indirectly through a group of new but related characters: through the narratives of Joe Williams who is Janey's brother, Eveline Hutchins the 'best friend' of Eleanor Stoddard, Dick Savage the young Harvard intellectual who becomes Ward's assistant and thus throws a new light on the group, and through the 'Daughter' of '1919' who in turn is to throw a very dubious light on Dick Savage. And through this shifting focus — beau-tifully manipulated to take advantage of every weakness in his people, of each ignominious trait in them which their own view of themselves hardly reveals but now very clear to these others — Dos Passos obtains great subtlety of character illumination, if the subtlety often holds little compassion. The people as a whole in '1919' are better drawn than those of 'The 42nd Parallel.' (With the exception of Joe Williams, perhaps, the central life of the novel again, the little man, the ordinary sailor for whom, as with the 'Mac' of the earlier book, Dos Passos has the most sympathy, as indeed we have also, and yet a sympathy which does not quite convert Joe's chronicle of despair into an artistic success.) Yet, held as we are by this intricate and well-managed craft, the shifting illuminations which Dos Passos throws upon his people, and the increasing validity of the people themselves, we realize at the end that these lives also are still weighted by the author. Their hu-manity is still moulded by the pattern of Dos Passos's American critique which in '1919' shows the sharpening disintegration of our society. As the Newsreels portray the war scene (Army Wife Slashed by Admirer, Fertilizer Industry Stimulated by War), the Biographies provide the indices of the war's tension upon the key American figures. But this is now a tension which not only degrades our national talent as in 'The 42nd Parallel,' but now has actively turned our talent away from American society. The index to this phase of Dos Passos's American critique lies in the portrait of the Morgan fortune, at once the most detailed and perhaps the most brilliant satiric biography in '1919' (though it is difficult to select the best of them), compressing with an admirable art the growth of a dynasty, an economic empire, into its six pages:

> By 1917 the Allies had borrowed one billion, nine-hundred million dollars through the House of Morgan: we went overseas for democracy and the flag;
> and by the end of the Peace Conference the phrase *J. P. Morgan suggests* had compulsion over a power of seventyfour billion dollars.
> J. P. Morgan is a silent man, not given to public utterances, but during the great steel strike, he wrote Gary: *Heartfelt congratulations on your stand for the open shop, with which I am, as you know, absolutely in accord. I believe American principles of liberty are deeply involved, and must win if we stand firm.*
> (Wars and panics on the stock exchange,
> machinegunfire and arson,
> bankruptcies, warloans,
> starvation, lice, cholera and typhus:
> good growing weather for the House of Morgan.)

But the growth of such an economic empire within the framework of American democracy in turn is a symbol for Dos Passos of the disease of our democracy itself. The biography of Wilson views him as the academic reformer whose liberal eloquence was the high-toned publicity of the financial interests whose war we fought. (This is of course the economic devil-theory of the First World War; the single-truth analysis upon which a generation was raised; and which made such a neat pattern, sometimes accompanied by a pacifism that sought to end all wars by inserting advertisements in the popular magazines.) And reading the tragic history of Woodrow Wilson in '1919' we become rather uncomfortably aware that for Dos Passos, Wilson is hardly tragic. There is a curious emphasis here of the semi-farcical as in the narrative of Dick Savage at the Versailles Peace Conference. On the Woodrow Wilson around whom the history of '1919' centers, there is in the end no full effort to appraise his significance in terms of American democracy, the liberalism for which he stood, the stresses to which he was subject, or indeed the errors which he committed — but those errors which in recent years have begun to seem more not his but his country's, as Gerald Johnson has remarked with great acumen in 'The Ghost of Woodrow Wilson,' the ghost which today walks again in prophetic robes. 'If you hit the words,' the narrator of the Camera Eye says, 'democracy will understand, even the bankers and clergymen.' But for the Dos Passos of '1919' it was no longer American democracy within its modern shell of finance-capitalism. The shell has destroyed the republican institutions. The tense is that of the past. We recall now the phrase in the portrait of La Follette. 'With the death of the 65th Congress representative government died in this country, if it had ever been alive.' The phrase on Paxton Hibben —

> no more place in America for change, no more place for the old gags: social justice, progressivism, revolt against oppression, democracy. . . .

That on Jack Reed, 'the last of the great race of warcorrespondents,' the 'last,' that is, from this view —

> Life, liberty and the pursuit of happiness;
> not much of that round the silkmills when
> in 1913,
> he went over to Paterson to write up the strike. . . .

And like Reed, no wonder, then, that the more talented sons of American democracy, those who were not crushed by it, like Bourne, or Joe Hill, or Wesley Everest, in the war years, turned their thoughts to a new direction; for —

> The windows of Smolny glow whitehot like a bessemer,
> no sleep in Smolny,
> Smolny the giant rollingmill running twentyfour hours a day
> rolling out men nations hopes millenniums impulses fears,
>   rawmaterial
>   for the foundations
>   of a new society.

Thus, against the post-war hopes for the foundations of a new society, the novel is portraying the dissolution of the old. The American critique in '1919,' and the analysis of the war, are not conducted from within the framework of American society; nor, as with Wilson, with any full attempt to examine the contradictions of capitalistic democracy, its strains and its strength, nor with any effort to see the bases for future progress. It is conducted from without: a revolutionary view which is discarding the democracy with the capitalism, and is ignoring for the most part (though never altogether fully) our own republican heritage of reform and indeed of revolution. In the words of the familiar cautioning, we may almost say that any resemblance in '1919' to living American institutions is purely coincidental. The final historical tone of the book (showing as much growth as it does of Dos Passos as artist, his insight as novelist; as exciting as '1919' is as a novel, and the closing sections of it quite magnificent) is not of life but of death. Or of a sick watch, as it were, over American society, in which there is often little sympathy for the diseased body, and describing which the historian selects the more absurd and incongruous details, often again brilliant in their effect, but details which hardly portray so much as they betray. It is this process, moreover, the recording of a disintegrating social order whose orgiastic revelries are the portents of its death, and a process of dissolution viewed largely from a fixed point outside of the social order itself, of which 'The Big Money' forms the last chapter.

Between the second and third novels of 'U.S.A.,' however, Dos Passos publishes another play, 'Fortune Heights,' in 1934, and the latest of his travelogues, 'In All Countries.' What we see in these two works is a sort of briefer recapitulation of the point of view we have been tracing in the 'U.S.A.' trilogy. Among all the countries Dos Passos is discussing, his American notes are the least reassuring. It is an America hardly lovable which Dos Passos studies over these years, an America he hardly loves. In the earlier section of 'In All Countries,' the discussion of the Sacco-Vanzetti trial, the post-war decade in the United States is viewed again as one of repression and reaction:

> While far away across the world new eras seemed to be flaring up into the sky, at home the great machine they slaved for seemed more adamant, more unshakable than ever.

By contrast, we get the European hope of social change: Sacco who wants the people of the world 'to walk straight over the free hills, not to stagger bowed under the ordained machinery of industry.' While Vanzetti, the Italian anarchist, shares the hope which has grown up in the Latin countries of the Mediterranean Basin that

> man's predatory instincts, incarnate in the capitalist system, can be canalized into other channels, leaving free communities of artisans and farmers and fishermen and cattlebreeders who would work for their livelihood with pleasure.

Here the antithesis which underlies Dos Passos's thinking has become explicit: his critical intelligence operating remorselessly upon his native American society, while his sympathies go out into the Spanish, the Italian, the Latin cultures and their human types and revolutionary idealism. (The Russian notes of these travels are also sympathetic, but again more hesitant, reluctant, and finally evasive.) And in the last sections of 'In All Countries' the basic dichotomy of Dos Passos is further clarified. For this is now the United States of social crisis which Dos Passos studies. The United States of labor 'agitators' and riot guns, of deserted, idle factory towns and mills, of men and boys 'standing still, saying nothing, looking no-where,' of the Harlan miners and breadlines. The 'great ma-chine,' so adamant, so unshakable a few short years before, is indeed shaken. But the Dos Passos who reports on the Washing-ton of 1932, the Hunger Strikers, the B.E.F., and Anacostia Flats, the heart of this democracy in chaos, is himself not changed. The Dos Passos who wanders through the House of Representatives (of the 'sovereign wardheelers'), the anti-quated scene of the Supreme Court, the early offices of the New Deal with their 'rosy smokescreen'; who compares Delano the Magician with Hoover the Ventriloquist; this author has little apparent concern with his social system, now so disorganized and trembling. 'Roosevelt or Hoover? It'll be the same cops.' As in his description of the Republican Convention, Dos Passos, indeed, sees the machinery of democracy in crisis chiefly in terms of spotlights and microphones, of theatrical fixtures pro-jecting an empty illusion:

> but the grand climax, when His Master's Voice poured out of the loud-speakers, and a moving picture of the rotund features of the Great Engineer flicked vaguely on two huge screens was a flop. . . . The Presence failed to materialize.

And for the Dos Passos of 1934 the Presence of democracy itself had failed to materialize.

'Fortune Heights' in the same year, the third and best of Dos Passos's plays, presents the story of a typical real-estate develop-ment of the boom era, Fortune Heights itself. In the outline of the American prosperity ethics, the first section of the play represents Dos Passos in his most penetrating satiric illumina-tions. And by contrast the last act, where Dos Passos expounds again his revolutionary thesis, seems perhaps all the more melodramatic in tone and moralistic in its exposition. As Fortune Heights crumbles away under the impact of the de-pression, its promoter, Ellery Jones, simply changes his occupa-tion to politics, his salesmanship to political oratory. But the speculator still operating behind the front of the reformer, the people in 'Fortune Heights' and by inference the author of the play himself reject the legal processes of political change for those of direct action and 'mass pressure.' In crisis, Dos Passos argues here, the American system changed its language, but not its beliefs. It presents a new façade for the old dealings. The government is still the same. The government is still the enemy. Thus, in the rather contemptuous disposal of our native American solutions for the economic depression of the nineteen-thirties which marks 'Fortune Heights,' Dos Passos reveals again the fundamental dissociation of the writer of this period from his own society. Both 'Fortune Heights' and 'In All Countries' carry forward the elaboration of his radical point of view — this American critique so indigenous in tone, well versed in our traditions, so much more learned, penetrating than any previous social study by any American novelist, and a critique nevertheless with its roots outside of the heritage and promise of our American traditions.

As Mac was the typical figure of 'The 42nd Parallel' and Joe Williams was that of '1919,' Charley Anderson becomes the symptomatic character of 'The Big Money' in 1936. Through him Dos Passos now shows the American social patterns in their most corrosive aspects. Returning from the war as an aviation ace, Charley, with his friend Joe Askew, starts the Askew-Merritt aviation company, finds himself thrown suddenly into the midst of the Lardnerian wealth. But material success hardly proves his salvation. Entering metropolitan life, Charley has a rather nasty love affair with Eveline Hutchins, now married and simultaneously opening her own career of illicit sexual relationships. From this Charley slips into a perhaps worse relationship with New York's Doris Humphries. Driven to torment by her tantalizing, frigid personality, Charley resorts to a series of drunken jags; in one of the worst of these he sells out his share of the Askew-Merritt Corporation. Now swiftly rising in the world, betraying the last few solid influences in his life — his partner Joe Askew, Bill Cermak his mechanic friend, and with Cermak the feeling of comradeship for the

mechanics in his shop, the feeling of craft Charley has had for
the shop itself — Charley leaves for Detroit. Stock market
gambling, a high society marriage with Gladys Wheatley, the
associations and values of the top flight of the American industrial order, lead him from one disaster to another. And
finally driven from his home by Gladys, driven out of his company by the financial manipulation of his friends the bankers,
and then out of the stock market itself, resorting in his declining
days to a commercialized sexual relationship with the gold-
digging Margo Dowling, Charley Anderson closes his glittering
career, amidst the ceaseless drunken fantasies which mark his
end, by cracking up in a motor car.

Around this central epic of disintegration in 'The Big
Money,' Dos Passos has concluded the lesser but no less appalling stories of his other central figures. Eleanor Stoddard has
become a refined shadow in the novel now as her life itself has
become a refined shadow. J. Ward Moorehouse has grown
older and emptier also in his own pursuit of Success; and with
his age he perceives his failure, cracks and dies. Dick Savage,
the ex-Harvard intellectual and potential radical who has succumbed in turn to the blandishments of the big money, takes
over Ward's rôle as publicity wizard. But what Ward did with
single purpose, Dick does with conflicts of spirit, accentuated
by sexual conflicts steadily growing more severe, ending with
the realization of his moral bankruptcy, and his terrible,
drunken surrender to the negro male prostitutes. Charley
Anderson's Margo Dowling is perhaps the worst of these
portraits — this child accustomed to deceit, thieving, sexual
depravity; this glamorous lady who would be deeply pathological if she were not totally amoral; who rises through the
ranks of prostitution, vaudeville, and the cinema to become
America's Sweetheart in the fabulous extravaganza of the
Success Myth which Hollywood typifies. Summarizing these
portraits of human disintegration which support his central
thesis, and which are presented as typical products of the
American pattern of aggression in the epoch of material opu-

lence, Dos Passos again places his Biographies — the key portraits now of a society which, having distorted all ordinary
human values for his competitive functioning, is itself apparently beginning to break down. Here in turn are Frederick
Winslow Taylor, the efficiency genius for whom his society
found no place; Henry Ford, the mechanical genius vainly attempting to recapture the world he had helped to obliterate;
Hearst gaining power 'out of the rot of democracy,' power but
never fulfillment; Insull, the breaking-up of whose baseless
utilities empire is symptomatic of that of an equally baseless
economic order; Veblen, drinking the bitter drink of America's
failure to use its talent, recording, as the chronicler of this disintegrating society, 'the last grabbing urges of the profit system
taking on, as he put it, the systematized delusions of dementia
praecox.'

The facts of 'The Big Money,' as we summarize them, may
seem bad enough. They are rendered appalling by the skill
with which Dos Passos now portrays them. Of the entire
trilogy here are the best of the Biographies and Camera Eyes,
the most pointed of the Newsreels, and here the flatness has
gone out of the Dos Passos people in the Novels. We can no
longer regard them as documents, as political puppets or as
sociological data. We are compelled by the author to identify
ourselves with them; they have become complex and convincing personages whose defeats we must share. In their disintegration, Charley Anderson, Dick Savage, Mary French, who
is the radical protagonist again and through whose narrative
we come to the drunken twilight of Revolution itself, now filled
with betraying memories and dissipated hopes — these figures
of 'The Big Money' have the vital drives sometimes lacking in
the previous achievement of Dos Passos. What a subject the
Lardnerian epoch makes for the novelist, more fully aware, as
Lardner was not, of its implications! And how wonderfully
'The Big Money' portrays that epoch.

It is a curious paradox of the 'U.S.A.' trilogy that as Dos
Passos's view grows steadily more despairing, his sympathy for

his people should steadily increase, his craft should develop, his entire equipment as a creative novelist should grow so much more effective — a paradox which leads to others. We have noticed the disoriented political view of the writer. In cultural terms there is very little center, moreover, to this historical study. Dos Passos shows us the heights and the depths of American society, the extremes of the Success Myth and those of revolutionary radicalism. But he omits, we may almost say, the bulk of the American people in his survey: those who live on the middle-ground, the mid-American citizens, those who are neither as rich nor as happy as they might be, perhaps, but who are also neither corrupted nor ground down by the prevailing patterns of society. So too in the individual presentation of his people, Dos Passos the novelist avoids any middle-ground of human actions, any common decency or happiness, or perhaps even the common facts of life. The story of Charley Anderson in 'The Big Money' is in extreme form the story of the behavior of all the Dos Passos people — these people who are apparently incapable of enjoying or keeping ordinary things in life, of maintaining ordinary human relationships, of gaining a minimum of ordinary human content which, being neither ecstasy nor despair, is still perhaps valuable. Looking over the entire range of Dos Passos people, indeed, what a gloomy picture confronts us! What women these are, steadily refining themselves away into respectable ghosts like Eleanor Stoddard, or steadily becoming sexually looser like Eveline Hutchins, or growing dryer, primmer, tighter like Janey Williams, or turning into revolutionary automatons like Mary French! 'Sleeping with a man,' Dos Passos records about her, 'didn't make as much difference in her life as she'd expected it would.' And perhaps we may add that with these Dos Passos ladies, apparently very little else makes very much difference in their lives. And what of the Dos Passos masculine figures? Sexually nil like J. Ward Moorehouse, having 'no time for that sort of thing'; stricken with homosexual conflicts like Dick Savage; pursuing these frigid or indiscriminate vampires like

Charley Anderson, and having captured one, turning to the
commercial and amoral wiles of his Margo Dowling. No
normal sexual releases apparently possible for these people, it is
perhaps idle to discuss their love relationships, or the non-
existent bonds of friendship in these modern American protagonists. With them there is no love, no friendship, no satis-
factions of family life, indeed very little family life at all, and
in the end very little human give-and-take in the common
business of living — no signs of flexibility in this vast, rigid, encompassing framework of human narcissism, perversion, and sterility.

The basic view of life in the 'U.S.A.' trilogy defeats itself in
one sense, of course. If these Dos Passos people are really as he
seems to want them to be, there would be little value in the
catharsis of social revolution which Dos Passos has been insisting
on. For such a revolution implies the freeing of human traits
which the present social order is crushing. But in these American protagonists, what is there to free? Where are the little
moments of human warmth, generosity, decency? Perhaps only
in the briefer Biographies, in the more historical, theoretical,
symbolic portraits. (And if these were turned into the full-
length Novels, we may wonder how much of their virtue would
remain in the Biographies also.) The total picture in Dos
Passos is that of inherent human weakness rather than crushed
strength, of barely restrained viciousness rather than of inhibited human potentialities. And the radical heroes of 'U.S.A.,'
indeed, who should perhaps reveal the promise of humanity
more fully, show it least. If this is an accurate portrait of the
race, then we may also say that the Capitalism which Dos Passos is attacking, if it is the cause of these social types, seems also
to be their proper orbit, their precise and poetical environment,
their logical inferno. Capitalism is what they deserve.

As the 'U.S.A.' trilogy comes to its conclusion, however, we
also come to see more fully that these Dos Passos people are not
in their entirety accurate historical creations, but very often the
symbols of a bleak and despairing view of life. Here again, behind the radical historian, is the American poet of dissolution,

comparable in these respects to our Hemingway, though working in such a different medium. If they are moulded by the social pressures of American culture, these Dos Passos people are
also being pursued by their Fate — by the internal view of the
writer now being projected outward into the patterns of our
society. In this respect the entire American critique of Dos
Passos may be viewed as the sociological embodiment of a point
of view: the bitterness of his social analysis, the despair of his
conclusions being not so much the historian's verdict as the
poet's lament, and the discontents of American civilization becoming in part the symbols for those of an indignant and disturbed soul.

In part. For despite the two central limitations in its view
which we have been tracing — the fundamental disorientation
of the artist from his society, and the fundamentally negative
view of life itself — how often also does the 'U.S.A.' trilogy
strike us as true and just, as both discerning and impassioned.
If despite the conversion of his early hero from aesthete to revolutionary, the promise of humanity is not very fully developed
in Dos Passos's work, what was there in the American twenties
to support such a promise? Despite his early return to the
American scene, his apprenticeship in the twenties, Dos Passos
is never able fully to integrate himself with the American society
he is describing; his sympathies remain outside it, his revolutionary idealism centers still in Europe. Yet what in the American prosperity decade could gain his sympathies and attract
his idealism? And if the artist of 'U.S.A.' confuses our democracy with the last extremes of our monopolistic finance, the
United States itself before the fortunate incidence of the depression seemed to be enjoying such a disastrous confusion. The
'U.S.A.' trilogy must be viewed as a study of our cultural weakness, of the dissonances, the dangers, and the strains which exist
in our society — a study which tends to ignore the factors of
strength and survival which reside also in our republican traditions. Yet who better than Dos Passos has caught these strains?
Who has illuminated more brilliantly the dark places of our so-

ciety; and recorded more intensely these dissonances of American life in the machine age? The 'U.S.A.' trilogy as a whole must be considered the most profound creative study of our cultural patterns given to us by an American novelist. Coming upon the heels of Dreiser's 'American Tragedy,' the last big product of a now obsolete tradition, Dos Passos has reinvigorated the novel of social criticism; and in the epoch which followed 'Broom' and 'Transition,' he has tied a dazzling but often empty tradition of literary experimentalism to a really tremendous study of the folkways of a continent. He has given a third dimension — society itself — to the older concepts of the novel of character; and very often this third dimension becomes rather more significant than the other two; for it is after all American society as a whole which is the real hero of 'U.S.A.' And steadily growing more skillful in craft and evocative in its emotions, the trilogy becomes in the end as aesthetically exciting as it is intellectually impressive.

Why is it, moreover, that despite the limitations of view, the cumulative effort in 'U.S.A.' to make a villain out of American democracy, why is it, repressed, evasive, apparently always the chronicle of our failure, the democratic myth nevertheless remains in the work of Dos Passos? Why is it that in the most eloquent passages of 'U.S.A.' it is again the American fate, always crushed, thwarted if not ridiculed, which nevertheless haunts the words on the pages of the novel and burns itself into the novel's structure?

> ... why not tell these men stamping in the wind that we stand on a quicksand?   that doubt is the whetstone of understanding is too hard hurts instead of urging   picket John D. Rockefeller the bastard if the cops knock your blocks off it's all for the advancement of the human race   while I go home ... and ponder the course of history and what leverage might pry the owners loose from power and bring back (I too Walt Whitman) our storybook democracy....

For Whitman, of course, our democracy was never a storybook one, and the decline of the democratic faith from Whitman to

Dos Passos makes perhaps a sad story — but is the story ended? 'U.S.A.' is the work of a maturing writer, of a growing writer, of a divided writer whose fundamental emotional stresses have yet to be resolved. We may say that the American apprentice-ship of Dos Passos is still continuing; his return to America until now has been, in one sense, a purely formal one. The process of his maturing, the clarification of the conflicts in Dos Passos, the start of a new view of American life, and indeed perhaps of life itself — these final meanings of Dos Passos begin to be revealed in his two latest works which indicate his reorientation as an American artist.

5. OUR STORYBOOK DEMOCRACY.   The two years after 'The Big Money' were again for Dos Passos a period of revision and consolidation.   In 1937 he published his three major novels as the single unit they were designed to be,'U.S.A.' In 1938 he published his collected travel notes revised, elabo-rated, with new material, as 'Journeys Between Wars.'   (It is significant as part of the self-awareness which marks Dos Passos that in his revisions he eliminates the weaker portions of his earlier work with an accurate eye for his own failings.)   And indeed these two volumes of collected fiction and travel jour-neys once again impress upon us the tremendous and distin-guished achievement of Dos Passos, the 'U.S.A.' trilogy perhaps even more effective as a unit than in terms of the single novels we have been considering.

These two years of revision and consolidation, however, are also a time of spiritual stress for Dos Passos which results in the disillusionment of his next novel. 'Adventures of a Young Man' in 1939 is the history of a young American radical, Glenn Spotswood, from the early forms of his personal revolt to his introduction into the American labor movements of the nine-teen-twenties, his conversion to Communism, his disillusionment and rejection of it, and his final death in the internecine struggles of the opposing radical factions during the course of the Spanish Civil War. Perhaps after the range of view and craft in 'U.S.A.,' the intensity with which a society is presented to us, any single volume traditional in craft and restricted to an individual's life would seem, for Dos Passos, less significant. We must add, however, that 'Adventures of a Young Man' lacks the sense of powerful human impulses however blocked and thwarted which mark 'The Big Money,' and the compassion heightened by fine satire with which they are viewed there. 'Adventures of a Young Man' is thus a sort of reversion to the earlier tone of Dos Passos, the more naturalistic chronicles, the colder and flatter people, closer to moralistic figures; but with what a changed moral!

If the Glen Spotswood of 'Adventures' is another of Dos Passos's radical protagonists, this time the lesson is not the failure of American democracy but rather that of the radical movements which, in the earlier work, were to offer us the salvation for our society. Perhaps we may say that Glen Spotswood is the last of Dos Passos's radical protagonists. And as a record of this total disenchantment, 'Adventures of a Young Man' is often perceptive and illuminating. If we were trying to tell, indeed, the typical story of our modern radical doctrines and parties, we could find few better source books of the human elements which are involved; the disastrous human elements; and the failure of the American Left. In the dubious origins of Glen's revolutionary ardor, the confusion and weakness of his own will, the failure of his personal relationships, which he never solves but escapes from to throw his energies into the workers' cause, Dos Passos's hero is of course typical of a certain sort of radical — and one who has seemed particularly to fill the ranks and often to distort the purposes of our American post-war movements. The 'Adventures of a Young Man' records these: the fusion of Bohemianism and Socialism, the meeting of Greenwich Village with Union Square, the rather terrifying mixture of glib Freudianism with supple Marxism, of free sex and free thinking, these theoretical barricades of the twenties which all too often became love nests. Upon the peculiar revolutionary ferment which marked the post-war American political movements of the Left, and traced by Dos Passos with a sort of honesty we must admit even while we are embarrassed by it, the miracle of Russian Communism descended. But if the Glen Spotswood of 'Adventures' also yields to this miracle, his disillusionment, encompassing that of a generation of American radicals, is sharp. The last half of 'Adventures of a Young Man' traces what Dos Passos believes to be the decline of the Marxist salvation in America. And with Glen's expulsion from the Party, his persecution by his former comrades, with the shooting of his Mexican anarchist friend Perez by the Communist Party, and the final destruction and death of Glen himself in the Spanish Civil War (through which Dos Passos reveals the climax of factional strife, the hatred of revolutionary for brother revolutionary, the struggle for power among the Leftist parties over the body of a dying Spain) the cycle of radical dissolution in 'Adventures' is complete. So Dos Passos records the follies and the failure of the American Left, the close of that international revolutionary ardor which illuminated his early work:

> C'est la lutte finale
>   Groupons-nous et demain
> L'internationale
>   Sera le genre humain.

For certainly the Marxist assumptions have held Dos Passos, have been the central framework of his thinking, the Marxist hopes and practices, if sometimes before the unknown Russian materialization Dos Passos has held back. And certainly this is now in 'Adventures of a Young Man' the destruction of the central framework of his work, of his own beliefs and hopes. If the accents of our writer are harsh in the novel, if in the immediate grasp of the disaster the novelist can hardly create a work to match the tragedy of his theme, we can see why. For if 'Adventures' is the record of failure of the American Left, it is by the

same token the admission of failure for Dos Passos himself.
What his protagonist Glen has done in deed, Dos Passos himself
— though he has always hesitated, always has drawn back before the final, conclusive step — has been, as we've seen, on the
verge of doing in thought. This caution perhaps has saved the
writer from the total disaster of his hero. But what is recorded
nevertheless in 'Adventures of a Young Man' is the final dises-
tablishment of the spiritual values and intellectual themes which
Dos Passos himself has built up over the twenty years of social
thinking and writing — this faith built, as we've seen, with so
much hesitation, reworking of themes and retracing of views, this
certainty which has come so hard to a spirit always testing its
faith on the whetstone of doubt. The real drama of 'Adventures' is beneath the novel then, the drama of the novelist now
facing, at his maturity, a major reorientation of his views. And
how indeed can we hope to portray the spiritual turbulence
which must lie in these three hundred pages of 'Adventures,'
artistically imperfect as they are, and nevertheless carrying
within them the destruction of the entire evolution of Dos
Passos, from the pallid aesthetes of his early work to the revolutionary protagonists of his later novels; the denial of the radical
faith which for Dos Passos has become the single positive pole in
his study of the disintegration of the American Republic — this
system of values, this hope and faith, this illusion which must
now be cast off?

That the climax of the drama should be placed in Spain
completes, of course, the sense of loss and tragedy. For if Dos
Passos's thinking has been linked to Marxist theory and the Russian Revolution, we have seen also how his emotions have always been drawn to the Spanish culture. From the origins of
his radicalism in the writings of Baroja in 'Rosinante,' through
the Spanish anarchist types who are always drawn so warmly in
his novels, to the Sacco-Vanzetti trial which became the catalyst of his mature work, we have seen Dos Passos's preoccupation with the Mediterranean cultures, the freeing of his feeling,
the warmth and intensity of his affections which he has never

been able to sustain in terms of Anglo-Saxon culture and American society. But now Spain, origin and center of his feelings, has been destroyed. Its destruction, moreover, as Dos Passos implies in the 'Adventures of a Young Man' is accomplished as much by revolutionary factionalism and internecine strife as by the external forces of German and Italian Fascism. The source of the novelist's affections is thus in a sense destroyed by the actual functioning of his radical beliefs. The object of love, as it were, is crushed by one's own contrivance. The fall of Republican Spain was a sort of double disaster for Dos Passos, in which one part of his spiritual beliefs destroyed both itself and the balance of his belief. Perhaps few writers have had to suffer such a blow at the summit of their career, and perhaps few writers could be so aware as Dos Passos of the full implications of this irony. No wonder then that the conclusion of 'Adventures of a Young Man' in particular should seem often flat and weary, as if the writer lacked the energy to conclude his story; such a story and such a conclusion.

It is hardly accidental, I believe, that the last of Dos Passos's revolutionary protagonists, the Glen Spotswood of 'Adventures,' though outwardly very different, should revert in his emotional patterns to the earlier heroes of Dos Passos: the young aesthetes out of whom, converting his values and his heroes, Dos Passos evolved his radical figures. In many respects Glen resembles and recalls these earlier heroes, these sad and good young men who are unable to find their place in humanity or society, and who at last, unable to make a meaning out of their lives, allow themselves to drift along: with the Martin Howe of 'One Man's Initiation,' awaiting the call of some beneficent sky goddess, with the Jimmie Herf of 'Manhattan Transfer' at the mercy of the post-war disillusionment, and now with the Glen Spotswood of 'Adventures of a Young Man' at the dubious mercy of radical factionalism. For with the intellectual and emotional framework of his career shattered, it is very natural for the novelist to return to his earlier literary patterns. And here we must state our own feeling that the early hero of Dos

Passos represents more than a literary pattern; the Martin
Howe and Jimmie Herf of Dos Passos are the literary symptoms
of a somewhat more basic spiritual complex. We must admit
our own belief, despite the total conversion of this early hero
which we have been tracing and the meticulous artistic eradi-
cation of his traits, that the emotional stresses which created the
earlier protagonists have remained with Dos Passos, underlying
his work — the sense of exile being heightened by his antago-
nism to his native society, and now the sense of despair returning
with the destruction of his radical faith.

But is our novelist then to be reduced once more, the cycle of
his radical education concluded in disillusionment, to the nerveless, rootless, drifting of his apprenticeship period? In the framework of Dos Passos's entire growth, we may see the importance
of his latest work, 'The Ground We Stand On' in 1941 — an importance the critics who marked the defects of the book have
perhaps tended to ignore. In terms of Dos Passos's best work,
'The Ground We Stand On' is not successful. Discussing now
as historian rather than novelist the roots of American republican traditions, Dos Passos treats freedom of conscience through
Roger Williams, civil rights through Jefferson, economic opportunity through Franklin (and much more than this of course),
the American literary spirit through Joel Barlow, and our early
political activities through Samuel Adams. The range of historical characters and episodes thus varied in 'The Ground We
Stand On,' we are again respectfully aware of the range of Dos
Passos's own interest and knowledge; here is another facet of
the most learned and thoughtful of our novelists. But we feel at
the end of the study also that it lacks enough concision in its
writing, certainty in its conclusions; the purposes for which
Dos Passos is writing his history are not always fulfilled. We
have the feeling that 'The Ground We Stand On' is written
more for its author than for his readers; it is the notebook now
of his travels in American republican traditions; here he is
reaching not formulating his conclusions. But in the words
which seem to indicate the failure of 'The Ground We Stand

On,' we see precisely how illuminating that failure is. As 'Rosinante' recorded the birth of Dos Passos's revolutionary idealism in the European tradition, Dos Passos is now recording his own new American explorations, his re-education, the building of a new system of values to replace those which ended in the 'Adventures of a Young Man.' Is it strange to find the biographer of the Smolny mills studying the white porches of Jefferson's Monticello? How long it has taken our artists, what a tortuous and weary road they have traveled to learn that America also has had its revolutions, its struggles to maintain human dignity against oppressive forces, its own seeds of that New Order which our radical thinkers sought everywhere but in America! The wave of the future once dashed against Plymouth Rock. America was once the beacon and flame of social regeneration for that Europe itself toward which our disenchanted modern children turned for their faith: our true heritage, much older, deeper, and more enduring than the finance-capitalism with which Dos Passos, like his generation, confuses it in 'U.S.A.' and from which now he must disentangle it so painfully. A De Tocqueville once visited the raw scene of the democratic revolution in much the same spirit as our Dos Passos surveyed the socialist revolution. And it is now the search for this heritage, our native republican traditions, our American as distinct from our monopolistic democracy which, however imperfectly formulated as yet, marks the value of 'The Ground We Stand On.' 'I, myself, believe ... that our peculiar institutions have a future, and that this country is getting to be a better place to live in instead of a worse.' However cautious the tone, and indeed almost grudging in its admission, this marks once again — as with the Hemingway we have studied, the Wolfe and Steinbeck we shall trace — the return of the American artist to his home. And with Dos Passos it is the true rather than the formal return: the formal return which preceded 'The Ground We Stand On' by some fifteen years; the magnificent American critique from 'Manhattan Transfer' on, which was nevertheless the product of a disoriented view and of estranged emotions.

The estranged emotions which seem to be so often the heritage of the American artist, and particularly our own generation, coming out of the Lardnerian twenties. For there is a curious discontent in the later work of Dos Passos, a weariness and bitterness of tone, a sense of strain, of effort hardly worth the achieving, which lies behind the artistic failure in both 'Adventures of a Young Man' and 'The Ground We Stand On.' How shall we define this last issue, whose intimations come to us from many sections of Dos Passos's work, and yet whose central structure is not altogether apparent? Is it the last heritage of the early Dos Passos hero — the echoes of that earlier 'failure of nerve' which had so preoccupied our writer? We have seen the sense of futility which marked the first literary figures of Dos Passos. We have said that they at least in part represented the final stage in the separation of the American artist from his society which came to its climax in the nineteen-twenties; that the sense of their own lack of function in life reflected that of their creator, the American writer surrounded by the Lardnerian materialism. With his introduction to the Spanish revolutionary faith, *la nueva ley*, in 'Rosinante,' Dos Passos dispels this earlier nervelessness from his work, casting off his earlier mood of disdainful isolation, converting his pallid, introspective hero of the twenties into the radical protagonist of the thirties. Now with the return of the familiar patterns of his hero in 'Adventures of a Young Man,' with the sense of weariness in the later work culminating perhaps in 'The Ground We Stand On,' is the failure of nerve returning also? As with Hemingway, are the Lardnerian twenties still exacting their price from the American writer, themselves being long gone and turned into historical ashes?

Yet the sociological explanation, however vital, seems also perhaps a little simple. Certainly reinforced by the cultural conditions of his literary apprenticeship, his sense of rebellion and frustration being the common heritage of his generation of American writers, there is also in Dos Passos himself a skeptical. a doubting, and often a negative strain; this archetype as he is of the rational and moral writer, this embodiment of the conscious and progressive forces. We have seen in him now how the exile disputes with the citizen, the social rebel opposes the reformer, and how always seeking his civilizational positives, Dos Passos is at his most brilliant in the despairing dissolution of 'The Big Money.' This seeker after Utopia is himself to be consumed by the fires of Inferno, we said, and we have noticed how the particular horrors of American finance-capitalism seem not so much the cause but the just reward of the Dos Passos people. And indeed there seems very often in Dos Passos an underlying doubt, not merely as to the social solutions he is seeking, but in the efficacy of any solution — a doubt in the efficacy, that is to say, of human life itself. It is perhaps a last and somewhat theatrical irony that the novelist, who has stood above all for mature values in his thinking, should in his emotions seem to question mature humanity. Thus looking back over the total achievement of Dos Passos which has come out of the basic struggle within the artist — the twenty years' total of conscientious and often painful progress, these two decades of innovation and bold experimentation which at their summit suffered disaster and once again had to be revised, this achievement in places imperfect but in its entirety so impressive — we may better understand, perhaps, the sense of fatigue in the last two works of Dos Passos.

But this fatigue is natural, and can only be temporary. For what marvels of work, nevertheless, what resolutions of intelligence and energy have been accomplished by the pallid and despairing young man hidden beneath the revolutionary intensity of Dos Passos! What nerve has been made manifest by the writer so concerned with the failure of nerve! By his own record Dos Passos has opposed the weaker elements of his temperament which one may surmise. By the exercise of the conscious will, the reasoning faculties, what we have called the positive and moral bent in Dos Passos, the writer has defied the negative strains within him. As they are within us all; what struggle has been made without them; what victory has not been their fusion and synthesis? It is the synthesis to which we look forward now in Dos Passos, as he merges his beliefs with his native traditions, exorcizing at last the opposing and weary exile, the failure of nerve giving place to the conviction of the writer who may fulfill, quite pre-eminently, his cultural rôle. 'And ponder the course of history and what leverage might pry the owners loose from power and bring back (I too Walt Whitman) our story-book democracy.'

Chapter Four

William Faulkner : THE NEGRO AND THE FEMALE

◇

1. UNRECONSTRUCTED REBEL   2. THE INCUBAE
3. THE NEGRO AND THE FEMALE   4. THE GREAT HATRED

Chapter Four

William Faulkner: THE NEGRO AND THE FEMALE

---

1. UNRECONSTRUCTED REBEL. We have noticed with Lardner, Hemingway, Dos Passos, the aversion of the writer in the nineteen-twenties to the patterns of his American society, the society which turned all the principles of its life into its principal, and demanded only interest. With the younger writers to follow, those moulded by the thirties like Thomas Wolfe and John Steinbeck, the process of cultural integration, the assimilation of American values themselves sharply changing, becomes less painful. There is less of the sense of traumatic shock which marks the American return of Hemingway and Dos Passos, and of the original almost schizophrenic cleft between the gifted individual and his communal existence. To the new writers, in fact, the anguish of their ancestors becomes a rather questionable speculation. The moving finger, having written, moves on. And if not all our piety and wit 'shall lure it back to cancel half a line,' it is nevertheless true that the historical script we read is never the one that was inscribed by the Eternal Sáki. 'Not even God can change the past'; nor our changing view of it.

Between these two literary movements William Faulkner stands, a curious author in a curious position. Born in 1897, a year later than Dos Passos and a year before Hemingway (what three distinguished talents those three years bore!), Faulkner seems to follow them in his early heritage as an American. Again the war experience would seem to be the central factor of Faulkner's youth. He joined the Canadian Flying Corps and served in the British Royal Air Force in France. He was wounded in an airplane accident. Yet with the common time and deed which Faulkner shares with his generation, there is an essential difference of setting. Here, as in all else, the American being the Everyman of the modern world, there is a variety of origins which helps to explain the variety of our American genius. While Hemingway derives from the middle-western town, and the urban origins of Dos Passos are part of his virtue and weakness, Faulkner is of course from the South which is both the clue and the scourge of his work. Faulkner was born in Mississippi, Mr. Millett tells us in his invaluable handbook of 'Contemporary American Authors,'

> of a family of governors, statesmen, and other public figures.... His great-grandfather, Colonel William Falkner, was the author of a popular novel, 'The White Rose of Memphis.' Early in his childhood he went to live in Oxford, Mississippi, and it has been his home almost uninterruptedly ever since.

These lines are to tell us more than Faulkner's European experience — this family tradition, this home uninterrupted except by visions of incest, rape, and murder, these ancestral halls in which echo only the sobs and shrieks of demons; a possessed gallery of the decaying and the demented who live in memory; memory which leads only backward in thinning circles of disaster until the cycle is wasted and spent in time; and memory itself passes into silence.

For in William Faulkner there is no such conversion as Hemingway and Dos Passos acquaint us with, no effort however imperfect at the integration of artist and society, or indeed of artist and modern life itself. With Faulkner the descending spiral of isolation, rebellion, and denial, the heritage of American negation, reaches its final emphasis. With him, we make our last study of the influence of the nineteen-twenties, forming, lasting over, and wholly conditioning the artist of the thirties. If the writing on the wall has already changed, each generation reading anew the chronicle of its origins and midwife to its own destiny, this one novelist stands and defies the vanishing script, like the Hightower of 'Light in August,' hearing still the thunder of martial hooves upon a cloud of phantom dust. The causes of this in Faulkner's work form an interesting sequence. Here is in some respects the history of a dissipated talent, but the history of the dissipation becomes as remarkable as the talent. So let us make our little pilgrimage to Jefferson, Mississippi (as certain respectable scholars are wont to visit Hardy's Wessex or the Lake district of the English romantics), though here we shall hardly glimpse a rugged yeomanry, thatched cottages, musing shepherds, pastoral games. The Faulknerian countryside has its own customs nevertheless — deep southern region of Baptists and brothels, of attic secrets, land of shadows and swamps alike in its interior and outward scene, presided over by its twin Furies, the odd conjunction in the Faulknerian epic of the Negro and the Female. Coming to Jefferson, Mississippi, we touch the capital of this world, which reaches backward in time to the origins of southern culture, forward to the horrid prophecies of its extinction; and ranges down in social strata from the Sartoris nobility to the new commercial aristocracy of the Snopeses; down to the last extremes of the modern dispossessed: the poor-white Bundrens of 'As I Lay Dying,' the criminal Popeye of 'Sanctuary,' the negro Christmas turned brute again by the society which had raised him from the animal. And even in these extremes and others — its overdone idiocy, its agglomeration of perverts and fanatics, all the excesses of disease, its labored anguish and fabricated horrors — the Faulknerian geography is often quite compelling, memorable, if hardly to the Wessex tourist, quite respectable. It is certain that William Faulkner not merely represents, but is the deep South as no other American novelist may quite claim to be. And whatever the sequence we shall trace here, it is certain that Faulkner remains in a double sense the unreconstructed rebel; living as he does in two pasts — that of his own youth, and in the other youth, tropical, cultivated, evanescent, of the South itself.

2. THE INCUBAE.   Like his generation also, Faulkner
starts his work with a dissonance, with another discordant overture to the post-war disenchantment. 'Soldiers' Pay' in 1926 is
of the same vintage as the tale of Hemingway's Krebs, Dos Passos's 'Three Soldiers,' or Tom Boyd's 'Through the Wheat.'
It is worth noticing how many traits these novels bear in common. As we read them we see that they are written by the
same historical mind, and a mind which is marked by the similar defects appearing in all these works. In 'Soldiers' Pay'
there is again no valid appraisement either as to the causes of
the First World War or the solutions of the Armistice. The
single heritage of the war is futility, the only response of the
post-war protagonist is alcoholic. Yet if 'Soldiers' Pay' is somewhat limited in its commentary on the world, it is revealing in
its comments on Faulkner himself. Anticipating Dalton Trum-
bo's 'Johnny Got His Gun,' the Donald Mahon of 'Soldiers'
Pay' returns from the European battlefield without the powers
of memory or movement; of all the traits of life, in fact, retaining
only one, the flickering, uncertain, blind clinging to existence
itself. 'The man that was wounded is dead and this is another
person, a grown child.' We must remember the opening emphasis also, in Faulkner's work, on the reversion to childhood.
And Donald Mahon, disfigured, uncomprehending lump of
flesh who may be called the central object rather than the central figure of 'Soldiers' Pay,' is thus the first of those peculiar
protagonists of Faulkner, from Benjy the aristocratic idiot of
'The Sound and the Fury' through to Isaac Snopes, the socially
parvenu idiot of 'The Hamlet,' whom Benjy would certainly not
talk to, we rather imagine, if Benjy could talk at all. These protagonists who at their best are mentally deficient, and whom we
shall see more often at their worst. Yet disgusting and degraded,
Mahon carries the mark of suffering, the remnants of human
dignity. We must learn to distinguish between Faulkner's
grades of imbecility, and Mahon, the result of society's crime, is
among the more sympathetic abnormalities of Faulkner's
work; the sections on him are not without compassion. And by

contrast with the Cecily Saunders who is engaged to marry him, we may say that Mahon, inanimate as he is, achieves almost a full human stature. Just as Mahon is the ancestor of the Faulknerian hero, the Cecily of 'Soldiers' Pay' is the first of those Faulknerian women in whose distasteful destinies lies a central meaning of the writer's work. Perhaps we may say of Cecily that no single attribute of hers is so odious as her total temperament. In appearance also there is nothing very alarming in the portrait of Cecily which the author gives us. Like the Patricia of 'Mosquitoes' and the Temple Drake of 'Sanctuary,' Cecily is the apparently typical Scott Fitzgerald post-war flapper, thin, flat, and emancipated, the prototype of the modern freedom of the sexes. But with Cecily and her Faulknerian sisters who follow her, this 'emancipation' is a euphemism for iniquity. To be free is apparently to be vicious. If Cecily is socially equal, she is also sexually insatiable. Infantile as well as precocious, sliding out of all her moral obligations without even being aware of them, as loose in her behavior as she is frigid in her feelings, using her charms as bait for the achieving of some purpose that she is quite indifferent to, dealing in all the physical pleasures without any gratification, Cecily starts out in 'Soldiers' Pay' as a curious adolescent and ends as a rather disgusting female. In the process of leading our curiosity about Cecily into this aversion to her, moreover, Faulkner surrounds her history with even more curious sexual references, sometimes oblique, sometimes direct. But whether uttered in jest or in venom, they lead to one conclusion, which is summarized in the reflections of Joe Gilligan who dislikes gardens:

> Whenever he was among flowers he always felt as if he had entered a room full of women: he was always conscious of his body, of his walk, feeling as though he trod in sand. So he believed that he really did not like flowers.

This is the sentiment, here expressed at its most favorable — a suspicion of women when it is not contempt, and contempt when it is not hatred — which dominates 'Soldiers' Pay.' We have here, of course, another reflection of the war of the sexes, most openly expressed perhaps by James Thurber, which occupies such a large part of the modern novel, which sheds a little more light on the nerveless young males of Dos Passos, and which Edmund Wilson has caught very acutely in relation to Hemingway's work. 'Soldiers' Pay' is as much or more an anti-feminine novel as an anti-war novel. And the portrait of the crippled, scarred body of Donald Mahon, intended to convey the horrors of the battlefield, seems to convey much more sharply the horror of the helpless male in the southern world of 'Soldiers' Pay,' dominated by these strange feminine temperaments. Reinforcing his central concept, moreover, with a good many details of sordid intrigue, already betraying his talent for the malicious (which Faulkner among contemporary writers retains perhaps in its purest form), and as early as 1926 gifted with an unusual technical facility, Faulkner makes 'Soldiers' Pay' a distinctive first novel, deserving in the United States at least some of the attention it received in England. It was Arnold Bennett, I believe, who remarked at this time that Faulkner 'writes like an angel,' though he neglected to mention what the angel was writing about.

Among Faulkner's three early novels, in fact, in the period 1926 to 1929, 'Soldiers' Pay' is the most effective. 'Mosquitoes' in 1927 (Faulkner had written some early poetry and paid homage to Sherwood Anderson, his early literary benefactor, as he does again in the dedication of 'Sartoris') develops what had been the imperfect aspects of 'Soldiers' Pay.' The studied badinage in Faulkner's second novel disturbs us, a heavy sophistication, an effect of wit which Faulkner carries off poorly (a genuine wit would save him from some of the errors he is to commit later). This troubled tone of 'Mosquitoes' is the synthesis of Aubrey Beardsley, Oscar Wilde, Aldous Huxley, and James Branch Cabell, in about this order, and with H. L. Mencken lurking behind the scenes. (These would seem the dominant influences on the early Faulkner, along with the Elizabethan poetry which he himself stresses, though his work will be much more nearly Jacobean in spirit.) The scene of 'Mosquitoes' is a luxurious but disabled yacht aboard which a group of New Orleans bohemians talk out their own luxurious but disabled existences. More precisely the formula of the novel is the early Huxley mixture of free thoughts and free love; or, as it amounts to here, of disjointed thoughts and disordered love. For the 'discussions' which mark the course of 'Mosquitoes' lack the intellectual validity of Huxley if they share a similar cynicism, and end by becoming smart rather than significant; which is the usual fate, I suppose, of Huxley's disciples or our own American followers of H. L. Mencken. What concerns us more particularly in 'Mosquitoes' is the further amplification of the themes inaugurated in 'Soldiers' Pay.' The Patricia of 'Mosquitoes' is again the Faulknerian flapper with her 'boy's body which the poise of it and the thinness of her arms belied. Sexless, yet somehow vaguely troubling.' Again elaborating the history of Patricia in the novel are the hostile references. 'This is my feminine ideal,' says sculptor Gordon pointing to his statue which has been compared to Patricia, 'a virgin with no legs to leave me, no arms to hold me, no head to talk to me.' And Fairchild, another of these philosophic spokesmen for the views of the young Faulkner, adds that the new type of woman is 'not satisfying any more; just exciting and monotonous. And mostly monotonous.' But women are never stupid —

> Their mental equipment is too sublimely sufficient to do what little directing their bodies require. . . . When women have more intelligence than that, they become nuisances sooner or later. . . . After all they are merely articulated genital organs with a kind of aptitude for spending whatever money you have; so when they get themselves up to look exactly like all the other ones, you can give all your attention to their bodies.

Thus Faulkner takes the post-war female and turns her for his purpose into a special figure. The flapper has become a sort of incubus. For there is no mistaking the special aura almost of dread with which Faulkner surrounds these creatures. But is this all directed against merely a type of post-war femininity? The Jenny of 'Mosquitoes,' in the sexual fantasies which mark the early Faulkner novels, might appear to compensate for all the limitations of Cecily and Patricia; Jenny, with her

> soft placidity, her sheer passive appeal to the senses . . . an utterly mindless rifeness of young, pink flesh, a supine potential fecundity lovely to look upon: a doll awaiting a quickening and challenging it with neither joy nor sorrow.

Yet in these words, of course, starting so pleasantly, we feel the change of attitude before the phrase itself has been completed; what starts, in fact, as desire ends as denigration. In Jenny, so sensual, sweet, and senseless, Faulkner introduces the second and apparently distinctive view of womankind which marks his novels. But is the second view superior? At her highest, the Jenny of 'Mosquitoes' will become, like the Lena of 'Light in August,' a genial case of arrested development, and at her lowest, the vicious sexual drug that Belle represents in 'Sartoris.' And we notice in both of the early Faulkner novels, how distasteful most of the characters are who surround the central figures, if they are not malicious or evil; how cold the emotions are for this young writer who seems to lack all the spontaneity of youth. The only passages of affection, indeed, in 'Mosquitoes' are those between Patricia and her brother Josh — these passages, with their tones of sibling intimacy, in which Patricia, this enigmatic female, gains an emotional warmth as a child which she hardly sustains as a woman.

Against this background of cold emotions and cheap people, the opening of Faulkner's third novel, the 'Sartoris' of 1929, comes as something of a shock For here in the chronicles of the aristocratic Sartoris line and of the pre-Civil War South which they typify, here are suddenly all the feelings of affection, of human grace and decency, and indeed of human nobility which have been hitherto so sharply missing in Faulkner's work. Is the fine old Miss Jenny of 'Sartoris,' in fact, almost too fine — shrewd, sarcastic and wise old southern belle who embodies all

the legendary merits of a departed epoch? Does she recall that
line of tottering but gallant viragoes, who for a while in the
annals of the motion picture were certain to rule with rod of
iron and heart of gold every American family brought to us by
the grace of the cinematic myth-makers? Old Sartoris himself,
the last of the old-fashioned southern gentlemen, with his hound
dogs, hunting horses, his keg of Bourbon and study of Dumas,
drowsing away his Indian Summer in memories of a better
past, Old Bayard is also a little synthetic. From Huxley, Faulkner has moved backward to Galsworthy, a strange recession.
Yet despite the overtones of sentimentality in 'Sartoris,' Faulkner has sometimes caught in it the evocation of a life that holds
at least some virtue, and whose vice has at least a certain grandeur. And why is it, against the departing scene of the Sartoris
aristocracy — with their military exploits, their deeds of daring
and devotion, their Mechlin lace and Toledo rapiers which had
brought civilization out of the southern wilderness, their silver-
mounted dueling pistols, frogged Confederate coats and ancient
brass-bound Bible — why is it that against all these remem-
brances of a vanishing splendor, Faulkner's modern tale in
'Sartoris' sounds even more inharmonious? Like the Donald
Mahon of 'Soldiers' Pay,' young Bayard Sartoris returns from
the First World War indifferent to life, his whole present activity being the hardly veiled effort to destroy himself. But
whereas Mahon was physically, Bayard is spiritually mutilated,
obsessed as he is by the death of his twin brother John in the
war, and by the ties of their childhood love for each other: 'the
young masculine violence of their twinship.' In the face of this
haunted love, the efforts of Narcissa Benbow (another aristocratic line, hereditary friends and relations of the Sartoris family) to nurse Bayard back to sanity are of little use. After her
marriage to Bayard, the birth of their son, Narcissa finally realizes this. 'Are you worrying,' Miss Jenny asks her, 'because
maybe he don't love you like you think he ought to?' 'It isn't
that.... He doesn't love anybody. He won't even love the
baby. He doesn't seem to be glad, or sorry, or anything.' Again

we have curious frigidity of the adult emotions in Faulkner's work, his people lost in their past, in their childhood affections. Miss Jenny, in her long knowledge of the Sartoris blood, affirms this. 'Bayard love anybody, that cold devil ... He never cared a snap of his fingers for anybody in his life except John.' But the emotional pattern in Faulkner's work is hardly restricted to the Sartoris blood, as Miss Jenny seems to believe. Tending and nursing Bayard, marrying him, bearing his son, Narcissa's affection goes out in turn to her brother, Horace Benbow. We have again in 'Sartoris' those curious scenes of brother and sister love, reminiscent, intimate, almost sexual, half tender and half embarrassing, which are to form a dominant theme of Faulkner's work. These are the genuine scenes of feeling in the novel, couched as they are in terms of the past, in the loving tones of infancy which takes on urgency in the face of a cruel maturity. Defeated at last in her effort to awaken Bayard Sartoris from his memories, Narcissa returns to Horace. 'This should be Horace's day, and her own too — surcease from that ghost-ridden dream to which she clung, waking.' That ghost-ridden dream to which not merely Narcissa but almost all of Faulkner's characters are to cling, waking. For Horace Benbow also must return to his sister to gain the few positive affections which after all contain the pleasure of existence. If Narcissa is now linked to a sort of masculine automaton, possessed by the past and destroying the present, Horace himself has married another of the Faulknerian incubae. The Belle Mitchell of 'Sartoris' is the Jenny of 'Mosquitoes,' sensuous and luscious, but a Jenny turned dangerous. How sharply now does Faulkner's hatred emerge around the portrait of Belle, as Horace is trapped and devoured by her!

> As he removed his clothes it did seem that that heavy fading odor of Belle's body clung to them ... and clinging, shaped in the darkness beside him Belle's rich voluptuousness until within that warm, not-yet-sleeping region where dwells the mother of dreams, Belle grew palpable in ratio as his own body slipped away from him. ... Just before he slept, his mind ... reproduced with the

startling ghostliness of a dictaphone an incident which at the time
he had considered trivial. Belle had freed her mouth, and for a
moment, her body still against his, she held his face in her two
hands and stared at him with intent, questioning eyes. 'Have
you plenty of money, Horace?' And 'Yes,' he had answered immediately, 'of course I have.' And then Belle again, enveloping
him like a rich and fatal drug, like a motionless and cloying sea in
which he watched himself drown.

That Belle Mitchell is a 'rich and fatal drug' we know from her
subsequent history in 'Sanctuary,' a drug whose fatality de-
scends to her daughter, the young Belle of the later novel whose
sexual aberrations contribute to the final disintegration of Horace. And here, of course, shearing away the mannerisms of his
earlier writing, and the attempts at smartness, touching on his
mature tone, Faulkner achieves one of his first noteworthy portraits. But what a disturbed emotional content the passage
brings us! As 'Sartoris' itself, opening with gallantry and idealism of a vanishing past, of voices 'proud and still as banners in
the dust,' now closes on the accents of terror. For we can't deny
that the scene which Faulkner has sketched in through the
course of his three early novels — this setting of distorted emotions and blocked human relationships, of present horrors and
happiness only in the past, whether in the childhood of the individual or that of the South itself, is now to become the world of
the mature artist; is to be pursued by Faulkner until at last we
can hardly tell whether he is controlling his métier, or if indeed
it has come to conquer the artist. The year 1929, the publication of 'Sartoris,' was also that of 'The Sound and the Fury,' an
even more disturbing but undoubtedly a magnificent novel,
marking the emergence, in the precise fateful year when so
much else seemed gone, of a major voice in American literature.

In its prelude to the big work of Faulkner, 'Sartoris' thus
gains an added value, itself in the end an interesting but hardly
successful story. For with Bayard Sartoris and Narcissa Benbow
we have been brought to Jefferson, Mississippi, proper, the
geographical, the psychological center of all Faulkner's future

writing, his tales of fallen grandeur, of a modernity which is loutish when it is not lewd, his estimates of future ruin. Jefferson! Now a series of legends will flow without cease, tragic and splendid, malformed and misbegotten, spectacular, horrific, and catastrophic. Jefferson, the deep southern heart of that southern web of fancy, the creation of which becoming Faulkner's major achievement, or obsession, marks him as extraordinary; a talent often raveling itself out in wasted chance, which nevertheless makes us pause and take note of this town, and these tales.

3. THE NEGRO AND THE FEMALE.   It is typical of Faulkner's talent that the three years between 1929 and 1932 should contain three of his major works, 'The Sound and the Fury,' 'As I Lay Dying,' and 'Light in August,' that these years contain, as it were, an explosion of virtuosity. But 'The Sound and the Fury,' if it has elements of the *tour de force* in it, is much more than that. Long after the shock of its dazzling experimentalism has subsided, and the coteries who espoused it turned into the dust their aestheticism sniffed at, a full decade later 'The Sound and the Fury' remains a fascinating novel of its class. In this career, indeed, which possesses so much of the meteoric, 'The Sound and the Fury' was the first, flashing, luminous arrival, and with it the brilliance began to tarnish.

The technic of the novel is the Joycean interior monologue, employing free association, the shifting sequences of time and place, the personal frame of reference. But until 'The Sound and the Fury,' we dare say, no writer had used this technic, itself so ambiguous, to convey the private psyche of an idiot. The Benjy Compson of the story, speechless, howling, carting around his dirty slipper and his perfume bottle, is the idiot, and the novel opens with his meditations on the morning of his thirty-third birthday. But clinging to the Compson gate, watching the returning schoolgirls, pursuing the nearby golfers, treated or rather mistreated by the negro Luster who is searching for his lost twenty-five-cent piece, Benjy Compson is himself living in the past. The past is 1900 when Benjy was five years old and surrounded by the Compson children, Caddy his sister, the brothers Jason and Quentin, Luster again, Dilsey who is Luster's mother and the negro family servant of the Compsons, and various odd negro children who are then part of the Compson retinue. (I must assure the reader that I am attempting to summarize in two sentences the facts and names and relationships, and time and place sequences, that are hardly clear in the first hundred pages of Benjy's astounding reverie.) But the reverie itself compels our attention, as well as by the mysteries we perceive in it, by its profound sense of loss and anguish. What is Benjy's loss, the anguish which we feel in his moronic behavior and confused speculations, this bitter pang which strikes Benjy anew each time the name of Caddy is mentioned? Caddy who smells like the rain, like leaves, like trees; Caddy who loves Benjy as a child, and understands him, and takes care of him, who will never leave him and is gone forever; Caddy who is the source of Benjy's moaning and slobbering; these overwhelming manifestations of his grief which, like the nearby river, flows unendingly through these obscure and poignant pages.

The second section, the reflections of Quentin Compson at Harvard on June 2, 1910, eighteen years before the opening date of 'The Sound and the Fury,' begins to clarify some elements of our confusion. Through the story of Quentin, perhaps the single most sympathetic piece of writing Faulkner has ever done, as the following section on Jason is Faulkner's most brilliant satire, we reach further into the enigmatic family relationships of the Compsons. Quentin's thoughts deal with Caddy again, her young kindness and sweetness, his own childhood passion for her. And with Quentin's discovery that Caddy has had love affairs; that she has become sexually loose; that she is pregnant and marrying Herbert Head for his money; with

Quentin's pathetic amateurish efforts to take the blame for
Caddy's condition, this sister whom he loves and whose vice is
destroying his life, we reach the center of his conflict:

> *we did how can you not know it if you'll just wait I'll tell you how it was*
> *it was a crime we did a terrible crime it cannot be hid you think it can but*
> *wait   Poor Quentin youve never done that have you   and I'll tell you*
> *how it was   I'll tell Father then itll have to be because you love Father*
> *then we'll have to go away amid the pointing and the horror the clean*
> *flame I'll make you say we did I'm stronger than you I'll make you know*
> *we did you thought it was them but it was me listen I fooled you all the*
> *time it was me you thought I was in the house where that damn honeysuckle*
> *trying not to think the swing the cedars the secret surges the breathing*
> *locked drinking the wild breath the yes Yes Yes yes . . . did you love them*
> *Caddy did you love them When they touched me I died*

But it is impossible in a single passage to summarize the cumulative intensity of 'The Sound and the Fury.' Seen first through
Benjy's eyes and then Quentin's, the portrait of Caddy is superb.
Quentin's own early love for Caddy, the shock of his disillusionment, his later affection for his sister which feeds on his despair,
his jealousy which becomes so much the more intense as it is tormented — these complex emotions form the memorable scenes
which convey the relationship between brother and sister. And
what makes the narrative perhaps even more effective is the
tone of naïveté which Faulkner has been able to maintain in
its telling. Throughout the recital of human debasement,
brother and sister alike maintain an innocence, a quite unique
purity of spirit. And thus lost as they are in the tortured au-
tumn of decline upon which still rests the dew of their spring-
time, around them moves the external world of 'The Sound and
the Fury.' Here is the Harvard campus scene to which Quentin has come with so much expectation, and which is felt so
vividly; the more phlegmatic Canadian Shreve, Quentin's
friend who is half aware of what is happening; the series of
fights in which Quentin engages to avenge his sister's name (he
is always beaten up); the fine witty portraits of Gerald Bland
the collegiate roué, Mrs. Bland, Herbert Head the rotarian

And finally, there is Mrs. Compson herself, the neurasthenic mother of the novel who regards the entire tragedy of 'The Sound and the Fury' as a malicious plot to interfere with her health.

Since all these events are still not altogether clear in the second section of 'The Sound and the Fury' (Quentin's reverie is half-mad, in turn, occurring just before his suicide), the third and last sections of the novel, becoming successively simpler in their technic, and more logical and objective in their view, round out the story of the Compson family line. Through Jason, the envious and bitter brother of Quentin, and through Dilsey the negro servant, we get still other perspectives on the tragedy and its subsequent events. Now we learn of the death of Quentin's father, the later history of Caddy after her marriage, and that of her daughter, the girl Quentin, who pursuing the same course as Caddy herself, repeating the entire cycle of the novel in miniature, as it were, returns us once more to Benjy the idiot: Benjy still clinging to the Compson fence, watching the schoolgirls and the golfers, moaning and slobbering, still waiting for his Caddy to return. If all this sounds somewhat complex, I can only assure the reader that it is. But does our admiration for 'The Sound and the Fury' proceed only from solving the intellectual mystery of the novel? This is a new process in Faulkner's work, a sort of detective story of the emotions which will appear from now on, to reach its apotheosis in the hushed, secret, shadowy unravelings of 'Absalom, Absalom!' Certainly the craft of 'The Sound and the Fury' is brilliantly planned. Once the central structure is arrived at, every detail falls into its place with a sort of astounding precision. Like the opening of a safe, given the combination, we can hear all the bolts clicking into place; and we may suspect that Faulkner has added a few extra bolts just for the satisfaction of making them click. Is it a somewhat juvenile pedantry (of which James Joyce himself is often guilty) for the artist to reveal to us that Benjy is pursuing the golfers in his furious anxiety simply because they cry 'caddie'? Or not to reveal to us that there are two Quentins in the novel? Yet we discover with some pleasure that the search of the negro Luster for his lost twenty-five-cent piece in the first chapter of 'The Sound and the Fury' is to buy his ticket for the circus show then playing in Jefferson; that ticket which Jason tears to pieces before the pleading eyes of Luster in the third section of the novel; that circus which has brought about the final degradation of Caddy's daughter Quentin, and that final degradation which is aesthetically necessary to complete the tragic history of Caddy herself. Very often the use of these details at once so mathematical and dramatic is justified in 'The Sound and the Fury,' marks a sense alike of architecture and histrionics which is quite superb here. For in 'The Sound and the Fury' the technics of the novel, and its pyrotechnics, are after all subordinated to its meaning — to the history of the degenerating Compsons, and the new commercial South, avaricious, prejudiced, 'practical,' of which Jason, both the Lardnerian slicker and sucker at once, is the product; and within this social framework the magnificent study of a drama of innocence. Here we draw close to the central meaning of 'The Sound and the Fury.' For beneath the technical virtuosity of the novel, beneath the portrait of a decaying Southern landed aristocracy and the emergence of the modern industrial order (with acumen Faulkner here establishes these new social values, and with what hatred!), the theme of the novel is basically the disenchantment of an evil maturity. What we feel in 'The Sound and the Fury' is all the comfort and affection of a childhood world at the moment of its impact with adult values; at the moment of its realization of sin. Thus the novel is a sort of allegory of the fall of man which takes place, in some measure, in each generation and with every individual. The 'incestuous' love of Quentin for his sister Caddy, the love affair which forms the most eloquent passage of 'The Sound and the Fury' and is incestuous merely because these childhood emotions have been placed in adult personages, is the embodiment of such innocence becoming aware of its own corruption. And the idiot Benjy is not so much the moron as the child again, not merely living in the past but never having emerged from it. Seeing the drama of the Compsons from this view, moaning and slobbering instead of speaking, but inarticulate rather than uncomprehending, Benjy is filled with the obscure passions of childhood: the lawless emotions which pervade his being, without our logic and morality, are primitive and profound. For the early emotions which Benjy typifies are those, as we know, which remain longest and deepest with us, hidden, if we are fortunate, but nevertheless forming the real basis of our 'mature' actions — a maturity which we usually continue secretly to fit, as Benjy does more obviously, into the design of our own desires. And 'The Sound and the Fury' remains vivid to us, in the end, because of the tenderness with which Faulkner endows these early feelings. The bawling and rejoicing of our infancy, the warm memories of our nursery infatuations, and underneath the deep drives and tensions of childhood, these accents, as it were, from the edge of the womb, and which make the world of the child in a sense deeper, more passionate than our own relatively recent and superficial realm of adult behavior — in the novel, these emotions touch and stir *us*: recall and draw up from the abyss of the past our own forgotten memories. Here is the achievement of 'The Sound and the Fury.' No other single contemporary novel can surpass it, I believe, in the evocation of our infantile origins. And Faulkner himself has never been able to equal it.

It is appropriate, moreover, that Faulkner's major achievement should spring from the semi-savage orbit of the infant. If Faulkner is not again able to portray this scene in comparable terms, if he is rather to lessen and exploit it, it will remain as the frame of reference for the work which follows. The element of exploitation, as a matter of fact, enters Faulkner's record hard upon the heels of 'The Sound and the Fury.' 'Sanctuary,' written in the same year though published in 1931, is his next and worst work. As far as possible from the splendor of its predecessor, it reveals now, as the big novel illuminates the furthest reaches of Faulkner, all the imperfect aspects of his talent. We are not condemning here the obvious commercialism of 'Sanctuary,' which Faulkner freely admits in its preface (there is also bravado in his honesty). A series of shocks and thrills are thrown together to make 'Sanctuary' a best-seller, a perhaps dubious desire for a major writer, but the wisdom of which seems to have been confirmed by the decision of the Modern Library to enthrone this volume among its masterpieces. And we must admit that the raping of the college flapper Temple Drake by the gangster Popeye, Temple's subsequent career in a Memphis house of prostitution, the murder committed by Popeye upon one of his henchmen, for which another of them, Lee Goodwin, is framed by southern justice and then burned by the mob, these and similar events give Faulkner a good framework on which to hang his episodes of sadism and pornography, his scenes of blood and brutality. What concerns us more directly, however, is the curious tone of 'Sanctuary,' the fertility of its perversions which we can hardly do justice to, the sweep and flow of its fabricated horrors, the final impact of its disgust which goes beyond alike the niceties of sensationalism and the necessities of commercialism. What is the meaning of the accumulation of nasty tortures to which Faulkner subjects his 'heroine'? Temple Drake gains no stature through her suffering. Rather, she willingly submits to her own disintegration, and hastens it along. What a strange new scene for us to enter directly after the tenderness of the Compson household, a procession, so to say, from the nursery to the brothel: this new Memphis of cold and calculated corruption, and the lust for power which rules all these new Faulknerian characters at the price of all other feeling, a price which these people pay without qualms. This new Faulknerian stage on which strut only pimps and prostitutes of one sort or another, mothered by the drunken Madam, Reba Rivers, of 'Sanctuary' and begotten by the Senator Snopes of the novel, the modern politician, against whom Horace Benbow, as the last of the southern statesmen, struggles in vain. In 'Sanctuary,' directly after the love, however thwarted, of 'The Sound and the Fury,' we have the first full outpouring of Faulkner's discontent. And as we shall see, the significance of the novel in Faulkner's career is to be more profound than Faulkner implies in his confession of sheer commercialism. 'Sanctuary' is doubtless the 'cheap job' which Faulkner calls it. We might wish it were only that.

In 'As I Lay Dying,' in 1930, the sensationalism has subsided somewhat, but the virtuosity of Faulkner has increased. Through the story of the poor-white Mississippi mountaineers, the Bundrens, centering around the death of the mother, and the expedition to Jefferson in order to bury her rotting corpse, a pilgrimage which is as interminable as it is harrowing, Faulkner has given us the material for another tragedy of the South. The elements of a big work are here, the scene, the tone, the imaginative conception, built around the dying mother who is obsessed by the pain of living. There is a curious parallel, as a matter of fact, between the Bundrens and the Compsons in 'The Sound and the Fury.' Again the central characters are a close-knit family: Jewel, Cash, Darl, and Vardaman, the young sons, and Dewey Dell, the daughter who like Caddy is bearing an illegitimate child. Again Dewey Dell, sinning with Lafe, is emotionally involved, not with the father of her child (who is hardly more than a name in the novel), but with her brother Darl. But Dewey Dell, the ignorant mountain girl, becomes a sort of inferior Caddy, almost a parody of Caddy, an ironic victim of life, but herself not aware of the implications of her actions. So too the rest of the Bundrens never quite attain their real dimensions in the novel. Like the child Vardaman who believes his mother is a fish, or Cash who is concerned only with building the coffin for his dying mother, or Jewel with his horse, they have become so eccentric, in their poverty and ignorance, that they are hardly capable of receiving the tragedy which unfolds around them. It is the father Anse, lazy, helpless, hypocritical, poor-white trash, who emerges as the most vivid character of 'As I Lay Dying,' a comic character. At the close of the novel, after all the horror and pain which has gone into the death of Addie Bundren, Anse triumphantly emerges with his new Mrs. Bundren, and perhaps more important, his new set of false teeth. What should have been the drama of the Bundrens thus becomes in the end a sort of brutal farce. We are unable to feel the tragedy because the author has refused to accept the Bundrens, as he did accept the Compsons, as tragic. And failing in the central identification of the artist with his material, Faulkner must fall back on his virtuosity, and resort to the dramatic episodes, the fine writing, the scenes in 'As I Lay Dying' which often dazzle us with their brilliance, but hardly capture our sympathies. As we work through the technic of 'The Sound and the Fury' we become increasingly more interested in the novel. As we work through that of 'As I Lay Dying,' we become less interested. When we understand the feelings of the Compsons, they affect us; when we get to know the Bundrens, we realize there is very little to know.

The years from 1931 to 1934 are again rich in Faulkner titles. 'Idyll in the Desert.' 'These Thirteen.' 'Light in August.' 'This Earth.' 'Salmagundi.' 'Miss Zilphia Gant.' 'Doctor Martino.' Faulkner's volume of verse, 'A Green Bough,' in 1933, is perhaps a typical example, and recalls a passage in 'Mosquitoes.' 'Subject, substance, doesn't signify in verse ... the best poetry is just words,' one of the southern philosophers remarks, and unfortunately this definition seems to apply to Faulkner's late verse as to his early. The mastery of words is no doubt superb in 'A Green Bough,' but we are often unable to tell just what the words signify. As to Faulkner's specialized pieces, we must notice that as with 'Sanctuary' Faulkner's eroticism is in the end hardly erotic. The underlying view is not sexual, but a distaste for sex. It retards rather than arouses the sensual impulses, throws its blight, in fact, over all the natural passions, and perhaps for this reason, rather than any other, these selections should be restricted to the limited editions which hold them. Of Faulkner's volumes of short stories, the first, 'These Thirteen,' in 1931, remains the best, and his most famous story is also the most effective. 'A Rose for Emily' is a *tour de force* but a good one. And if this deals with a spinster hoarding the body of her dead lover (after she has killed him, we rather suspect), we remember also that 'Red Leaves' includes the digestion of ants, snakes, rats, with appropriate salivary discharges, and the proposed eating of humans. 'The Hound' in 'Doctor Martino,' later to appear as an episode in 'The Hamlet' (as some of these tales are put into Faulkner's novels, and many of them concern figures like the Sartorises or the Snopeses who are familiar to us), deals with Killer Mink Snopes who hides his corpse but loses its limb. 'Elly' treats of a young girl who compulsively seduces a mulatto and then has him killed, as 'Dry September' earlier told the story of another spinster whose sexual illusions condemn a negro to death by lynching. And with the emphasis on necrophilia and cannibalism, on misogynists and miscegenation, with these murderers and their dangling corpses, we are touching on the center of Faulkner's mature work, and the creation of 'Light in August' in 1932, which appears to synthesize all the strains of Faulkner's discontent.

In its scope 'Light in August' is certainly one of Faulkner's big novels. Here he has again penetrated more deeply into his people and created a more complex scene than that of 'As I Lay Dying.' Here too, in a curious way, Faulkner is closer to the central figures of his novel, though it is not easy at first for us to recognize just who the central figures of the novel are. Written as objective narrative rather than interior monologue, 'Light in August' is still not without complexity in its exposition. Through the story of Lena, another poor-white mountain girl, again pregnant, again wandering, again seeking the father of her child, and again, we are inclined to believe, mentally deficient, we come to Byron Bunch who falls in love with her. Through Byron's story, we come to Hightower, the minister, betrayed by his wife, driven out of his parish by his congregation, living in disgrace with the town and among his memories of the Civil War. Caught by the dead who had conceived him, the son 'who grew to manhood among phantoms' dies among them —

He hears above his heart the thunder increase, myriad and drumming. Like a long sighing of wind in trees it begins, they sweep into sight, borne now upon a cloud of phantom dust. They rush past, forwardleaning in the saddles, with brandished arms, beneath whipping ribbons from slanted and eager lances; with tumult and soundless yelling they sweep past . . . are gone; the dust swirls skyward sucking, fades away into the night which has fully come. Yet . . . it seems to him that he still hears them: the wild bugles and the clashing sabres and the dying thunder of hooves.

From the story of Hightower, held by that moment of thundering hooves and wild bugles in which his life, Faulkner tells us, had begun and ended, we come at last (I am simplifying the exposition, since these narratives within narratives are also broken in time and place) to the murder in Jefferson. Working backward in time from that, we reach the relationship of Joe Christmas and the Miss Burden of 'Light in August.' And what a romance this is, the central love affair of Faulkner's maturity — this colored Romeo and abolitionist Juliet of Jefferson, Mississippi; the amoral mulatto and the starved spinster; the brutal criminal and the aging nymphomaniac. We come at last to the vicious conjunction in Faulkner's work of the Negro and the Female, the twin furies of Faulkner's deep southern Waste Land; but a waste land, quite unlike Eliot's, of demons and incubae rather than pallid clerks, one which is built on diseased fury and ends, indeed, not with a whimper but a bang.

Which of these entwined partners of evil seems to earn more of Faulkner's opprobrium? It is the woman, Faulkner implies, who has been responsible for the fate of Joe Christmas, the new Faulknerian hero, orphan and outcast, hunted by the world and venting his own hatred on it, semblance of a white man who carried the taint of his own knowledge that he is negro. It is worth while noticing the sequence of female actions which have conditioned the history of Christmas. There is his mother, begetting him illicitly from his negro father, and so condemning him at the start. There is the dietitian at the orphanage where

Christmas is left, with her 'natural female infallibility for the spontaneous comprehension of evil.' If the phrase is a little verbose, the dietitian is not. When the boy catches her in the sexual act, she drives him away from the orphanage with a minimum of discussion. There is now the waitress with whom Christmas has his first love relationship, her cramped appearance moulded by some 'inner corruption of the spirit itself.' Christmas first learns about women from the waitress, these 'victims of periodical filth.' For her the youth is nevertheless willing to steal, lie, deceive his benefactors, and so distort his whole future, until the waitress throws him off, 'womanfilth' which destroys his youth. Yet Christmas cannot escape from the curse of this 'abomination and bitchery.' Like the 'bodiless fecundmellow voices' of the negro women, it pursues him —

> On all sides, even within him, the bodiless fecundmellow voices of negro women murmured. It was as though he and all other manshaped life about him had been returned to the lightless hot wet primogenitive Female. He began to run, glaring, his teeth glaring, his inbreath cold on his dry teeth and lips....

And fleeing from the huts of the negro women, from the habitation of the lightless hot wet primogenitive Female which they symbolize for him, and in a larger sense from the entire social order which by inference they have spawned, Christmas can find some relief only with the animals. 'He was thinking now, aloud now, "Why in hell do I want to smell horses?" Then he said, fumbling: "It's because they are not women. Even a mare horse is a kind of man."'

The Miss Joanna Burden of 'Light in August,' however, is apparently a respectable northern lady, devoting her life and fortune toward helping the southern negroes out of their bondage of poverty and ignorance, and attempting, in fact, to reclaim Christmas himself for the society she believes in. This is surely praiseworthy, and why is it that after such a sympathetic preface, Misss Burden becomes not the exception to the Faulknerian female principle, but the cardinal example of it? Why,

having hardly met the virtuous northern lady, are we plunged
into her viciousness? It is not, indeed, the brutalized, amoral,
tortured negro, by now hopelessly lost, condemned to his crime,
who violates the spinster, but now the virgin who corrupts the
criminal. 'It was as though,' Faulkner says, 'he had fallen into
a sewer,' though we should have thought Joe Christmas had
stumbled long ago.

> At first it shocked him: the abject fury of the New England glacier
> exposed suddenly to the fire of the New England biblical hell.
> Perhaps he was aware of the abnegation in it: the imperious and
> fierce urgency that concealed an actual despair at frustrate and
> irrevocable years, which she appeared to attempt to compensate
> each night as if she believed that it would be the last night on
> earth by damning herself forever to the hell of her forefathers,
> by living not alone in sin but in filth.

We shall omit here some of the details which Faulkner takes
care not to omit. During this period, Faulkner says, 'it could
not be called a honeymoon,' Christmas watched Miss Burden
'pass through every avatar of a woman in love.'

> ... sometimes he would have to seek her about the dark house
> until he found her, hidden, in closets, in empty rooms, waiting,
> panting, her eyes in the dark glowing like the eyes of cats. Now
> and then she appointed trysts beneath certain shrubs about the
> grounds, where he would find her naked, or with her clothing
> half torn to ribbons upon her, in the wild throes of nymphomania,
> her body gleaming in the slow, shifting from one to another of
> such formally erotic attitudes and gestures as a Beardsley of the
> time of Petronius might have drawn. She would be wild then,
> in the close breathing half-dark without walls, with her wild hair,
> each strand of which would seem to come alive like octopus ten-
> tacles, and her wild hands and her breathing: 'Negro! Negro!
> Negro!'

It could not be called a honeymoon, but can we really call it
love? The relationship of the northern woman and the emancipated negro has no affection, only corruption. As Christmas is
caught and then destroyed by the female, 'like a man being

sucked down into a bottomless abyss,' as the negro begins to fear, then hate her, and attempts to cast her off, and still caught, must murder her to free himself, we should feel that at last Joanna Burden has atoned for her crimes. Yet the precise point that 'Light in August' seems to make is that she does not. There is no catharsis for the Faulknerian sense of evil. It is through vice that we may, if we wish, illuminate the depths of the human soul, and paradoxically envision its grandeur. But with Faulkner's work there is no pattern of such guilt and expiation, as with our own Nordic Dostoevsky of a Hemingway: no crushed tenderness here, no redemption through suffering, or through any other chalice of grace. There is indeed no redemption. Only as in 'Light in August' the continuing sense of destruction, the incessant breeding of evil by evil. Faulkner like Hemingway has been compared to the Russians in his emphasis on sin, but the critics making the comparison have forgotten the alternate and inextricable emphasis of the Russians on salvation. The Russian perversions are a sign of God's mystery; the Faulknerian perversions are the mark of man's disgrace. The negro Christmas also must die at the end of 'Light in August.' He dies brutally, as he had lived. He is shot and mutilated while still conscious. And he dies unchanged, or even untouched, made only harsh by his agony. But this double brutality on the part of victor and victim alike in 'Light in August' seems to Faulkner hardly so outrageous as satisfying.

We have noticed, then, over the mature period of Faulkner's work a curious progression. From the troubled but tender and intensely human world of 'The Sound and the Fury' (looking back at this early scene now, it seems almost impossible for Faulkner to have created it), the writer has moved steadily toward the perverse and the pathological: and the denial of humanity which he uses his inversions to convey. From the touching drama of innocence, he has advanced to that of corruption. In the sequence of Faulkner's thought, the idiot Benjy Compson, who evoked in us all that was compassionate, has been replaced by the pervert Popeye, who represents all that is diseased. And we must notice the meaning of Faulkner's new phase. Faulkner is still describing the world of childhood, but now a very different aspect of it: the world of human perversions whose precise nature is that they also are infantile emotions; they are the reflection of our early animal instincts which have been blocked and forced out of their normal channels of maturing. This is the alternate half of that realm of tender young emotions which Faulkner caught with such integrity in 'The Sound and the Fury.' It is the destructive side of our primitive nature, coming so easily and richly to Faulkner, which is now being manipulated to portray a world the writer condemns. This is childhood, as it were, taking its revenge upon the maturity which had dissolved its faith. For now painting his people in these gruesome colors, seeing humanity only in terms of its aberrations, Faulkner has come, with 'Light in August,' to show us the full range of his discontent: his contempt for modern maturity which displays itself so eloquently in the variety of perversions which the writer contrives for his characters. The defiance of modern society is pervasive, as we have seen, in the works of the American writers in the nineteen-twenties. But Faulkner may be seen as perhaps the supreme example of it — a hatred of life so compelling with him that there almost seems to be an inability in the writer to reach maturity itself.

We are about to trace the course of this great hatred a little further. But meanwhile we have also noticed where the crux of Faulkner's discontent has come to rest. As the series of women in 'Light in August' are the factors of Joe Christmas's degeneration, we have seen how Faulkner himself has focused his anger on the feminine portraits which mark his work as a whole. We recall Cecily Saunders, the 'papier-maché Virgin' of 'Soldiers' Pay.' This 'Virgin' turned into a vicious prostitute, the Temple Drake of 'Sanctuary.' The neurasthenic Mrs. Compson of 'The Sound and the Fury,' who is perhaps the most purely contemptible character in the novel. And even Caddy herself, the object of such intense devotion, on the part of Benjy and Quen-

tin, whose sexual weakness is nevertheless the direct cause of
their destruction. We remember the Belle Mitchell of 'Sartoris,' whose effect, like that of Joanna Burden, was of a rich
and fatal drug, 'a motionless and cloying sea' in which the
Faulknerian male watches himself drown. And as Faulkner has
been steadily concerned in the past with these female incubae,
so now, and drawn like these later women toward the black
male, he will view the negro with perhaps even greater bitterness. The negro, who in the person of Joe Christmas has already begun to dominate Faulkner's work, whose shadow falls
across not only the white writer, but in the Faulknerian view,
the whole white race:

> I thought of all the children coming forever and ever into the
> world, white, with the black shadow already falling upon them
> before they drew breath. And I seemed to see the black shadow
> in the shape of a cross. And it seemed like the white babies were
> struggling, even before they drew breath, to escape from the
> shadow that was not only upon them but beneath them too,
> flung out like their arms were flung out, as if they were nailed to
> the cross. I saw all the little babies that would ever be in the
> world, the ones not yet even born — a long line of them with their
> arms spread, on the black crosses.

What, then, is the meaning of these twin Furies of the Faulknerian deep southern Waste Land, this odd, and to Faulkner
quite horrifying, conjunction of the Female and the Negro? Of
these symbols which he has taken to convey the entire complex
of his southern revolt against modern society, and even maturity itself? In the work of Faulkner's latest period, we may at
last identify this theme.

4. THE GREAT HATRED.   'Pylon' in 1935, concerning
a group of fliers celebrating the Mardi Gras at a New Orleans
airport, is relatively slight. From his own history we know of

Faulkner's concern with aviation, yet in this case his stunt pilots somehow seem more exciting to ride with than to read about. There is a sort of virtuosity in 'Pylon,' to be sure. This time Faulkner decides to use a variation of Dos Passos, as very often he can turn out what looks like most adequate Hemingway, as the school teacher Labove in 'The Hamlet' is to be Wolfian, and as Joseph Warren Beach, in his acute study, notes Faulkner's technical affinity with Conrad. By now our author is equal to any technic; perhaps in sheer craft facility Faulkner is superior to any other American; he can be like anybody else that he chooses to be like. And we notice again that the central relationship of 'Pylon' is triangular, the woman of the novel, Laverne, living with two men, Shumann the racer and Holmes the parachute jumper (the consistent triangular pattern of Faulkner's literary relationships with the homosexual implications is interesting, though we may almost add that homosexuality is too adult an inversion for Faulkner to deal with directly). Having her child, moreover, apparently by Holmes, Laverne implicitly drives Shumann to his death through her pressing need of money. But thus, casually as it were, giving us another facet of his anti-feminine bias, Faulkner himself appears hardly very concerned with his thesis, and we can hardly pretend that we are.

With the 'Absalom, Absalom!' of 1936, however, we come to a different matter, the third of Faulkner's major works, the typical novel of his latest period, as 'The Sound and the Fury' culminated his apprenticeship and 'Light in August' embodied the increasing discontents of his middle period. The plot of 'Absalom' served as the occasion of one of Clifton Fadiman's wittiest philippics:

> One may sum up both substance and style by saying that every person in 'Absalom, Absalom!' comes to no good end, and they all take a hell of a time coming even that far. The story runs from 1807 to 1910, with the major action concentrated between 1833, when Thomas Sutpen appears in Jefferson, Mississippi, and 1869, when he is rather regretfully murdered by an old family retainer.

Thomas Sutpen is a monomaniac, known familiarly to the other characters as The Demon. . . . The Demon's second wife, Ellen Coldfield, gives birth to two children, Henry and Judith, goes dotty, and dies after a while. Her younger sister, Rosa, is insulted by The Demon and also goes dotty, though it takes her much longer to die. The father of Rosa and Ellen goes nuts when the Civil War arrives, nails himself up in a garret, and perseveringly starves himself to death. Now, young Henry, upon finding out that his best friend, Charles Bon, engaged to be married to his sister Judith, is (a) his half-brother and (b) part Negro, also goes dotty in a complicated way, and finally shoots Charles dead. By the end of the story Henry has been reduced to straight, simple idiocy and is kept shut up in the attic. Judith, after some years passed in a vacant-eyed trance, passes out as a result of smallpox, a death so natural as to strike a rather jarring note.

Continuing with his résumé, Mr. Fadiman adds his criticism of the novel's structure:

. . . Then we have what may be called Anti-Narrative, a set of complex devices used to keep the story from being told. Mr. Faulkner is very clever at this. He gets quite an interesting effect, for example, by tearing the Sutpen chronicle into pieces, as if a mad child were to go to work on it with a pair of shears, and then having each of the jagged divisions narrated by a different personage: the author, Rosa, Quentin, Quentin's father, Quentin's grandfather. All of these people do a neat job of mixing up the time sequences, delaying climaxes, confusing the reader. . . . I should add that everybody talks the same language, a kind of Dixie Gongorism, very formal, allusive, cryptic. Apparently the entire population of Jefferson, Mississippi, consists of rhetoricians who would blench at the sight of a simple declarative sentence. On the other hand, it is only fair to say that there are a score of pages . . . full of remarkable prose poetry, beautiful in itself, if magnificently irrelevant.

There would seem very little to add to this summary, except that Mr. Fadiman has understood both the plot and technic of the novel, which is no simple feat. The publishers of 'Absalom' themselves, after confessing their belief that it is Faulkner's

major work — 'his most important and ambitious contribution
to American literature' — talk, on the jacket of the novel, about
'demonic Stephen Sutpen' when they obviously mean Thomas
Sutpen. The Faulknerian genealogy of 'Absalom' is complex
enough without the publishers adding their own characters.
And in one sense 'Absalom' deserves Mr. Fadiman's rebuke.
It is certainly the most pretentious of Faulkner's works, which
all have their degree of pretense. It is the most self-conscious,
technically the most elaborate product of this rather self-conscious technical virtuoso. There seems to be a Henry Jamesian
influence at work here too in the polished writing, the involved
patterns of behavior which circle around an enigmatic horror
story. 'Absalom' is in this respect a kind of Mississippian 'Turn
of the Screw,' and like the later Henry James, sometimes its
effect of mystery seems a little strained; it pants intricately with
suspense; it becomes a gothic novel of the emotions. Yet once
'Absalom' has been subjected to this deflationary process, and
the air let out of it, the novel does get the 'interesting effect'
which Mr. Fadiman allows it, and its remarkable prose is not
always so irrelevant. Once we have worked through the pretensions of 'Absalom' the story holds us, at times moves us, and
certainly provides the last missing pieces in the pattern of
Faulknerian discontent. 'Absalom' is indeed a mystery story we
must solve, and the mystery is that of the author as well as his
work.

Once again it is the Negro who is the fundamental source of
Thomas Sutpen's destruction, and with Sutpen his southern
dynasty, and with this the whole framework, for which it stands
in the novel, of Southern culture before the Civil War. It is, in
fact, the 'monkey nigger,' barring the door of the great southern
estate, who starts the poverty-stricken and ignorant young
Sutpen off on his monomaniacal vision of himself building such
an estate and founding a dynasty to inherit it — the vision to
which all else was sacrificed during Sutpen's life, but which as it
was induced by the negro was thwarted by him: the monkey
nigger barring the door at the end of Sutpen's mad and indom-

itable life, as at the start. For the woman whom Sutpen marries in Haiti, Eulalia Bon, proves to have negro blood in her. In a curious pattern, partly accidental, part design, seeking his revenge on the father who has disowned him, but also the father's recognition and love, Eulalia's son, Charles Bon, meets young Henry Sutpen in college. Through his own volition Bon corrupts Henry; against his volition he becomes Henry's close friend, almost lover; meets Henry's sister Judith; and the tragedy opens which will destroy the Sutpen line. So here Faulkner has joined his twin Furies. It is Eulalia Bon, both the female and the negro, who is at the root of the disaster, the original cause of that 'dread and fear of females which you must have drawn in with the primary mammalian milk.' In many passages of 'Absalom' Faulkner makes quite implicit the evil which proceeds from the 'female principle which existed, queenly and complete, in the hot equatorial groin of the world long before that white one of ours came down from trees and lost its hair and bleached out. . . .' But if the Faulknerian complex of the Female and the Negro has been fused in 'Absalom,' is the prime movement of the novel, there is here a sort of elevation to the action, in contrast to the pollution which marks 'Light in August.' Charles Bon himself, the active instrument of the drama, if he is biologically akin to Christmas, both of them apparently white with the hidden negro blood, is temperamentally very different. Where Christmas is the brutish and criminal negro principle, Bon is complex, civilized, and tragic. And as we read 'Absalom' we realize that not only Bon, but all the central figures in the novel have a human stature which has been missing in Faulkner's work since 'The Sound and the Fury.' This comparison arrests us in 'Absalom,' puzzles us — until we realize also that these figures are closely related to those of 'The Sound and the Fury.' The Quentin who tells the story here is the same Quentin Compson, the Sutpens are part of the same lineage as the Compsons and the Sartoris family, and, in short, Faulkner is once again dealing with the aristocratic South of the Civil War. And returning to the old South, endowing

'Absalom' with the mark of genuine tragedy which has been lacking in his writing for seven years, Faulkner has dropped off the bitterness, the stale perversions which characterize his portraits of the new South. He has once again caught, on this odd sabbath, the sense of human grandeur, where for a long and harsh aesthetic tilling he has been able only to feel that of human bondage.

It is worth noticing how closely the pattern fits. If the negro Charles Bon of 'Absalom' is the curse again of the white Sutpen dynasty, Bon is nevertheless the product of the old South, as compared to Joe Christmas, the 'emancipated' new negro, who must be punished with all the devices of Faulkner's hatred. And now we see also the cause for all the indignities which Faulkner heaps upon the Miss Burden of 'Light in August,' this respectable, decent, well-meaning abolitionist spinster. Miss Burden is respectable. She is decent and well-meaning. But she is also the abolitionist spinster who is attempting to raise the freed negro, the pair seeming to symbolize for Faulkner all the evils which have befallen his land. And what better expression of his scorn can the southern writer produce than to have the sterile female accept the emancipated negro as her sexual partner, to have her humiliated by the negro, and to have her murdered by the negro. We see now, if Faulkner is the misogynist (we shall come to the root of this a little later), it is the modern woman, and particularly the 'northern' woman who is the special object of his venom. Thus the Miss Coldfield of 'Absalom' differs radically in her fate, though it is not either a very pleasant one, from Miss Burden — both spinsters, equally frigid and neurotic, and equally deserving, one should think, of Faulkner's sympathy or aversion. But the southern lady in her historical setting retains at least her dignity, while the northern woman retains nothing, not even her life. Judith Sutpen in 'Absalom,' if she is hardly very compelling as a person, being much more the vehicle through whom the affection of Henry and Charles Bon is being consummated, nevertheless has a 'serene, tranquil repose' befitting the southern belle.

Judith reminds us of the Narcissa of 'Sartoris' who had equal poise, if as little charm, so long as Faulkner described her within the aristocratic tradition. But transposing Narcissa to the new South of 'Sanctuary,' he turns this musing madonna (Faulkner's single type of 'good' woman, and usually a madonna of somewhat imperfect mentality) into the malignant shrew. We recall now the significance of 'Sanctuary' itself beyond its commercialism. Presenting us with the first flow of Faulkner's modern discontent, the new stage of Memphis society on which strut only pimps and prostitutes, it also portrays the losing struggle of the aristocratic Horace Benbow, the old-fashioned liberal statesman, against the new southern corrupt politicians. We see more clearly now why, holding as it does all the elements of tragedy, 'As I Lay Dying' was not after all tragic, since the poor-white Bundrens were not capable of receiving tragedy. The pattern fits, so perfectly, so mechanically, so rather inartistically for a major artist dealing with the complexities and not the simplifications of life, that we may feel it to be an almost unconscious expression of Faulkner's feelings — as if the writer were in the power of these deep prejudices rather than their master.

And the Thomas Sutpen of 'Absalom,' ragged, ignorant, poor boy whom Faulkner paints, is he not very comparable in his origins to these same Bundrens? Or his rise to state not without equivalents to the modern Snopeses whom Faulkner castigates? Violent, rapacious, marked by the same lust for power, Thomas builds his Sutpen's Hundred out of the virgin forest by tricking his friends and intimidating his enemies, Sutpen who is after all the type of Robber Baron of the old South, as Snopes is of the new. But against the lecherous idiocy of the new southern mercantile rulers, what dignity does Faulkner invest his Sutpen with! What iron will (lost to the modern epoch) working out its tragic rôle, and thwarted, gaining the grandeur of a defeat which for Faulkner seems attributable only to the past, belonging only to that bygone 'high (and impossible) destiny of the United States.' A destiny high only to these Sutpens, Sartorises, and Compsons of Faulkner's ancient mythology; impossible for their heirs. For indeed they have no heirs. Closing, the chronicle of 'Absalom' holds this message also. We see the new age implicit in the country store which Thomas Sutpen now runs, returned home, broken by the 'bloody aberration' of the Civil War; we see this 'ancient varicose and despairing Faustus' fling his final main now —

> ... with the Creditor's hand already on his shoulder, running his little country store now for his bread and meat, haggling tediously over nickels and dimes with rapacious and poverty-stricken whites and negroes, who at one time could have galloped for ten miles in any direction without crossing his own boundary, using out of his meagre stock the cheap ribbons and beads and the stale violently-colored candy with which even an old man can seduce a fifteen-year-old country girl. . . .

With this country store, of course, we are back in the land of the Bundrens, a country girl, a human life, worth only cheap ribbons and beads. How Faulkner's imagery itself conveys his moral, the despairing Faustus and the stale candy! But this last desperate effort of Sutpen's to gain a son and carry on his line is blocked also. The woman of the post-Civil War South bears Sutpen no male. And the aristocrat himself is killed by the girl's father, Wash Jones, gangling, malaria-stricken, imbecilic poor-white Jones who is now to inherit the southern earth.

Or at any rate the southern earth of Faulkner's novels, as in 'The Hamlet' of 1940. Between 'Absalom, Absalom!' and this, however, Faulkner published another volume of short stories and another novel. It is interesting to notice that even the stories in 'The Unvanquished,' mostly written as money-makers for the popular magazines, confirm the Faulknerian thesis, though obviously in rather theatrical and sentimental terms. Again the Sartoris family about whom the stories center show dignity, a sense of morality, and nobility. As Percy Boynton notices in his 'America in Contemporary Fiction,' Faulkner recognizes here 'that the demands of something higher than respectability reduced depravity to its place as an incident and as an obstacle to a desirable life.' This is an acute observation about our writer, who has however built the major part of his work around these 'incidents.' And Ringo, the negro slave in 'The Unvanquished' who is the close companion of Bayard Sartoris, is loyal, intelligent, and in some respects more admirable as a person than Bayard. But Loosh, the negro who wants to be free and to help the Yankees, is bad. 'The Wild Palms' of 1939 has its interest also as an exception to the rule, as one of Faulkner's few excursions into a modern love relationship which shall not be depraved, and is part of a desirable adult life. It appears as if here Faulkner were attempting to break out of the mould which he has made for himself. But the love of Harry Wilbourne and Charlotte Rittenmeyer in 'The Wild Palms,' if it is not infantile, is unfortunately merely adolescent. Threatened by the destruction of their love, Charlotte cries:

> No!... No! No! Jesus God, no! Hold me! Hold me hard, Harry! This is what it's for, what it all was for, what we were paying for: so we could be together, sleep together every night: not just to eat and evacuate and sleep warm so we can get up and eat and evacuate in order to sleep warm again! Hold me! Hold me hard! Hard!

Such a speech, which we may find more embarrassing than passionate, is typical of the central relationship in 'The Wild Palms.' And despite Faulkner's efforts to make the love of Charlotte and Harry constructive, it is Charlotte who drives Harry into their life together and becomes pregnant; it is Charlotte who insists that Harry perform the abortion which leads him to the penitentiary. Yet the penitentiary, Faulkner implies, is after all preferable. In the subordinate plot of 'The Wild Palms,' the convict of the novel has also been sent there because of a robbery committed for the sake of a woman who does not love him. And being freed during a flood, becoming involved with another woman, the convict's frantic struggle is to escape from the woman and return to the safety of the prison.

In his next novel, moreover, Faulkner returns from his brief excursion into romantic love to write the latest chapter of his southern epic. 'The Hamlet' is the explicit story of the rise of the southern mercantile aristocracy whose future was prophesied in 'Absalom, Absalom!' Here is the full account of those Mississippian Snopeses, brokers and blackmailers, perverts, murderers and idiots, senators and horse-thieves, poor-white trash elevated by cleverness and corruption into a ruling financial oligarchy — those southern Snopeses who have been haunting the corners and shadows of all of Faulkner's novels of the new era, and are now thrown into the center of the stage and exposed to the light. We need hardly say more. Yet it is worth noticing, at the very last, that the typical woman of 'The Hamlet' is Eula Varner, mentally retarded like the Dewey Dell of 'As I Lay Dying' and the Lena of 'Light in August'; that the highest lyricism of the novel occurs in the description of the idiot Snopes's love affair with Jack Houston's cow; and that 'The Hamlet' ends with the rise to power of Flem Snopes who cheats the inhabitants of Jefferson into believing there is buried treasure on Flem's acres. Worthless land, and worthless people. Thus Faulkner fills the pages of his latest novel with the folklore of imbeciles.

What is curious, however, is the tone in which this last account is rendered. The sense of tragedy in 'The Sound and the Fury,' or that of disgust which lies behind the morbid action of 'Sanctuary' and the inversions of 'Light in August,' these have been succeeded by a sense of comedy, even gaiety, in 'The Hamlet.' Faulkner seems now to accept the antics of his provincial morons, to enjoy the chronicle of their low-grade behavior; he submerges himself in their clownish degradation. And in one sense why should he not? If the Snopeses are all the writer can discover in the modern world, the descendants of the gangling and giggling Wash Jones, if they now tread omnipotently the southern acres where Sutpen had his vision of dynasty, they are after all the victims and not the victors, they are the blind vessels of the final wrath. For in the Faulknerian mythology, the

Wash Jones of 'Absalom, Absalom!' will himself be superseded by another sort of Sutpen, the illegitimate Sutpen from the colored branch, the Jim Bond of the novel, the final type of brutish negro idiot:

> I think that in time the Jim Bonds are going to conquer the western hemisphere. Of course it won't quite be in our time and of course as they spread toward the poles they will bleach out again like the rabbits and the birds do, so they won't show up so sharp against the snow. But it will still be Jim Bond; and so in a few thousand years, I who regard you will also have sprung from the loins of African kings.

And tell me one thing more, says Shreve to the Quentin Compson who we know is about to commit suicide,

> 'Why do you hate the South?'
> 'I dont hate it,' Quentin said, quickly, at once, immediately; 'I dont hate it,' he said. *I dont hate it* he thought, panting in the cold air, the iron New England dark; *I dont. I dont! I dont hate it! I dont hate it!*

So we see, just as Faulkner was punishing the northern woman in 'Light in August,' now he threatens the entire western hemisphere with the rape of the Negro. And what better images, after all, could the artist have found to express his discontent — this great hatred of the entire complex of modern northern industrial society — than the Negro and the Female? The emancipated negro who to the southern writer is the cause of the destruction of all he held dear. And now showing this negro as Joe Christmas, as Jim Bond, as the inhuman criminal, the degenerate who will dominate the civilization which freed him, Faulkner proclaims at once his anger and his revenge upon those who have destroyed his home. What more appropriate symbol than the woman, who to the southern writer is the particular treasured image of the bygone, cavalier society he is lamenting and lost in: the southern Lady, elevated and sacrosanct, the central figure of the southern age of chivalry, of those gallant agrarian knights who, very much like Quixote.

went forth in 1861 to perish in combat with the dynamo. How
shall the artist better show the universal debasement of modern
times than to turn the pure Lady into the contemporary Female,
now wanton, graceless, and degraded? The woman is both the
homemaker (this new home in which the southern artist feels
himself the exile) and the original source of life itself (this new
life against which all of Faulkner's work is the incessant protest). How shall the artist more aptly convey his total protest
than to portray the Female source of life as itself inherently
vicious? And as the last step in his sequence of discontent,
Faulkner mates the Female with the Negro, the savage as
Faulkner feels for whom the southern Lady was sacrificed, and
spawns out of his modern union the colored degenerate who is
to reign supreme, the moronic emperor of the future.

As against his discontent, we have now reached the complex
of that double childhood in which apparently the positive emotions of Faulkner are caught: by contrast, all his affection, hope,
and sense of human grandeur. There is first the pattern of the
writer's personal involvement in childhood, in early family relationships. We have noticed in Faulkner's work the continual
warmth of his childhood ties, the passion of siblings, the affection of brother for brother and brother for sister — Bayard and
John Sartoris, Horace and Narcissa Benbow, Caddy and Benjy
and Quentin Compson, Henry and Judith Sutpen and Charles
Bon the half-brother in 'Absalom' where the nature of Faulkner's love becomes quite explicit:

> Perhaps in his fatalism he (Bon) loved Henry the better of the
> two, seeing perhaps in the sister merely the shadow, the woman
> vessel with which to consummate the love whose actual object
> was the youth. . . .

Yet, however distorted or infantile in its forms, this *is* love as
against the always unsatisfactory nature of Faulkner's mature
relationships, and at its best Faulkner's achievement is that we
may ignore the form of his emotion and are moved by its content. And beneath his personal emphasis on childhood values,

and reinforcing it, there is Faulkner's involvement with a cultural past, with the birth and early growth of all those southern aristocratic values which the Civil War and the modern industrial age were to shatter — his involvement, as it were, with the youth of his southern society itself which never came to its destined maturity, which was cut off in its own early blossoming. But in this curious complex of a double childhood in which our writer seems caught, we must admit our own belief that it is the sociological rather than the personal patterns which dominate. For the meaning of Faulkner's work comes directly out of that whole web of historical southern emotionalism which colors the thought even of so fine a traditionalist as Allen Tate and so extreme a rebel as Thomas Wolfe. Disentangling themselves from this web, treating similar themes, but their ideas often in direct opposition to Faulkner's, we may nevertheless find out Faulknerian connections also in the plays of Paul Green or the stories of Erskine Caldwell. The symbolism in Faulkner comes, as it were, out of a cultural psychosis of which his work manifests the extreme hallucinations, but which still colors the dreams of those who seem most free of it. In his total rejection of the modern South, portraying it only in terms of bestiality, Faulkner is held by the historical southern myth as surely as that great-grandfather of his, whose 'White Rose of Memphis' would now find itself blooming from such strange soil. The great-grandson is perhaps the greater romanticist. For while his ancestor delineated the graces of an age which never quite existed, Faulkner is caught by one which now can never possibly exist. And we may now say that Faulkner's characters never grow up because there is no world for them to grow up into.

Held in such reversionary superstition, moreover, to what distortions can the psyche not bring itself? What a strange inversion it is to take the Female and the Negro, who are if anything the tragic consequence, and to exhibit them, indeed to believe them as the evil cause! This turning of the logical coin is psychological prestidigitation which ends with the head be·

coming the tail, and all respectable sense lost! The using of the one object that is certainly not responsible for our woes as being the single creator of them (so the Fascists use the Jew) — this is an inversion all too familiar to us today in other areas, another symptom of the confused emotions of our time. What genuine ills can be ignored by this again infantile preoccupation with scapegoats (so the child blames its mother), the infatuation with chimeras, what terrible ills can be created by it. Here is a dangerous quirk of the psyche, a trick once learned never wholly forgotten, a temptation once indulged in perhaps never to be wholly denied, a trick which may end by deceiving the trickster. I have used the title of Maurice Samuel's penetrating study of the Fascist superstitions, 'The Great Hatred,' to best describe Faulkner's work as a whole. For it is in the larger tradition of reversionary, neo-pagan, and neurotic discontent (from which Fascism stems) that much of Faulkner's writing must be placed — the anti-civilizational revolt which has caught so many modern mystics, the revolt rising out of modern social evils, nourished by ignorance of their true nature, and which succumbs to malice as their solution. It is not accidental that in Faulkner's novels we have watched the retrogression from the affecting era of infancy to that of infantile corruption; and that returning in 'Absalom, Absalom!' to the only society he can believe in, Faulkner's affection is nevertheless thinner, and the pretension of his novel greater. Hatred, as we know, feeds upon itself, while living in the past is apt to be an attenuating process.

Yet these are dangers dormant in parts of the Faulknerian reversion rather than immediate. It would be a tragedy if the major talent of Faulkner were to yield to any such gross chicanery, or to any other smaller trickeries. But it would be unjust to claim that on the whole, really, it has. (And it is a vital fact that no major American writer has as yet succumbed, in the manner of Knut Hamsun, to the Fascist ethics, even though some of our popular entertainers have shown the signs.) If we notice the dangerous possibilities of Faulkner's position, moreover, we must remember it is still the southern world of the nineteen-twenties that the novelist rejects. It is the earlier impact of the American industrial ethics he denies, the ethics embodied so brilliantly in the Jason of 'The Sound and the Fury,' whose final citadel is perhaps Mississippi, and whose last deity is Snopes. In the repudiation of our society from 1860 to 1929, Faulkner thus presents another aspect of the total cultural rejection of the American artist over this epoch. Alone among the major writers of the twenties Faulkner has remained without change, our unreconstructed rebel, like the Hightower of 'Light in August' still bemused in the vision of a nobler southern past where his life began and ended. Yet to Faulkner as to Lardner, viewing the modern scene, what may have seemed like perpetuity was after all only an American adolescence. The new age, as it reached the Michigan woods of Hemingway and the metropolis of Dos Passos, may yet rout the phantoms and ghouls of Faulkner's Jefferson. The crisis and indeed the new world war may bring another glimpse of that high and impossible American destiny which for Faulkner was ended by the Civil War. A developing American maturity, this maturity that Faulkner despairs of, must at last penetrate even to Jefferson, even to the Snopeses; and may awaken in our artist that magnificent compassion which he has vouchsafed only to the children of a disintegrating aristocracy. Like his Hightower, waiting, our author may once again hear 'the wild bugles, and the clashing sabres' and the thunder of martial hooves, but not dying now nor forever lost in the phantom dust. And, like Hightower, will he also find then 'something to pant with, to be reaffirmed in triumph and desire with'?

Tragic consequences ——— inverted and seen as causes of evil

The negro & the female seen as the causes of the fall of the Old South

Chapter Five

Thomas Wolfe : THE UNFOUND DOOR

◇

1. TORRENTS OF A YOUNG MAN'S SPRING   2. DIARY OF A
PROVINCIAL   3. THE ENFABLED ROCK   4. THE DOOR

Chapter Five

Thomas Wolfe : THE UNFOUND DOOR

1. TORRENTS OF A YOUNG MAN'S SPRING.   Something to pant with, to be reaffirmed in triumph and desire with. This, indeed, is the story of the nineteen-thirties, as now we reach the younger authors most clearly conditioned by our own decade, and in particular this is the meaning of Thomas Wolfe's struggle. It is interesting that two of our six key figures should be southern; and perhaps also provocative that out of the social degradation of the Faulknerian Waste Land should have come a sort of modern literary awakening. Faulkner and Wolfe, of course, are merely two figures out of a larger group that in some respects is more stimulating than any other recent literary movement, including such names as Paul Green, Allen Tate, Erskine Caldwell, Elizabeth Madox Roberts, John Crowe Ransom, Herbert Agar, and the younger people like Cleanthe Brooks and Robert Penn Warren.

Yet if we say that Wolfe and Faulkner are both Southerners; and Wolfe illustrates in his own early life some of the cultural ills which Faulkner portrays; and that condemning, and escaping from the South, Wolfe is also, in his moments of error and prejudice, still caught by the web of southern emotionalism which we have noticed in Faulkner's work — here the resemblance stops. As with Hemingway and Dos Passos, these two, starting from a somewhat similar basis, come to stand at opposite ends of the creative world. While Faulkner works steadily backward, Wolfe's movement is continuously forward; one

exploring the dissolving reaches of memory, the other will come
to face the urgencies of the future. Faulkner marks the final and
fullest expression of the artistic despair evoked by the American
twenties; Wolfe becomes perhaps the fullest expression of the
new hope evolving from the thirties. Wolfe, indeed, the product
of the southern rising middle class which the aristocratic writer
excoriates, becomes the precise symbol of the American maturity that Faulkner denies; and of that 'northern' emancipation
which to Faulkner contains the seeds of all his horrors. In some
respects, too, Wolfe reminds us more of Ring Lardner. With
his elaborate and impossible 'plans,' his ego-bound affections,
theatrical pronouncements, and his black rages, Wolfe does
recall the tumescent yokel of '29. Yet in his vitality, his passion
for experience in all its endless ranges, in the extremes of his
aspiration, and at last in the value of his achievement, Wolfe
rises above the Lardnerian caricature. This torrential youth is
from a deeper source than boomtime, and as such deserves careful scrutiny. Yet on Wolfe such restraint is hard to achieve.
Can we talk of Niagara Falls with circumspection? Wolfe carried sheer energy to greater heights than ever before in American letters. His haunting trails are likely to become super-
highways; a Wolfian whisper is never inaudible and usually
inescapable.

Aware of this, as Wolfe came slowly and painfully to be aware
of much else that was true about his own temperament, he
decried at last the turgescent aspect of his writings. So far as
the artist is concerned, Wolfe tells us, the unlimited extent of
human experience 'is not so important for him as the depth and
intensity with which he experiences things.' He has learned,
Wolfe says, that it is more important

> to have known one hundred living men and women in New York,
> to have understood their lives, to have got, somehow, at the root
> and source from which their natures came, than to have seen or
> passed or talked with 7,000,000 people on the city streets.

But the use of the word 'somehow' is a grudging concession to
the limits of the artist's endurance. It is with a sigh that Wolfe

relinquishes his earlier goal of unlimited human experience. And did it occur to him in his moment of dawning sobriety to have known merely one hundred living men and women, to have got even 'somehow' at the root of their natures — that in itself this is no tiny task?

Yet Wolfe, of course, was writing no ordinary novel. The early version of his projected 'October Fair' was about twelve times the average length. It was only appropriate for such a work that in one minor scene the conversation of four people consumed eighty thousand words. The first chapter of the original manuscript was eliminated because it was not a true beginning for the book, but 'merely something which led up to the true beginning.' Through his entire career, indeed, in one sense Wolfe was always leading up to a 'true beginning.' Compiling 'gigantic and staggering' lists of the 'towns, cities, counties, states, and countries' he had visited, Wolfe tells us again, he would ask himself, not merely for the population of Europe and America, but for the 'total combined population of all the countries in Europe and America.' He would recall all the people he had ever seen. With how many of them had he had some vital and illuminating experience? And again, hardly content with that, Wolfe would elaborate his experiences into those of 'joy, pain, pity, love, anger, or simple casual companionship.' And finally completing his plans for his novel (which by now had grown into a series of novels) Wolfe realized that he was dealing with material covering a hundred and fifty years in history, demanding the action of more than two thousand characters, and including in its final scope 'almost every racial type and social class of American life.'

Wolfe is thus rather like one of those raconteurs we all know who are prepared to render everything but their conclusions — who approach their destination with the courage of circumlocution, who are prepared to deviate at the slightest provocation, or at the suspicion of some possible or probable provocation. Yet, if we are attracted to Wolfe by our amazement at his spectacular peregrinations, in the end, of course, we are held by our appreciation of their value. For with the literary man, as with the rest of us, his destination is never so vital as the journey there. The message of his work can be related in a phrase of it, and there is no purpose to a novel if the purpose is not on every page. Literature is not like logic, each syllogism of which makes an inevitable sequence, though, indeed, our assumptions may be purely hypothetical and our conclusions entirely erroneous. Nor is it like the trader, for the consummation of his bargain gathering all the resources of his cunning. Literature must be closer to the underlying pattern of our lives, where, if we look only to our immediate ends, we lose the pleasure of their gaining for the always dubious values of conclusion; and seeking our ultimate end, we do but view the grave; that underlying pattern of our existence we all acknowledge and seldom follow, but which a Wolfe, in his passion for pure experience, brings back to us again.

It would be inappropriate if Wolfe's errors, like all the rest of him, were not gigantic. Like our American earth he is often so unduly fertile that he needs plowing under. Correcting themes, Wolfe has told us, he would scribble his comments on their margins, on the backs of the pages and on new blank pages which Wolfe would insert, until at last the teacher's essay was longer than the student's. For Wolfe, in fact, the blank page was an everlasting temptation. And the power in him which thus soared across new distances as well as pages, a power blind, indiscriminate, has in itself a sort of natural splendor. It is a kind of syllabic Mississippi, the Wolfian phrases flowing and boiling every which way, often beautiful, often penetrating, and like the Mississippi too, often stagnant; the tides of Wolfe's writing flourishing and swirling as well around some piece of useless spiritual driftwood or some ancient buried hulk of an idea.

It is our function to study this amazing energy with reference to Wolfe's life and culture. And indeed from the outlines of his history it would seem impossible to prophesy the massive tomes which commemorate it. What was there in this life which produced this vast and often seemingly eternal flow? Wolfe was born in 1900, in Asheville, North Carolina, of laboring people, he tells us. The impulse to be a writer was strong in him, but to him and his people a writer was an obscure and remote figure, 'somebody strange and peculiar, like Sir Walter Scott.' Thus diligently pursuing an uncertain aim, Wolfe went to the University of North Carolina and then Harvard, wrote plays, and failed. As to the making of his first book, 'Look Homeward, Angel,' Wolfe has told us in 'The Story of a Novel' his perplexities as he wandered in strange lands, the false beacons which guided him along a dark and uncertain path to the destiny he felt within himself. Published in 1929, a symbolic date with Wolfe too, 'Look Homeward, Angel' brought him recognition as a new voice in American letters. But where Wolfe's struggle should have been concluded, it began.

Over the entire nine years of Wolfe's creative maturity there lie the accents of torture and turmoil. 'I had committed my life and my integrity so irrevocably to this struggle,' Wolfe says, 'that I must conquer now or be destroyed.' He wrote furiously, interminably, twelve to fourteen hours a day. The words mounted up, the characters multiplied by the hundreds. He wrote

> about night and darkness in America, and the faces of the sleepers in ten thousand little towns; and of the tides of sleep and how the rivers flowed forever in the darkness. I wrote about the hissing glut of tides upon ten thousand miles of coast; of how the moonlight blazed down on the wilderness and filled the cat's cold eye with blazing yellow. I wrote about death and sleep, and of that enfabled rock of life we call the city. I wrote about October, of great trains that thundered through the night, of ships and stations in the morning; of men in harbors and the traffic of the ships.

A magnificent fragment! But Wolfe's feeling persisted that his work was after all composed of just such fragments; and his life. Where was the pattern, the meaning that would pull it all together? And though Wolfe's fragments mounted up to three or four hundred thousand words, and more, though 'Of Time and the River' appeared in 1935, a massive document of such words, characters, descriptions, and it was simple enough to put more of them together into a volume of short stories and sketches ('From Death to Morning'), still there was no resolution of Wolfe's internal battle.

The blood of Wolfe's novels thus flowing from his psychic wound, it was only in 1938, with his last two works, 'The Web and the Rock' and 'You Can't Go Home Again,' that the details of his creative process became complete. Around Wolfe's personality, his massive, awkward frame, his tremendous eating, his talking, his suspicions and his antics, a host of legends have sprung up. Around Wolfe's history, however, there are more basic and indigenous properties we must examine: this malformed titan, untutored, extravagant, pierced through with error. The sprawling provincial, so much the prey of his own delusions, lost in the quicksands of his uneasy spirit, bound down by superstition, fighting giants of his own creation. But always giants! Even the figments of Wolfe's imagination were augmentations. And if in his wealth of resources Wolfe reminds us of his American land, so too is he comparable in his little knowledge of them, of their proper use and conservation; in the tragic misalignment of capacity and function which so often, in his case and his country's, led to disaster.

In many such respects Wolfe is strongly American, our own — backwoods poet emerging from the dark of 'the buried life' to the dream of the American future. In his origins, in his less praiseworthy aspects, and in his unsteady direction he is one of us. And there are indications, too, that he half-envisioned the allegorical quality to his life, the deep belonging of himself to his society, the possibility of being the writer of his time, the Whitman, or even, as it were, a sort of literary Lincoln of his society. Embryonic, untried, ostentatious in his fears, through ignorance debasing his art, he was at the end approaching this strain in himself. He was nearly ready. This is a particular and poignant phrase with Wolfe, with him perhaps more so than

with all our human intentions; and in Wolfe's struggle which
we are about to discuss: a conflict so histrionic and inadequate,
imbued with the pretenses of Wolfe's society and himself, creating improbable hindrances and impossible goals. And yet with
enough of reality too. This stone, this leaf, this unfound door!
The door which Wolfe was forever seeking, the 'unspeakable
and incommunicable prison' he was escaping.

2. DIARY OF A PROVINCIAL. 'All serious work,'
Wolfe says in the preface to his first novel, 'is autobiographical,'
but with him more than conventionally so, his work is his life.
When he attempted in 'The Web and the Rock' to write a more
'objective' novel, the Webber hero becomes progressively more
and more Wolfian, and by the last sections the novel almost
abandons the attempt at anonymity. In the recounting of his
life, moreover, we are fortunate that Wolfe had few false reti-
cences. The artist, as Somerset Maugham has noticed so nicely
in 'Cakes and Ale,' is the only free man. The treachery of
friends, the departure of his beloved, the unaccountable malice
of acquaintances — these are the grist of the writer's mill.
Whatever blows life deals him, he alone can repay them with
profit to his soul, and often indeed to his pocketbook. And if
through his writing Wolfe did not always gain this complete
artist's freedom (which, by the way, has its ambiguous aspects
for the beloved, the friend, and even the acquaintance) he at
least achieved a wonderful frankness. Nothing was to Wolfe,
but writing made it more so. His novels are the diary, tremendous, often inchoate and very possibly unique in our time,
of the artist in America. And more particularly of the writer
in our provincial America. Here, indeed, is the local origin of
Wolfe's 'unspeakable and incommunicable prison,' the Pentlands of Wolfe's first novel, in which, enchained, his broken
angel looks vainly homeward.

In the old myth, as we know, man himself, as the broken angel, has his memories of an earlier heaven before his fall. We remember Milton's paradise, with its modest claim of

> things unattempted yet in prose or rhyme

— or Eve's garden itself. With our more analytic modern sense we have come to see that the haunting feeling of man's better past derives in part at least from the peace of the womb in the individual's life, and that perhaps of sheer inanimate matter in the race's memory of its existence. How strong a theme this is in our history! So cruelly pointing backward to its ultimate goal of death, and perhaps even so ironically the hidden and despairing cause of all our infinite progress. We find many traces and currents of the theme in European literature, from Plato to the Wordsworthian infant trailing his clouds of glory. And too few traces of it are found in American culture, where this idyllic garden is never in the forsaken and haunting past, but, as we all know, immediately ahead of us: paradise and prosperity right around the corner. No melancholy mysticisms for our pragmatic optimists in a land where work, not recollection, will prove our salvation.

Wolfe is perhaps the only major modern author who has seized upon the theme of the lost paradise for his first novel, and he had his reasons. If we for the moment ignore the soaring rhetoric which marks 'Look Homeward, Angel,' we may see in it a very realistic portrait of Wolfe's society. Out of its calculations and pretensions Wolfe has fashioned a sort of heroic scene. But the calculations and pretensions remain. He embellishes the provincial rudeness with poetry, but the ornamentation also accentuates the frame. It is Gant, of course, with his memories of rich meadows, corn, plum trees, and ripe grain, of the old rich pioneer America, who is the exile in the Reconstruction South. It is Gant who recalls the 'great, forgotten language, the lost lane-end into Heaven.' Why here? O Lost! Lost indeed the Gantian South with its gray and withered Altamonts, its squalid Toytown cities, the 'pasteboard pebbledash' hotels.

The muddy clay roads. The slattern people. The rows of yokels strung like apes along the fences. The drunken Mc-Guires (the more talented souls of Wolfe's South are the drunkards) and the Pentland dwellers. But is there only the southern idiocy to oppose Gant's northern madness? The Pentlands, Wolfe says, by marriage and intermarriage among their own kin, 'could boast of some connections with the great, of some insanity, and a modicum of idiocy' — for once a Wolfian understatement. For Bacchus Pentland, Armageddon was due any day now, and for his family, as a matter of fact, it seems to have arrived. We remember the first reception of Gant by the Pentland clan, this tribe 'who saw one another only in times of death, pestilence and terror.' The males with their birdlike winks and nods, the children with their lapping idiot grins, the roaring of the wind outside, 'remote and demented.' Was it a time of joy for the northern Gant, his marriage with the daughter of this clan? It proved in fact a time of death, pestilence, and terror, for it marked his union with them, the prelude to his long and painful conquest by them.

And for the young Eugene of the novel, these Pentlands are the South with variations. There are two characters who stand out in some contrast: the younger brother Ben, whom Wolfe tries unsuccessfully to create as a tragic and lovable person, and the teacher, Margaret Leonard, who is perhaps the only character in the book possessing a genuine warmth. And here, of course, we come upon the major fault of 'Look Homeward, Angel.' The writer who is fully himself is certainly the rebel. His nature, his obligation, his essence is the civilizing spirit which evaluates and condemns. In the midst of Utopia the writer, as it were, must protest the divine injustices, and in the context of, as yet, an imperfect and mortal society, he must remain continually sensitive to human abuses. He is at once society's irritant and antiseptic. Yet to become wholly this, to lose the sense of loyalty to one's origins, of devotion to one's land or of faith in one's neighbors, to lose this basic sense of a creative if always skeptical affection for his material, is for the writer and his society equally sterile. The most brilliant satire which has no focus within our human hopes leaves us its victims, perhaps, but not its followers. The writer who in his intelligence forsakes his humanity — an Aldous Huxley, for example, in the manner of 'After Many a Summer Dies the Swan' — loses his own purpose as a writer.

It is incorrect to mention Huxley and Wolfe together here, and only as the extreme may illustrate the mean. For Wolfe's entire struggle, as we shall see, becomes the attempt to remedy the emotional deficiencies he felt within himself. But in the range of his first novel, which always arouses our interest, the moments which also compel our sympathy are few. With all Wolfe's marvelous faculty of characterization, he omits the essential of our identification with these people of 'Look Homeward, Angel.' We see them brilliantly and we hardly feel them at all. We are the outsiders watching a variety of human specimens operating in their milieu, which should be ours. We recognize Wolfe's Altamont, but we are bound to it by few ties of affection, nor those of mere companionship, common neighborliness, nor by any mutual concern for our collective achievement. We exist in it merely, as it were, by proximity. Just so, Wolfe was born in the South, but he shared with it little except the accident of birth. A strange irony, and one which we must return to later, that this writer — so American in his temperament, so filled with the necessity of his belonging to his land in order to fulfill his destiny — should be denied the ordinary heritage of a home, of a place and people to love.

Yet what was there in Wolfe's early life to evoke this obvious loving-kindness, this ordinary and basic attribute of art, the common identification of a writer with his brothers, which the critic is almost ashamed to identify, such is our period, and must speak of with bated breath? If Margaret Leonard is the one person in Wolfe's portrait of his youth who gives out some humanity, who has some interest in Wolfe's hero, Eugene, can we say as much for her fellow teachers? 'What is an Epode, Mr. Leonard?' asks Eugene's friend of the drawling, stupid schoolmaster. 'Why,' said Mr. Leonard reflectively, 'it's a form of poetry.' 'Hell,' said the boy, 'I knew that before I paid tuition.' Is there very much in fact which these boys didn't know before they came to school? The dry and distorted forms of Cicero, Ovid, Lucretius, which John Leonard presented to his adolescent audience, squirming in its seats, projecting petty obscenities to divert itself from such intolerable boredom — what connection have these 'classics' with Eugene's actual life? Nor was Leonard an unusually stupid man, Wolfe tells us. He was indeed

> an example of that sad liberalism of the village — an advanced thinker among the Methodists, a bearer of the torch at noon, an apologist for the toleration of ideas that have been established for fifty years.

The ludicrous Shakespearian pageant, one of the finest scenes in 'Look Homeward, Angel,' and in which Wolfe shows very sharply the satiric gift which was later to constitute his most impressive achievement, is the logical symbol of the false values of Eugene's education. And just so Wolfe himself sums up his impression of the more enlightened thinking of the 'university':

> The appraisal of personality, like all other appraisal with them was coarse and blunt. They were suspicious of all eminence. . . . The vast champaign of the world stretched out its limitless wonder, but few were seduced away from the fortress of the State, few ever heard the distant reverberation of an idea. They could get no greater glory for themselves than a seat in the Senate, and the way to glory — the way to all power, highness and distinction whatsoever — was through the law, a string tie, and a hat.

Such is the verdict of our hero upon his total provincial education. It is harsh, biased, no doubt, but there is reason for its bias. Even Margaret Leonard, who encourages at least Eugene's avid hunger for knowledge, though without much discipline or discrimination in the sort of knowledge, has perhaps little sense of Eugene's real needs. His hunger is also for human relationships as well as poetry, for some knowledge also of his

own physical and mental development, this hero tormented by
his family's disgrace and by his own adolescent sexual fantasies.
'She was an inspired sentimentalist,' Wolfe writes of Margaret
Leonard. 'She thought she "knew boys"' —

> In fact, however, she had little knowledge of them. She would
> have been stricken with horror if she could have known the wild
> confusion of adolescence, the sexual nightmares of puberty, the
> grief, the fear, the shame in which a boy broods over the dark
> world of his desire. She did not know that every boy, caged in
> from confession by his fear, is to himself a monster.

Yet the 'fear' which cages in Eugene is not at all a necessary condition of a boy's education except within the strait limits of the
provincial-puritan view of youth. From the insistence, indeed,
with which these 'sexual nightmares' intrude upon Eugene's
life, it might almost seem that his education had in the end only
one major function: the stimulation of his prurience. But if
Eugene's formal education cannot thus be viewed as highly
constructive, what can be said of his sexual education itself?

Only, I am afraid, that it was compounded, in a pattern familiar to our society, of secrecy and salaciousness, and of ignorance which is no bliss. The colored prostitute, Ella Corpening,
with her pathetic Kewpie dolls and calendars from the Altamont Coal Company, her moaning, undulating, writhing
'Jelly Roll,' is in fact an advance for the young Eugene, at least
from the classroom obscenities, the sneaking sexualism of his
white companions; for Ella's passion, if commercial, is also honest. The little waitress, Louise, may add something further to
Eugene's amorous sophistication, but hardly to his sense that
often a human relationship may accompany the sexual one.
From Louise, the young Eugene moves to Lily Jones in her
house in Exeter, Lily Jones with her 'coy and frigid modesty' —

> She yielded her kisses with the coy and frigid modesty of the
> provincial harlot, turning her mouth away.... She chafed him
> with rough, embarrassed professionalism. In a moment she rose
> impatiently. 'Let's git started,' she said. 'Where's my money?'

Is the pursuing of such affection, then, the lost language Wolfe seeks, the lane-end into paradise? If love should be the core of the adolescent's growth, is this to be the love which rewards him? In Eugene, Wolfe writes, the ghost turned grievously away. 'The lost bright wonder died.' Based on such premises how can Eugene's final affair with Laura James, the climax of 'Look Homeward, Angel,' if it attempts to be idyllic, have any genuine substance? It seems, despite all of Wolfe's efforts, artificial and empty; so too is the young Eugene in respect to any previous knowledge of a sound relationship. It is literary, and D. H. Lawrence; what other standard can Eugene create for himself? Certainly not that of reality. And if in it the pornographic again often replaces the passionate, this has been the essence of Eugene's sexual education.

Love like charity begins at home. Of course, Eugene's family should have created the emotional security which might compensate for the terrors of these other areas of his learning, but it is among the members of his family that we find the greatest indifference toward the facts. It is precisely this family, indeed, which contributes most to the sense of shame, fear, disturbance underlying Eugene's youth. Eliza, Eugene's mother, we recall, since her husband is a tombstone cutter, declares that death is not remunerative. 'People,' she thought, 'died too slowly.' With Eliza's entrance into real-estate speculation, she gains 'a freedom she had never known.' But this 'freedom' is that of materialist America, of Lardner's U.S.A., the freedom of possession and power which in the end is only a superior sort of bondage. What does Eliza not offer up as human sacrifice to this insensate freedom? — her husband, her children, her home, and, of course, herself. A Rockefeller is reputed, in Matthew Josephson's 'Robber Barons,' to have stated the classic American dictum of family life: that he cheated his sons every chance he could. 'I want to make 'em sharp. I trade with the boys and skin 'em and I just beat 'em every time I can. I want to make 'em sharp.' But to Wolfe's Eliza we cannot even attribute this rather primitive parental concern. Tending her property, she could not also tend to her children. Hoarding old string, empty cans, paper, anything she may retail at a profit, symbol of the property psychology which a Balzac flayed in France, she is the twentieth-century version of Shakespeare's 'snapper-up of unconsidered trifles.' Sometimes she attains a comic dignity, grandly ascribing to her tubercular clients 'a little bronchial trouble.' But lacking at last any warmth and ease of personality, we feel only her increasing sterility, a woman who lusts only for money. We share with Eugene his gradually perceptive hatred, first of Eliza's effect on her husband Gant, and then on the boy Eugene himself:

> He felt, rather than understood, the waste, the confusion, the blind cruelty of their lives . . . the conviction that their lives could not be more hopelessly distorted, wrenched, mutilated and perverted away from all simple comfort, repose, happiness, if they had set themselves deliberately to tangle the skein, twist the pattern. . . . He saw plainly by this time that their poverty, the threat of the poorhouse, the lurid references to the pauper's grave belonged to the insensate mythology of hoarding.

And the growing perception of the actual conditions of his existence, the young Eugene materializes a little later in a perhaps less rhetorical but more convincing statement to Eliza on Gant's dying agonies:

> My God, my God, where are we going? What's it all about? He's dying — can't you see it? Don't you know it? Look at his life. Look at yours. No light, no love, no comfort — nothing. . . . Mama, mama, in God's name what is it? What do you want? Are you going to strangle and drown us all? Don't you own enough? Do you want more string? Do you want more bottles? . . . Do you want the town? What is it?

As though, indeed, all the young men of America were crying such phrases to certain other industrial Lords of Creation!

Such, then, are the outlines of 'the buried life' from which a Thomas Wolfe slowly and painfully extricated his spirit. If we are accused of simplifying the picture Wolfe gives us, it is simply because the grim outlines are softened by the lyric passages of 'Look Homeward, Angel.' It is precisely this other strain in his first novel which we must now for a moment examine. The rich meadows, corn, plum trees, the ripe grain Gant forever mourns, and for the splendors of which, now forever lost, he may only substitute the tides of his preposterous rhetoric, a richness of words for the vanished richness of fact — this is Gant's memory of a different America. And Wolfe's long, rich elaborations of food throughout this book and his later novels also, the orgies of tremendous feeding, the hunger for richness not only of food, but of personality, action, knowledge, sensation, of words and life itself — these are Wolfe's desire. Memory and desire: what power resides in these attributes of the human temperament, and especially when they are denied their realization by the facts of our life! Then indeed they rise triumphant to their extremes, and their excesses, just when they are most evidently betrayed by the realities of our existence, to demonstrate beyond doubt the dominance of the wish over the statistic. Wolfe's passion for the sensuous wealth of life, his repeated invocations to black, wet, spermy earth, existence oozing, bursting, with fertility —

> huge, frosty apples, whole hogs, smoked bacons, great bins full of flour, dark, recessed shelves groaning with preserved cherries, peaches, plums, quinces, apples, pears . . .

— we must surely establish this as not the truth of his own life, but its hunger; and a hunger based exactly on the material and spiritual poverty of the life he describes in such harsh and condemnatory terms. The excesses of Wolfe's quest for abundance are in short attributable to its absence in his early environment.

We must mention in this respect Wolfe's affinity (which was surely a southern sacrilege) for the Jews of his novels, an affinity which was to lead him to such strange terminating conditions of his life. Like him the Jews are the outcasts of society, the exiles, the strangers. But they often seem also to possess the very qualities denied to Wolfe by his own existence: laughter,

ease, a generosity of temperament. Thus the ridiculous and
ironic excesses of gaiety and warmth with which Wolfe later
endows his New York Jewish friends, and which to a large degree led to catastrophe when Wolfe was faced with facts rather
than his romantic and wishful imagination. For the Jews are,
as Dorothy Parker noted, just like everybody else, only more so,
and even they could not measure up to Wolfe's exorbitant demands. In the meantime, Wolfe was to preserve his special
affection for them, those Jewish students of his, as he tells us in
'The Story of a Novel,' who stood first even in the accusing
circle of his dreams of guilt; the little Jews of 'Of Time and the
River,' with their swarthy faces, sensuous beings, full of the life
and laughter lacking in Wolfe's own. And they also are, as
Wolfe is, alone, imprisoned. Like him, alas, they also sought
their lost, forgotten language, their lane-end into paradise,
strove to escape the unspeakable and incommunicable prison
of this earth.

A prison indeed if we may trust Wolfe's portrait of his youth.
Early, if somewhat absurdly, echoing Wordsworth's omniscient
infant, he saw himself as the sad one, 'caged in that little round
of skull, imprisoned in that beating and most scared heart,' his
life forever walking down lonely passages —

> He understood that men were forever strangers to one another,
> that no one ever comes really to know any one, that imprisoned
> in the dark womb of our mother, we come to life without having
> seen her face, that we are given to her arms a stranger, and that,
> caught in the insoluble prison of being, we escape it never, no
> matter what arms may clasp us, what mouth may kiss us, what
> heart may warm us.

And if this is perhaps a little prescient for the baby, it is certainly evident to the mature Eugene.

Is it likewise so evident to all the rest of us, the common condition of our existence, the inexorable terms of our own being?
If the dominant theme of imprisonment, which is the framework of 'Look Homeward, Angel,' certainly is to a large extent

the immutable analysis of our worldly activity, it is just as certainly true that the characteristic of the human, as against the brute, spirit lies in the effort to defy it: to break the bars of our savage bondage, to escape from this brutalizing loneliness. To communicate and share, to depend on and support our fellow exiles and prisoners, to fuse through our common experience and effort a communal unity — these are the defiant aims of the progressive forces in humanity. Civilization is the attempt to escape from this prison. And long ago the poet's song reminded us

> Stone walls do not a prison make,
> Nor iron bars a cage.

But what was there in Wolfe's provincial culture to support such a faith? The instruments of our salvation from the Wolfian tomb are precisely those which, as we have seen, were denied to him: family, friends, love, and knowledge. These, like Ariadne's 'clue of silk' which rescued ancient Theseus from the labyrinth, are the slender but nevertheless sufficient thread to lead us from the domains of our own modern solitude, but for Wolfe the thread, the clue, was missing.

The pilgrimage of a Thomas Wolfe from this point onward is the attempt, often misdirected, sometimes even lacking consciousness of his problem, and yet in the end with a sure purpose, to solve this enigma for himself and his work. Meanwhile we should notice that Eugene's farewell to his Altamont has, for this prison-pent soul, a certain degree of vigor. Years later, Wolfe tells us, his hero was still afraid of his South. Even —

> when he could no longer think of the barren spiritual wilderness, the hostile and murderous entrenchment against all new life — when their cheap mythology, their legend of the charm of their manner, the aristocratic culture of their lives... made him writhe — when he could think of no return to their life and its swarming superstitions without weariness and horror, so great was his fear of the legend, his fear of their antagonism, that he still pretended the most fanatic devotion, excusing his Northern residence on grounds of necessity rather than desire.

But finally, Wolfe concludes, it occurred to Eugene that his education, his family, his friends, these people of the South had given him nothing —

> that neither their love nor their hatred could injure him, that he owed them nothing, and he determined that he would say so, and repay their insolence with a curse.

The 'curse' was, of course, 'Look Homeward, Angel,' but what Wolfe owed to the South was not in fact so easily concluded.

3. THE ENFABLED ROCK.   Perhaps we have sounded rather like Pollyanna among the Encyclopédists, harping as we have upon the familiar virtues in the very midst of an age which in its skepticism is close to that of Diderot and Voltaire. And the absence of these homespun traits would not, indeed, be so significant in Wolfe's life if they did not so seriously affect his work. We have seen how his excessive striving for vitality and richness in living springs directly from his sense of their loss in his youth. We must recall that in his first novel he felt no loyalty or sympathy with the society which had denied such qualities to him. And the issue would, moreover, be hardly so significant with Wolfe, if it did not also concern the range of major American writers among whom he stands.

Is it at all true that great literature must have as its base the identification of the writer with his audience — some feeling of the artist for his land, his people, or as a last resort some ordinary affection for humanity in general? Then we must almost rule out from this definition much of our contemporary fiction. We are not espousing now any spurious patriotism, nor are we lamenting the perfidious ingratitude of our literary sons. But surveying American literature from this aspect, we are obliged to confess that even chauvinism would have its charms. Where are the Whitmans of our world? Thoreau liked Walden if not

Boston. Emerson, for all his rather chilly abstractions, had an American sense; he loved his origins, though perhaps in the end he loved learning more. Our writers have followed, rather, the path of Henry Adams who despised his age, or of Henry James who was half-ashamed of it. We have seen the troubled course of Ring Lardner and Hemingway. We know again the one quality which prevents the 'U.S.A.' trilogy of Dos Passos from commanding its true position, written as it surely is with the cultural insight missing in so much of our literature, with eloquence and wit, and the indignation which Henry Adams never had quite the strength to admit; and lacking only love. What is there, once more, to redeem the often empty brilliance of Faulkner's technic? Certainly not, as we know, the community of his interest with his characters. We have spoken of this, and shall speak again when we reach the sometimes fabricated emotions of John Steinbeck. Our subject, indeed, forces us to speak of it: of those who early had affection and lost it; of those who grew without it; of those who have yet to learn it, such is too frequently our melancholy chronicle.

We shall come a little later also to a fuller statement of the American literary hostility. But in Thomas Wolfe at least we can see the effect of his provincial environment on his emotional development; the upbringing which now leaves him in the dubious position of Mr. Van Wyck Brooks's 'half-artists' — those who have broken away from the tribal laws and have not as yet gained an inner discipline to replace the outer superstitions. Isn't this the explanation of 'Of Time and the River,' least impressive though the most voluminous of Wolfe's works? Carrying forward the hero of 'Look Homeward, Angel,' Wolfe's second novel certainly adds to his quantitative achievement. It is marked again with the vitality, the range and extent of Wolfe's experience — along with the familiar hunger for experience which scorns even the astounding quantities of it which Wolfe encompassed. It adds, as Wolfe proclaimed his purpose, the hundreds of characters and almost a thousand pages to his already none too modest chronology. It describes what is very

likely the longest train ride in literary history. It has in it some
biting sections and portraits, including that on Harvard academic society with its Professor Hatcher, Scoville, and Seth
Flint the newspaperman, both sour and pathetic, who brings a
sort of fine vulgarity to the refinements of Cambridge dramaturgy. Who can select a better book to suggest, at least, the
varied flavor of American life, holding within it, as 'Of Time and
the River' does, a dozen strains of this life, a dozen literary
manners for its recording. It is in short a sort of résumé of what
is happening in the American scene: Harvard professors and
New York university students, Boston tradesmen, lawyers,
waitresses, poor Irish, eager Jews and hyper-English middle-
westerners, slums, inns, high-society estates on the Hudson —
all this recorded in so many varieties of romanticism, realism,
satire, lyricism! No wonder that the visiting Englishmen, like
J. B. Priestley, were 'impressed' by such a talent, seeming to be
working out through one mind what all the other American
minds were dealing with separately. Perhaps anybody but a
visiting Englishman would have been overcome.

Saying this, we must nevertheless admit 'Of Time and the
River' is disappointing. If it accentuates certain good traits in
Wolfe's achievement, it seems almost defiantly or compulsively
to emphasize certain other traits of Wolfe which were pardon-
able in a first novel and irritating in a second. Wolfe's approach to his material is too often topographical. There is little
effort to break his new experiences down, to penetrate through
them, to interpret them in other terms than the Wolfian quest
for sheer experience. 'Of Time and the River' is vital, sometimes superb reportage. But what we must demand from a
writer of Wolfe's potentiality is a gain in his discrimination as to
what kind of experience is worth more, and which less, of his
attention. And this gain isn't very noticeably recorded in his
second novel; something of the opposite, in fact. For released
at last from the binding confines of Altamont, faced with the
society of Cambridge and Boston, two whole new cities with
their innumerable new types and personalities, buildings,

streets, books, sounds, smells, ideas, food, the young Eugene is
faced by a temptation he cannot resist. He must devour them
all, and (in this he is very American, of course) immediately.
What a challenge to the Faustian provincial! What insufferable
effrontery that Fate should place him among all this new life
and not expect him to possess it!

> That first impact of the city had stunned him with its huge and
> instant shock and now, like a swimmer whelmed in a raging
> storm, he sought desperately among that unceasing flood of faces
> for one that he knew.

And Wolfe's 'one face,' as we know, is merely the prelude to ten
faces, a hundred, or a thousand. The notable scene in the
Harvard Library, whose shelves drive Eugene to despair, since
no matter how fast he reads, they contain books he hasn't read,
is very typical. And how can he rest in this library, since outside, on the streets passing the library door, there are a million
souls he has not met, studied, known? And this is only Boston.
What of New York? Paris? An extra and entirely new continent of Europe? This mad desire for instantaneous and total
possession, however appealing it may often be, in the end, of
course, results in no genuine possession at all. Emitting such
undigested loads of experience, Wolfe confuses us by his sheer
abundance. On which of the innumerable pages was it that we
left the young Eugene with his innumerable Harvard faces, his
New York faces, his Paris faces, or the nameless faces in the
nameless cities on the nameless continents he has yet to conquer?
   The lack of discrimination in the experience Wolfe sought so
eagerly, and whose surface texture, indeed, he often recorded
with such brilliance, is made clearer if we notice Wolfe's European sources: Joyce, as Wolfe tells us in 'The Story of a Novel,'
and Dostoevsky, as he relates in 'The Web and the Rock.'
Wolfe talks in fact of basing 'Of Time and the River' upon
his hero's 'search for a father,' which is the quest of Stephen
Dedalus in 'Ulysses,' but a comparison of Joyce's immeasurably
subtle imagery with that of Wolfe's will show the difference in

the layers of meaning attached to the symbols. Wolfe was too often content with the first meaning of things, even if Joyce, perhaps, is too often not content. And modeling his eccentric characters upon the Russian, Wolfe often catches their peculiarities in action without the paroxysms of their spirit. In the inchoate mass of Wolfian experience, Eugene himself, at least, remains one constant force among the multitude of variables in 'Of Time and the River.' Yet Eugene, as he prowls day and night among the myriad, swarming humankind of Wolfe's second novel, is not in himself sufficient to hold our sympathies, gigantic if somewhat theatrical in his desires —

> He would wait for night to come with furious impatience, and would feel his hands grow weak, his entrails numb, his heart begin to pound, and his throat to swell with this intolerable exultancy of joy . . . his whole body would be stirred with such a shifting iridescence of passion, happiness, hunger, triumph, music and wild exuberant humor that he felt he could no longer hold the swelling power of ecstasy that he felt in him.

Just as we cannot hope to comprehend, with the final comprehension of identification, the tremendous scope of Wolfe's material in 'Of Time and the River,' we may marvel somewhat at the diversity and intensity of his hero's emotions, but we cannot accept them, after all, except as a sort of remarkable travesty of our own less ostentatious human desires.

When we recall Eugene's provincial origins, however, we understand his apparently grotesque hunger for sensation. His temperament so rich, eager, warm, curious, and starved, how could he arrive in Boston except in a torment of impatience? Haunted by the specter of Altamont's harsh and sterile existence, Eugene indeed must look to the culture of New England. Here may lie his lost happiness, his forgotten language; Harvard his little lane-end into the paradise of the life he was seeking. No wonder his novel includes such a vast range of new life, that he seizes upon the most trivial of events, when the secret of a better life may lie, who knows, everywhere around him. Certainly Wolfe did not know. His consuming and almost compulsive feeling that everything is important, if it has certain psychological roots, is strongly supported by his sociological environment. It was all too easy to include everything. The immense amount of detail, fattening and often swelling his work to sometimes almost absurd proportions — this tremendous drive for knowledge but without moderation, balance, or discrimination — is the penalty he paid for his provincial education, and which, reading his massive work, we must pay also.

It may be questioned whether a Francis Starwick was in fact 'that rare and tragically gifted creature who was one of the most extraordinary figures of his generation.' Overcome by a sophistication and an intelligence superior to, a personality remote from, his earlier life, Wolfe makes Starwick interesting but hardly in the end worth the elaborate attention we must pay him. Yet Starwick, cultivated, assured, tasteful, with all the values of critical discrimination Wolfe himself lacked, and by this contact began to realize his lack; perhaps Starwick with his beautiful, precise English is the very guardian angel of Wolfe's new heaven? Just as the lady in the fabulous castle on the Hudson, the Rosalind Pierce of the middle sections of 'Of Time and the River,' with her 'warm, sweet, lovely and affectionate voice' — and notice how Wolfe's spiritual needs are revealed in his adjectives — her salons of artistic and metaphysical chatter, her wealth, her easy references to Paris, Rome, Berlin, Bucharest, this lady perhaps, like Ariadne herself, might lead Wolfe out of his tortuous maze:

> 'Look here — if I live to be a million years I'll never — the way the river was tonight, the moon, and the way Joel met me and then finding you and your mother and your friends there in the moonlight — and the river down below — and now this walk with you — this road — the field — and all those cows there in the field — and you here — why, by God!' he cried thickly, incoherently, 'you are the finest girl I ever saw in all my life! — this place — tonight here — the most wonderful —'

We realize that Wolfe, looking back upon the exploits of his Eugene, has already gained enough perspective to express this declaration in a fine satiric vein. It is also true that to Eugene this Rosalind Pierce was 'the finest girl he ever saw.' Remembering his sister Helen Gant, Ellen Corpening, the waitress Louise, the house of Lily Jones at Exeter, the provincial and vapid Laura James of Wolfe's first novel, why this is most obviously so. And it is quite as obvious that the stuttering, groping incoherence of Wolfe's hero in this passage, dazed and bewildered as he is before this first spectacle of the rich and cultured life in this castle on the Hudson, typifies the deeper artistic incoherence of 'Of Time and the River.'

We see clearly, too, that it was the girl's life rather than the girl which attracted the young Eugene.

> . . . it was the feeling that this life of wealth and luxury and comfort was so beautiful and right and good. At the moment it seemed to him to be the life for which all the men on the earth are seeking, about which all men living dream, toward which all the myriads of the earth aspire.

But Eugene's quest for the good life of wealth and luxury and comfort was not yet concluded. It was indeed barely started. It was to form the theme of his next novel. It was to lead Wolfe to a strange termination of his illusion, and to the central crisis of his life. And with what high hopes does the Monk Webber of 'The Web and the Rock' approach the Magic City of New York, still on his illusioned quest for a life superior to the provincial existence he has known. For despite Wolfe's change of his hero's name, who will doubt that here is the same personage, the same search? And perhaps no other modern American has caught so well as Wolfe the excitement of a provincial's search, and his meeting with the city's enchantments and terrors. In the flowing, vivid passages which inaugurate this section of 'The Web and the Rock,' Wolfe illuminates the meaning of the metropolis, the whole complex fabric it has woven around itself in our entire provincial society, this new web of shining gossamer, of promise and illusion which is, we are told, to replace the confining web of rural society.

> There is no truer legend of the world [Wolfe writes] than the one
> about the country boy, the provincial innocent, in his first con-
> tact with the city . . . Hackneyed by repetition, parodied and bur-
> lesqued by the devices of cheap fiction and the slap-stick of vaude-
> ville humor, it is nevertheless one of the most tremendous and
> vital experiences in the life of a man, and in the life of a nation.

And for the moment, at least, it was. For in Esther, beautiful,
wealthy, talented, the Monk Webber of the novel has surely
found the guide who will lead him at last into the city's pageantry and culture, its pinnacles and labyrinths. How full the
novel's pages are of Webber's breathless meetings with theatrical society, famous tradespeople, artists, publishers, critics,
poets. These are the destinies he has been seeking, this at last
must be the true version of that life of richness and goodness
toward which the myriads of the earth aspire! Poor Rosalind
Pierce now is only a shadowy memory, her castle on Hudson
a poor beacon beside this brilliance. The 'Community Guild'
theater, the gay and cultured parties Webber attends, the speakeasy society of the twenties whose barred and secret entrance
Webber's Esther so easily penetrates — experiences enough
for Wolfe's young provincial innocent! The 'celebrated columnist' Webber meets is perhaps typical of the meaning of all
this experience, these new and glittering personalities, this hope
of a new direction, more gracious, and full of meaning, in
Webber's life:

> The celebrated columnist whose winged jest, whose subtle wit,
> whose jabs and praises, whose graceful lyrics and whose clever
> limericks had flashed forth for more than twenty years — this
> man whose daily chronicle of the city's life he had so often
> feasted on in his own college years, reading into that diary of
> the day's activity the whole glamorous pageantry of that distant
> Babylon, cloud-capped and rosy-hued there in the smoke of his
> imagination.

And this 'celebrated columnist' (whose initials are easy to de-
cipher, as indeed we recognize very well the other prototypes

of the literary personages Wolfe here illuminates so incisively),
this 'Aladdinlike enchanter,' upon whom a thousand other
American youths in a thousand other little towns also feasted,
dreaming forever of a better life, there in 'the smoke of their
imagination' — this, for Webber, almost mythical figure now
calls Esther by her first name.

And what shall we say of Esther herself, mistress of such circles, holding in herself the dazzling abundance Webber has
been seeking, Esther now in love so deeply with the naïve and
gross provincial? How shall we treat the celebrated romance
which is at the core of 'The Web and the Rock,' this modern
idyll of Baucis and Philemon, in a penthouse: this strange
romance in which blintzes alternate with bliss; in which both
participants are so fervently seeking their emotion to be recollected in tranquillity, but to be recollected in a detail which
would have astounded Wordsworth. For the gargantuan
love affair sprawls its length over 'The Web and the Rock,' and
as if hardly content with that, throws its bitter shadow over
Wolfe's last novel also. Here we discover every thought, action,
sensation of these lovers carefully recorded in their memories,
and perhaps, we suspect, in their diaries too. In this strange but
absorbing love relationship, a little domestic quarrel becomes a
feud, a battle, a major engagement, and in the end a sort of
Hundred Pages War.

For our purposes, however, we must be content to show how
Webber's relationship with Esther contains — or rather, is —
the summation of his history, the resolving pattern of his early
desires. 'Place! That was the word he had needed,' Wolfe says
of his hero. 'The East Side was a Place — and that was the
thing that made it wonderful. It was a Place that people came
from, where men were born and lived and worked and sweated
and died.' And the sense of belonging, of home, of roots, and
identity with a larger group which Wolfe, the rebel who dis-
owns his own land, has been seeking is now gained for him with
his Esther. She is the 'great lady' of his provincial erotic fantasies. And, glamorous, mysterious, inviting, she is actually the

city itself — as Wolfe himself realizes in an acute moment of self-perception:

> It was not merely that he was in love with her. In addition to that, through his association with her, it seemed to him that now at last he had begun to 'know' the city. For, in some curious way, the woman had come to represent 'the city' to him. To him, she was the city he had longed to know.

Though perhaps we must add that this has come about not at all in 'some curious way' but in a strictly logical way, according to the logic of Webber's (or Wolfe's) entire emotional history.

But if this central love relationship of 'The Web and the Rock' embodies in it the climax of Wolfe's provincial education, so it reveals most sharply the final defects of this education: the illusionary nature of his lifelong dream. Wolfe was incapable of sustaining such a relationship in fact, or even, as yet, of creating it effectively in his literary work. Who does not see how 'literary' this love affair is also, reminding us again of the Laura James of his first novel, how pretentious, artificial, lacking the traits necessary to make it as convincing as it is copious. It is, as we say, a make-believe love affair. But how could it not be, compounded of a lifetime of make-believe, the fruit of frustration and of fantasy? And in this context it is impossible not to know that their love — accounted so immortal by its participants — must inevitably fail.

With its failure came Wolfe's great crisis, the dark period of the novel, and the start of his bitterness: the venomous attacks not at all on the rightful origin of his failure, his own limitations, but rather on the urban society which is now forcing him to realize them. Much of what Wolfe wrote on the disappointments of the metropolis is certainly true. His invective against the literature, the art, the drama, and the merchant society of New York — in short, the whole pattern of its society — is not entirely governed by his disillusionment. But what Wolfe did not realize is that the Magic City itself is merely another projection of the provincial yearning. We know the false temper of

American culture in the years of Wolfe's growth: the adoption by so many of our intellectuals of foreign values and ideologies, a seeking almost frantic in its haste and thoughtless in its possession. Our scholars wrote biographies of Hardy, or if they were emancipated, studies of the French decadents. Our painters were imbued with the surrealism of Vienna and Berlin. Our writers dealt with Spanish bullfighters or Corsican idylls. And as the last outgrowth of this movement turned into political channels, and even now persisting, our social thinkers turned their devout and distracted gaze upon the Russian Utopia, while indeed the Russians often turned and gazed equally devoutly upon our capitalistic splendors.

If this were true of the first rank intellectuals, what was not true of their followers in the salons of the American city. The bohemianism of the twenties, the parlor freudianism, the radicalism without roots, dilettantism of every variety, even the orientalism of every mystic shade — apparently the farther we wandered from our own sources, the more distinguished we might be. Only so long as there was nothing in our thinking from our own past, nothing that might be marked as merely contiguous. If Wolfe earlier showed us how the American provinces rejected the spirit, here he shows us how the American spirit rejects the provinces. The historians of Wolfe's era, the Beards, Frederick Lewis Allen, the Lynds, all record this strange phase of our cultural adolescence; the same sad and distraught search for foreign roots. Like Wolfe, all the other American rebels, whom he thought so cosmopolitan, looked back upon their sources with suspicion and defiance. Realizing this at last, the knowledge was to prove another step in Wolfe's own growth. But now, still caught in the new web of his first intimation that the metropolis, cloud-capped Babylon of his imagination, was also human, and the entire pattern of his future crumbling away upon this realization, Wolfe loses his balance. In the end, his criticisms, so subjective, so colored by his own disappointment, and spiritual turmoil, reveal not so much about the city, more about its critic.

For the city world of Wolfe's day was vain, arrogant, thin, annoying. But it was hardly, as he implies, sinister. Nor obscene, 'intolerable in its damnable injustice.' 'It shone there,' Wolfe tells us, 'written on the face of night, like a lurid and corrupted sneer.' The refrain enters into the dark portion of 'The Web,' until we can no longer evade its impact. For these are the words of petty and ignorant prejudice, not those of the balanced and civilizing artist. These are the slogans of the small mind rejected by the society it has aspired to; slogans all too familiar to us today in our world dominated by just such prejudice. These perhaps are not far from the turgid and malicious accents of a Hitler, meditating venomously in the pages of 'Mein Kampf' on his own Viennese culture. To such a pass has his heritage brought our Wolfe, great as his genius is, and now forced back into the pattern of the ugly provincial who takes his revenge, indeed, on the illusioned city for not being the illusion he has nourished.

If Wolfe had left his South, we see, the South had not left him. In his developing disillusionment with the enfabled rock are revealed his prejudices at their sharpest. The fruit of his provincialism is here. His salvation by the city — surely a strange path of redemption — vanished, now we see most clearly his manias and follies, the total pattern of the traits which have held him back, and which are both so tragic and so degrading for a major artist as we have noticed with Faulkner: the insecurities and the hatred born of his ignorance, the denunciations, interminable and almost paranoiac, rising out of his fears. Even Esther, once to Webber so full of health and hope and morning, Esther herself must now take the brunt of Webber's despairing violence:

> And yet, indubitably, she was a part of this thing too — of this Midas world of night, of this reptilian wink, its criminal corruption and inhuman privilege, the impregnable arrogance of its living sneer.

Indubitably, Esther was part of 'this thing.' But even more indubitably, 'this thing' was not the horrendous city world that

Wolfe imagined he saw, now that the city had failed in its hope of redemption for his anguished spirit. 'This thing' was a monster of Wolfe's own creating.

And of his society's. For we have seen how almost tritely Wolfe follows the pattern of our provincial artists, and indeed of many other young provincial souls. In the course of his struggle here, and in the pages of 'The Story of a Novel,' we notice Wolfe's sense of 'naked need and utter isolation,' his feeling that no one can help him, a fanatical and morbid preoccupation with his problems. Yet what in Wolfe's origins was given him to balance the continuing sense of exile? Certainly not the ties of family, as we have also seen, nor the value of human relationships, nor any relationship with his society or its institutions. Even the literature, the 'culture,' that Wolfe devoured were not to sustain him in the midst of life, but rather to feed his special hunger. Through this, too, he was to feel only the more an exile. The young Eugene had around him only the examples of the provincial rawness, he had before him only the tragedy of Gant's fruitless exploration or the alternative frustration of Eliza's implacable drive toward material power. Thus there is a sense of 'utter desperation' running through Wolfe's life. The only beliefs he could accept from Altamont were those of rebellion, and, without harbor in the North, the only winds he could as yet trust were those of his own achievement.

His ambition, as yet unqualified and undirected, his solitude, his rebellion, were poured forth into his work, without restraining bonds. The artist we know to be the egotist. Narcissism is his occupational disease. By his temperament and calling he must continually invoke his faith in himself. But our Lardner has already shown us the dangers of excessive egotism in its more outward aspects, and surely here Wolfe shows us the torments of its inner dialogue. The harm it brought to Wolfe's achievement, through the extraordinary reaches of its swollen desires, his resultant despair when his work, no matter how tremendous in scope, still fell below the demands of his ambi-

tion — these are equally clear. Toward the last, indeed, Wolfe
came to realize that he had been consumed by his own flames,
impaled on the hook of his own 'furious and insatiate desire':

> I knew . . . that one bright cell in the brain or heart or memory
> would now blaze on forever — by night, by day, through every
> waking, sleeping moment of my life, the worm would feed and
> the light be lit — that no anodyne of food, or drink or friendship,
> travel, sport, or women could ever quench it, and that never-
> more until death puts its total and conclusive darkness on my
> life, could I escape.

The darkness of death may not be quite so conclusive as Wolfe
here imagines, the uncertain confines of our existence have yet
to be established, but it is certain that Wolfe's tortures will
extend to the limits of his present existence. And for the writing
itself, into which alone he could pour the entire ferment of his
life, his provincial education had again not given him enough
tools. The qualitative standards lacking in his work so far, the
sociological as well as psychological insights which he needed,
even the details of an outmoded craft which he was soon to re-
linquish — these also Wolfe had to learn for himself, almost
learn every new syllable of the language he was seeking.

The total stress of Wolfe's early life should now be clear.
Altamont placed its mark upon a temperament already holding within itself more than usual conflicts. For in any society
Wolfe's would have been a disturbed personality. He is without
doubt close to being what we have termed a compulsive neurotic. But how much of this is due to his early life itself? And
certainly the social forces which might have restrained his temperament, directed it and balanced it, which might have given
him the security, the sense of 'place,' the belonging, the friendship and the faith, in short, the precise emotional and technical
equipment for his creative work — these are not only lacking,
but everything, indeed, in Wolfe's life seems to accentuate his
troubles.

We see with Wolfe the weight that sociological patterns may

lay upon the writer, already trembling with his sufficient burden of inherited and psychological woes. And if this American heritage has harmed our writers in the past, how fatal it may be in our own time! In the present moment of our crisis, we look back upon the harshness of Henry Adams's day, the thin and compensating refinement of Edith Wharton's, the gross lavishness of Lardner's, with something close to nostalgia. How fortunate they were who fought only local corruption, false gentility, or sheer materialism! For today, when the whole destiny of our era lies open, ready, for the human will to transform it, now there must be nothing narrow, local, or ignorant in our responses. The answers of sectional insight, or prejudice, or of blind self-interest may lose us, not a writer, but a world. Today, just when this provincial thinking in the persons of the totalitarian dictators (who are the apotheosis of ignorance joined with genius) is apparently commanding our destinies, the writer has his special responsibility.

With his narrow evaluations, his denunciations of every aspect of the city's culture, with his conclusions based upon his own insecurities which the city has revealed — with this return, in short, to all his provincial prejudices just when he has finally abandoned his provincial home — Wolfe thus debases his work and himself. 'The Web and the Rock,' in these sections, reveals not his emancipation but his enslavement. For all his high hopes, he shows himself still caught in the web of his heritage. And now his 'rock of life' crumbles away. The sense of Place, which Wolfe so much wanted and needed, which he had thought he had gained with his Esther and her life, is still wanting. Esther, Webber had thought, had at last given him a frame and purpose in his life —

> a kind of target at which his tremendous energies, so long exploded, scattered, misdirected, or diffused into thin air, could now be aimed.

But now this frame is broken, his purpose gone, his energies merely wasted but turned bitter and destructive.

Was Wolfe to become, like so many past American artists, homeless in spirit, and perhaps in fact, a hotel-child? We understand Wolfe's fascination for travel, when every trip may bring perhaps his true and lost destination. And now that his great illusion of the metropolis is broken — this one illusion which was to restore all the missing values of his life — must we then leave him on his trains roaring across the American continent? Or with his hero, Webber, 'approaching the town of Boulogne' on his Channel steamer? Must our Wolfe always be 'approaching,' then, always setting up new hopes of home and purpose and love, which in turn will always be broken?

Or perhaps we should leave young Monk Webber in his luxurious house of prostitution in Paris? It is not by chance that Wolfe makes this scene so vivid among the last pages of 'The Web and the Rock.' For this is the true conclusion of Webber's pilgrimage to this point. His love for the lady of the city destroyed, Webber resorts once more to the commercial love of his youth, the bought love of Lily Jones's House in the Exeter of 'Look Homeward, Angel.' Artificial values must still suffice for genuine values. Yet the house in Paris is so superior to those that Webber has yet known — with its 'charged and secret stillness,' its crimson stairs, its passion, perhaps purchased, but yet so 'soft, secret, vicious and luxurious'! To what glorious climax, then, has the provincial hero's vision of the city's 'whole, glamorous pageantry' brought him!

4. THE DOOR.   'You Can't Go Home Again.'   In this phrase, the title of his last novel, Wolfe has fully defined the complex of personal and social issues which we have been tracing. He has gained a sense of self-realization we should hardly have thought him capable of, and which, if Wolfe had written nothing more of consequence, might still make him remarkable.

Through his own solitary, tortured, and interminable struggle, the series of revaluations forming the sequence of his novels, and each of them in turn always advancing a little farther than the previous view, Wolfe has at last reached the truth about himself and his society. It was Proust's work, I believe, that was described as a novel about a novelist writing a novel. In this sense, we might almost say that Wolfe's work is a novel about a novelist thinking about a novelist. And if this reaches the limits of subjectivity, if it holds within it a certain degree of literary incest, I do not mean to deprecate the significance of Wolfe's final catharsis. The critic's words, indeed, can hardly render our astonishment at the resolution of Wolfe's turmoil. Following the prosperity era, marked too often with the sense of our literary failures — the tragedy of Lardner, the dwindling inconsequence of Sinclair Lewis, and the thinning finesse of Willa Cather — Wolfe again gives us growth. In a period of social disintegration Wolfe again reaffirms the power of the creative human spirit to solve its problems; and like the leaven of Matthew's Loaf, one touch of this may redeem us all.

'You Can't Go Home Again.' To Wolfe, as he tells us, the phrase had many implications beyond the central fact that no return is possible for the race to its dark ancestral cave, 'the womb from which mankind emerged into the light.' So has Wolfe qualified, in the knowledge of our evolutionary past, his early, poetic visions of a better life! You can't go back home, he says,

> to your family, back home to your childhood, back home to romantic love, back home to a young man's dreams of glory and of fame, back home to exile, to escape to Europe and some foreign land, back home to lyricism, to singing just for singing's sake . . . back home to the ivory tower, back home to places in the country, to the cottage in Bermuda, away from all the strife and conflict of the world, back home to the father you have lost and have been looking for, back home to someone who can help you, save you, ease the burden for you, back home to the old forms and systems of things which once seemed everlasting but which are changing all the time — back home to the escapes of Time and Memory.

In a way, Wolfe says, the phrase summed up everything he had ever learned. And such a total renunciation of the errors that men live by sums up much knowledge indeed. This is a tremendous achievement of the spirit for Wolfe, and, as Mr. Brooks says in his 'Literary Life in America,' 'by what prodigies of alert self-adaptation, of discrimination, self-scrutiny, conscious effort, does the creative will come into its own!'

Reading the pages of 'You Can't Go Home Again,' it is almost a shock to come upon this new Wolfe, as if he, repeating the exploits of his Eugene in 'Look Homeward, Angel,' had stolen away from us to 'create a life of his own making,' even while we were in the midst of examining him. Yet within the framework of 'The Web and the Rock' are the elements which led, in the very middle of Wolfe's disillusionment, to this spiritual regeneration. If in his portraits of the city's culture Wolfe came close to being the provincial paranoiac, he, unlike many others of the class, also saw himself as being this. We must notice the part of Webber's Esther in this change. It is through the Wolfian hero's relationship with Esther that the smoldering embers of his provincialism are provoked. But it is also through Esther's commentary on these prejudices that the book's hero, if not the author, gains his clear view of himself. Esther's defenses of the city, its culture, her friends and their achievement are among the most penetrating sections of the novel. Their lucidity penetrates even the hysteria of Webber's emotions until he is forced to exclaim: 'I don't hate everyone the way you think — in spite of all I say. I hate no one but myself. Esther, in God's name, what's gone wrong with me? What's the matter with my life?' And Esther gives us those brilliant satirical passages which contain Wolfe's finest summary of his own temperament:

> 'Now,' she thought, 'I know exactly what he's thinking. There are still a few things in the universe which have not been arranged to suit his pleasure, so he wants to see them changed. And his desires are modest, aren't they? *Very!*' she thought bitterly. 'All he wants is to eat his cake and keep on having it forever. He's

tired of me and he wishes I would go away and leave him here
alone to contemplate his navel. He also wishes I would stay here
with him. I am the one he loves, his jolly little Jew that he adores
and could devour, and I am also the evil wench who lies in wait
for unsuspecting country boys. I am the joy and glory of his life,
and I am also the sinister and corrupt harpy who has been em-
ployed by the forces of darkness to kill and destroy his life. And
why? Why, because he is so innocent and pure — God! Could
anyone believe it if they heard it! — and all the rotten people
who hate life are staying up at night plotting how to wreck and
ruin him. The Jews hate the Christians, and they also love them.
The Jewish women seduce the pure young Christian boys because
they love them, and want to destroy them, and the Jewish men,
cynical and resigned, look on and rub their hands in glee because
they hate the Christians and also love them too, and want to
destroy them because they love to see them suffer, but really adore
them because they feel such sympathy and pity for them, and yet
say nothing because they get an obscene sexual satisfaction from
the spectacle, and because their souls are old and patient, and
they have known that their women were unfaithful for seven
thousand years, and they must suffer and endure it. Weave!
Weave! Weave! He weaves it day and night out of his crazy
and tormented brain until not even Einstein could make head or
tail of it — and yet he thinks it all as plain and clear as day! . . .
Weave, weave, weave!' she thought. 'Weave, you crazy and tormented weaver, until you are caught up and tangled hopelessly
in your own web!'

Wolfe's characterization of himself as a crazy and tormented
weaver is doubtless true. But just so, the crazy and tormented
weaver who could thus characterize himself, who could thus
penetrate into the core of his prejudices (and this passage is
one of the best refutations of anti-Semitism in our time) with
such wit, this weaver is about to cast off his web.

Coincidental with the gain of Wolfe's perspective about himself comes the change in his literary achievement. We notice in
'The Web' also the movement away from the usual Wolfian
'eccentrics,' such as those who occupy almost the entire scene
of his first novel, or the Uncle Bascom who occupies so many

pages of Wolfe's second novel, and perhaps so needlessly. Wolfe is moving into the sphere of common affairs, a good indication for a young writer. (For we don't after all deal with the abnormal to create pathology, but through it to illuminate the normal.) And this development is even more significant as it leads to another growing concern of Wolfe's. Now he has given up the talented, ambitious, and unique young hero of his early novels, this twentieth-century reverberation of the Romantics' 'Fatal Man.' Wolfe is no longer concerned with one young man, but with young men; not merely with his own experience in society, but with his society. He has begun to identify his life and work with the life and work of his American brothers. Often indeed his new direction is but a beginning, or an afterthought. 'The youth,' Wolfe says, 'if not the type and symbol of the period, was yet a symptom of it.' It takes more than such a phrase, however, to establish such a connection. And often it may seem as if Wolfe has merely projected his own neurotic symptoms into those of his nation. Yet it is in one sense better to be neurotic, I suppose, over large issues than small ones, better to lament for a nation than for our own dissolving entities.

For the transference of our own temperament, whatever its peculiarities, into a larger sphere is obviously a preliminary sense of the larger world. Through this, however imperfectly, we may establish the contact with a reality which in turn may transform our own values. And whatever the imperfections of Wolfe's early concern with American society, the relationship gives a new strength to his mature work. The world of the 'mountain grills' in 'The Web and the Rock,' this nightmare town of poverty; the portraits of Jim Randolph, Jerry Alsop, Preacher Reed, to whom Christ was a Varsity Man — these are distinguished passages indeed. The increasing sense of Wolfe's social realism, his acute perceptions — when he frees himself from his own subjective emotions — of typical and normal life are not to be underestimated. Here they form a notable evidence of his progress and of his potential achievement.

And where in his first novel Wolfe had complained, rather vaguely, that his education had lacked genuine content —

> There was no word here of the loud raucous voice of America, political conventions and the Big Brass Band, Tweed, Tammany, the Big Stick, lynching bees and black barbecue parties —

this content had seemed valuable to him almost chiefly for its picturesque value. Now his demands have greater certainty:

> In fact, in spite of all this high-sounding talk about 'service,' 'ideals of leadership,' and 'democracy,' one could not see that it made much actual difference in the way things were. Children still worked fourteen hours a day in the cotton mills of the state. Tens of thousands of men and women and children were born, suffered, lived and died in damnable poverty, bondage, and the exploitation of the tenant farm ... Class after class of pure young idealists marched forth from Pine Rock, bearing the torch, prepared to bare their breasts and to die nobly, if necessary, at the barricades ... in defense of monogamy, matrimony, pure sweet women, children of the Baptist Church, the Constitution, and the splendid ideals of the Democratic and Republican parties; aye, resolved furthermore to die there at the barricades in the defense of the splendid institutions of child labor, cotton mills, tenant farmers, poverty, misery, squalor, damnation, death and all the rest of it. . . .

To his superb reportorial sense, his hunger for experience and his exultation in its recording, the marvelous evocations of place and time, such as the three-o'clock sections in 'The Web' and those again on New York streets, Wolfe has thus added an historical, a sociological sense — a deeper view of the origins, the underlying patterns, and the civilizational direction of the life he is dealing with. This process carried into 'You Can't Go Home Again,' we see in its pages that we are dealing with a much more thoughtful and a bigger author.

It is significant that we may trace the growth of these new Wolfian insights to the depression of '29 itself. 'Everywhere around me, during those years,' Wolfe tells us in 'The Story of a Novel,' 'I saw the evidence of an incalculable ruin and suffering.' Universal calamity had struck the life of almost everyone he knew. Prowling the pavements of New York, as he was then, in the throes of his own creative conflicts, he saw about him a greater darkness than his own. He saw acts of violence and corruption, the menace of privilege, cruel authority trampling the lives of the poor, the weak, and wretched of the earth:

> And the staggering impact of this black picture of man's inhumanity to his fellow man, the unending repercussions of these scenes of suffering, violence, oppression, hunger, cold, and filth and poverty going on unheeded in a world in which the rich were still rotten with their wealth, left a scar upon my life, a conviction in my soul which I shall never lose.

We see that Wolfe's tone here is that of rhetorical violence, obviously inappropriate for a ranking author, and recalling again the provincial accents of his diatribes against the city itself. The impact of '29 on him cannot, nevertheless, be ignored. However emotional, however ignorant Wolfe was, this was the start of his true education. And this time, correctly, he was, 'if not the type and symbol of the period,' a symptom of it. A new generation of American writers like Wolfe were also to carry this 'scar' upon their lives, this 'conviction' in their souls. Like Wolfe also, they were to be at first exorbitant and inaccurate in their protest. For they were a generation of writers faced by a crisis for which they had no training, for which indeed their entire social education had rather unfitted them. And in many cases, as we shall see particularly with a John Steinbeck, they, as Wolfe, could only hope to compensate for their ignorance by their intensity.

Thus we realize the total expression of Wolfe's new achievement — his gain in objectivity, perspective, restraint; his movement from the eccentric to the normal; and from the unique individual to the communal good; his growing sense of historical and sociological patterns; culminating in these, his last deep conviction of social maladjustment. And why is it that his new expression, this sharp and difficult changing of Wolfe's

values from those which formed the basis of 'Look Homeward,
Angel,' should also become dominantly satirical in tone? Is it
purely accidental that so many major voices among our novelists move in this direction also? His new work, Wolfe tells us,
will contain a 'strong element of satiric exaggeration,' not only
because this belongs to the nature of his story, but — 'satiric
exaggeration also belongs to the nature of life, and particularly
American life.' 'And particularly American life.' And particularly for Wolfe, may we say, what marvels of condensation are
contained in that phrase! What a miracle of summarizing! In
these four words we may read the history of Wolfe's inheritance,
the series of his illusions based on the provincial education, the
series of disillusionments, the absence in his life of the elements
he had been seeking. It is logical, then, that the satiric note
grows steadily stronger with him, until his last volume contains
such devastating critiques of American society. Every issue of
Wolfe's life which we have noted here forced him to use the
catharsis of humor. Looking at the surface of the American
scene, he must view it as satiric. If not, it was often outrageous.

Yet even the satirist, as we know from our Lardner, may lose
the catharsis of humor without its complement of faith. And
the last, the finest of Wolfe's new discoveries lies here, in the
formulation of an American belief. He must take the present
facts of American life satirically or he could not take them at all,
but he must also believe in another sort of American life.
'Gentlemen,' Warren Hastings informed the critics of his Indian
fortune, 'when I think of my opportunities, I am amazed at my
moderation.' But when Wolfe in turn thought of the opportunities of our national life, he could no longer confine himself
to this tone, to such a cynical realism which has been, indeed,
the dominant faith of our own industrial nabobs entrenched in
the bottlenecks of the promised land.

Early in his first novel Wolfe had felt his America as a world
of flimsy rickets stretching upon the 'terrific' land:

He felt suddenly the devastating impermanence of the nation.
Only the earth endured — the gigantic American earth, bearing

upon its awful breast a world of flimsy rickets. . . . O God! O
God! We have been an exile in another land, a stranger in our
own.

This view, coming out of his own inner turmoil, Wolfe was to
revise later. The period of his American discovery came rather
during the years which formed 'Of Time and the River,' when
he turned away from the fancy, aesthetic European-Americans
who, he says, became more Flauberty than Flaubert: 'The
Europeans say: "Oh God, where did these people, these aesthetic
Americans, ever come from?"' One must consider what a
decisive step this is for Wolfe, how in many respects these fancy
and involved Americans must have tempted the young provincial, just as Starwick did at Harvard — and how indeed so
many of our other Northerners, Southerners, and Westerners
have not all resisted this temptation, a Glenway Wescott, a Kay
Boyle, Stein, and even our Hemingway himself. He came
to understand, Wolfe tells us in 'The Story of the Novel,' that
these fleeing Americans were not looking for a place to work, but
a place where they could escape from work. They were not
fleeing from the Philistinism in American life, but from the
necessity of grappling with themselves. Yes, the place to work,
Wolfe adds, was Paris, or Spain, or Capri, but 'great God, it
was Keokuk, and Portland, Maine, and Denver, Colorado, and
Yancey County, North Carolina, and wherever we might be, if
work was there within us at the time.' From the renunciation of
the expatriate pattern so often marking our literature, Wolfe
began to fashion his new American myth. And from his exile's
dreams in Paris —

> the look of an old iron bridge across an American river, the sound
> the train makes as it goes across it . . . the sound of a milk wagon
> as it entered an American street just at the first grey of the
> morning

— from the lost memories of the land he had disowned, grew
the sense of America as promise which comes to dominate
Wolfe's last two volumes. Even when his hopes of the Magic

City are so sharply destroyed, the whole new life he has built around the shining towers of enfabled Babylon comes crashing down, there is nevertheless a larger vision beyond it. Just as Esther is in fact only the symbol of the enchanted metropolis, so, after all, the metropolis is only Wolfe's early and imperfect view of his true home. 'That place was America,' we remember Wolfe's hero said at the end of 'Of Time and the River,' 'that place was the reaches to the American coast, the approaches to the American continent.' And in 'The Web' these reaches and approaches grow far more sharply defined.

The ancient Columbus, Wolfe tells us, returned from the new world with a handful of foreign earth, 'the roots and herbage of unknown flowers,' as a token that there was beyond the hemisphere of his day 'the promise of another paradise.' His own adventurer, the Webber of his novels, had returned to the old world to recapture this early vision: 'there, from the leaden vacancy of foreign skies to derive the substance of his own America.' And now at last, renouncing the path of the European salvation, he returns home again, still seeking, so

> naked, lonely, so absurd — home, to find anew the home that he had lost — so naked, homeless, yet not utterly forlorn — here to return, still tongueless, still unfound, and still seeking — still seeking home.

And New York, for all its bitterness, brings him at last in a magic hour the vision he has been seeking, in unuttered tongues the song of the land:

> Smoke-blue by morning in the chasmed slant, on quickening the tempo of the rapid steps, up to the pinnacles of noon; by day, and ceaseless, the furious traffics of the thronging streets; forever now, forevermore, upbuilding through the mounting flood crest of these days, sky-hung against the crystal of the frail blue weather, the slamming racketing of girdered steel, the stunning riveting of the machines ... And across the plains the Overland, the continental thunders of the fast express, the whistle cry wailed back, the fire box walled and leveled on eight hundred miles of wheat; the stiff rustling of the bladed corn at night in Indiana;

down South, beside the road, the country negro, clay-caked, marching, mournful, and the car's brief glare; the radiance of the mill at night, the dynamic humming behind light-glazed glass, then the pines, the clay, the cotton fields again; fast-heard, soon-lost, the wheeling noises of the carnival; and sinners wailing from a church; and then dumb ears beneath the river-bed, the voices in the tunnel stopped for Brooklyn; but hackled moonlight on the Rocky Mountains, time silence of the moon on painted rock; in Tennessee, among the Knobs, down by the Houston River . . .

And the rustle of young leaves across America, and 'Say it! fierce, young, and low . . . and the leaves softly, "*say it, say it*" ' — and half-yielding, desperate, fierce, 'Then . . . if you promise!' — the leaves then, sighing, '*promise, promise*' — quickly, fiercely, 'Yes, I promise! . . . Darling . . . There! I said it!' — fierce, exultant, the boy's note, 'Darling! Darling! Darling!' — wild and broken, 'Oh, you promised!' — wild and fierce, 'Oh, darling, darling, darling, darling, darling!' — despairing, lost, 'You promised!' — and the leaves sadly, '*promised, promised, promised*' — 'Oh darling, but you promised!' — '*promised, promised, promised, promised, promised*,' say the leaves across America.

And everywhere, through the immortal dark, something moving in the night, and something stirring in the hearts of men, and something crying in their wild, unuttered blood, the wild unuttered tongues of its huge prophecies — so soon the morning, soon the morning: O America.

Thus the discordant strains of Wolfe, his great energies hitherto wasted in thin air, have found at last their framework in the triumphant song of the whole land. Who among our moderns has caught better the positive rhythms of America, now recalling the large and generous faith which marked Whitman, and for the next half-century was lost to us. It is not by chance, either, that Wolfe emphasizes the refrain of the lyric. Defeated by the present facts of American life, the realities forcing him into satire, it is exactly the American 'potential' he states — a potential, as the passage implies, also possibly to be betrayed, despairing, lost. 'Promised . . . say the leaves across America.' But if Wolfe's hope is colored by enough doubt, it is nevertheless this hope, this purpose and love, even of an abstraction, an expectation, which have brought a new meaning into his work. Given indignation and eloquence by such a view, Wolfe's satiric writing would very likely have been among the finest achievement of contemporary letters — as in fact we may look for our evidence to the many brilliant sections in 'You Can't Go Home Again.' The portraits of Libya Hill in the throes of mad speculation; those of the 'Federal Weight, Scales and Computing Company,' which in itself seems to typify every outrage of American salesmanship; that, in a lighter tone, but a fine evocation of a class and system, of Mr. Jack; the innumerable and acute portraits of ordinary life on ordinary Brooklyn streets — this is our evidence. The wonderful blending of satiric and affectionate elements in 'You Can't Go Home Again' leaves us upon a note never before obtained in Wolfe's work. Those critics who do not feel this must feel perhaps very little. Faced with their miracle, they lament the absence of life's mysteries.

For in the record of American letters, of course, such a growth as Wolfe's is all too unusual. The perils of our spiritual life, which Wolfe has here undergone, have too often conquered the spirit. I have mentioned Dreiser earlier. In many respects he is an early Wolfe, in his own excitement with American life, his passion for experience, his attempts to cope with the entire panorama of a new society. But with Dreiser, we see, his ignorance, obtuseness, the confusions of mind which mar his work, all these traits which, as with Wolfe, we can lay to the troubles of his education and his society; with Dreiser, very big too in his weaknesses, the dangers of American life at last defeat him. And Wolfe, in his conquest of the factors which lamed and then broke his Dreiserian brother, doesn't in the end rely on the sheer vague 'promise' of American life. The last sections of his last novel contain the formulation of the philosophical view which has contributed so fully to its writing. In the fine series of letters to the New York editor, who was very likely the single most vital factor in Wolfe's development, and perhaps even the factor of Wolfe's survival, we see that Wolfe has emerged much larger also in his intellectual stature. In these touching expressions of Wolfe's respect for 'Fox Edwards,' there is also contained, Wolfe tells us, a basic difference of belief.

> Your own philosophy has led you to accept the order of things as they are because you have no hope of changing them; and if you could change them, you feel that any other order would be just as bad. In everlasting terms — those of eternity — you and the Preacher may be right: for there is no greater wisdom than the wisdom of Ecclesiastes, no acceptance finally so true as the stern fatalism of the rock. Man was born to live, to suffer, and to die, and what befalls him is a tragic lot. There is no denying this in the final end. *But we must, dear Fox, deny it all along the way.*

Wolfe has perhaps never attained a greater simplicity than here. And in terms of Wolfe's personal values, this implies a complete reorientation. The worldly power of Eliza's sterile quest he had never sought. But now he must discard even that personal artistic 'Fame' which, nourishing the flames of his quest, had been hitherto his motivating force. Such success, even creative success, Wolfe adds to Lardner's theme, will not do — and Mr. Lloyd McHarg is the dreadful object lesson. This is the final shedding of Wolfe's American individualism, the relinquishing of his own vain personality, the merging of the artist with his material: humanity.

> Mankind was fashioned for eternity, but Man-Alive was fashioned for a day. New evils will come after him, but it is with present evils that he is now concerned. And the essence of all faith, it seems to me, for such a man as I, the essence of all religion for people of my belief, is that man's life can be, and will be, better.

The enemy, Wolfe says, the new Satan (but lacking the grandeur of Milton's which made it sometimes impossible for us to tell whether the English poet was justifying the ways of God or the Devil to man), the barriers in our path lie all around us. Fear, hatred, slavery, cruelty, poverty, the forces of European Fascism which at last seemed to Wolfe to embody all other evils. But the origin of this evil is single: 'compulsive greed.'

And reminding us that if there is a Lost Generation in the United States, 'it is probably made up of those men of advanced middle age who still speak the language that was spoken before 1929,' Wolfe sees also that the coming battlefield, upon which the forces of civilization and brutality in man's nature will play out their rôles, will be America:

> I believe that we are lost here in America, but I believe we shall be found. And this belief, which mounts now to the catharsis of knowledge and conviction, is for me — and I think for all of us — not only our own hope, but America's everlasting, living dream. I think the life which we have fashioned in America, and which has fashioned us — the forms we made, the cells that grew, the honeycomb that was created — was self-destructive in its nature and must be destroyed. I think these forms are dying, and must die, just as I know that America and the people in it are deathless, undiscovered, and immortal, and must live.
>
> I think the true discovery of America is before us. I think the true fulfillment of our spirit, of our people, of our mighty and immortal land, is yet to come. I think the true discovery of our own democracy is still before us. And I think that all these things are certain as the morning, as inevitable as noon.

This, then, is the full and last intellectual development of the view that the earlier and young Wolfe expressed in his song of the land. This is the spiritual sinew which sustains the vision. This is the love and hope, neither vague nor rigid, which Wolfe's work has needed, and for so long has been wanting. So long delayed, so falsely sought, accompanied by such catastrophes, through such almost infinite error Wolfe has at last reached the threshold of his home. The door — the door which no one can open for us, and which indeed will never open until we are ready, and open it — stood before him.

What a long journey it was! Where has he come, our very talented provincial, raised in the sick and dying culture of a lost South, in the blood and agony of the States, consumed, like Wolfe's Gant, by the cancer of their industrial revolution. The tumescent yokel, as we've said, struggling against both the

South and the States, with his psychological woes and cultural
bondages, seeking for the Magic City, and, finding it, becoming
once again the provincial paranoiac. This rural Faustian, so
antagonistic to his cultural values and yet with no others to
guide him, encompassing quite madly all of experience's
ranges in his frantic efforts; almost coping with the size of a
continent by the size of his manuscripts. Why should he not believe there was a better life than his, a Lost Language he had
yet to discover, another home toward which his broken angel
yearned?

Yet, if Wolfe's growth was thus slow, his movement hampered
by the fetters of his milieu; if still in recurrent prejudice and
repetitive error, and in his last book, his last statements too, he
disappoints us just when we are most hopeful; if with him the
vision often preceded by some distance the fact — so it does,
after all, with mankind in general. We have talked of Wolfe as
the mark of provincial humanity: what humanity is not? But,
if Wolfe remained even toward the end a provincial, he was
also at the end still struggling to free himself. His last agonies
were those of defiance and change. His virtue lies most clearly
in this sense of continued conflict. And the compassion with
which we must view his history rises out of the eagerness with
which we greet every human prisoner who emerges from the
chafing chrysalis of his ancestors, his birth and his life — to
assert himself as something fresh and in his own right free; to
defy the iron laws of human determinism; in some degree, at
least, to evidence once again the force of the human will.

This is what Wolfe did. This is what raises his history beyond
even the level of achievement he came to show us. That he
accomplished so much is of significance in the record of American literature. But that he was able to accomplish it at all is
perhaps of greater significance in the record of man's progress.
And in the sometimes terrible friction of Wolfe's spiritual mis-
alignments, moreover, his artistic inefficiency at which our industrial engineers would shiver, Wolfe's struggle has a sort of
grandeur. In it we may see the archetype of one strain of the

creative spirit in the United States. And perhaps apart from
social systems and chronological eras, we may behold one
source of the liberating human spirit itself. In his very slow and
stunted movement forward, Wolfe belongs to us, in the regressions that mark this movement, and even possibly in the last
regression of death.

For standing thus at the threshold of the door, Wolfe was
halted. Was this another blow of Fate, the bitter indication of
Thomas Hardy's blind and hostile Force? Perhaps so, yet in
our modern view this same 'Chance' or 'Fate' is always to some
degree, and sometimes to a large degree, the product of our own
natures. Though the element of chance in our lives may never
be eliminated, the more we know about it, the less it may seem
so purely chance. How much in the death of Thomas Wolfe
may be attributed not merely to a physical and sudden blow,
but to the cumulative effect of his life? How much of his sickness grew out of his great and insatiate quest for experience —
this quest without its proper qualifying media, which consumed Wolfe where it should have burned? How much of his
death lay directly in the excesses of his life and work? His sickness, we know, came after he had just completed his final two
volumes, those gigantic and troubled volumes which seem to
contain the turmoil of a dozen anguished spirits. And how
much of the exhausting psychological and sociological pressure
in Wolfe — this whole tremendous effort to learn everything
all over again by himself — was the penalty he paid for being
the American artist?

For if our actions are never quite what we think they are,
their true consequences flow from them nevertheless. 'Nothing
in his life became him like the leaving it,' as the bard said.
But then this 'leaving of life' may after all be inevitably the
end-result of its living. Our deaths are only too consistent,
perhaps, with the rest of us. We are informed, indeed, in the
melancholy tones of the great psychological thinker, that all life
is merely the effort of our organism to die 'only in its own way.'
And even the life forces themselves, the vital instincts of self-

preservation, power, self-assertion — 'even those watchmen of life were originally the myrmidons of death.' And certainly in a less prosaic sense, at least, we may say also that Thomas Wolfe's organism died 'in its own way.' For his ending was not only consistent with the penalties he paid for existing as he did. In a larger sense — that of Wolfe's final union with his land, the resolution of his long homelessness and exile into his American view — Wolfe has again a sort of prophetic and perhaps warning significance. In his living, as we have seen, he is so fully the American artist, in his great resources and in his ceaseless struggle to use these resources fully. And in his death, is he to be also the tragic and 'typical' American?

Wolfe being so like his land, is his land to be too much like Wolfe — this America with such great energy, such fabulous plenty, with its incomparable 'promise' that Wolfe at last saw, but only in a song? The 'promise' of Wolfe's America, rustling in the immortal dark from girdered steel to plains of wheat, from bladed corn to radiance of mills at night, from voices in the tunnel stopped for Brooklyn to hackled moonlight on the Rockies. And everywhere in Wolfe's America something stirring in the hearts of men, something crying in their blood: 'the wild, unuttered tongues of its huge prophecies.' 'O America!' Hailed by your own Thomas Wolfe, your life too much, certainly, like his, great resources disorganized like his, too often shattered, frameless, and wasted in air! In its own death is the American promise also to remain only Wolfe's vision, 'the wild, unuttered tongues of its huge prophecies' also stilled, like his, in premature and tragic silence? Or perhaps indeed worse, its prophecies lending themselves at last merely to that satiric exaggeration which belongs to the nature of life, 'and particularly American life.'

Chapter Six

John Steinbeck : OF WRATH OR JOY

◇

1. SUCCESS STORY, '39   2. THE CURSE
3. PIRATES AND PRIMITIVES   4. FROM HOBGOBLINS TO
HUMANITY   5. OF WRATH OR JOY

Chapter Six

John Steinbeck : OF WRATH OR JOY

---

1. SUCCESS STORY, '39.   In the year 1937 a new Young Lochinvar came writing out of the West with a little fable which dazzled Broadway. So faithful in man's love of man, and so dauntless in war (was it proletarian?), there never was writer like this young John Steinbeck, or so it almost seemed. His career itself was romantic. Ranch hand, carpenter, painter, by his own admission Steinbeck felt himself a loss to the building trades. Newspaper man, then writer of bitter chronicles, caretaker on lonely Lake Tahoe where the silent snows 'melted the hates out of him,' and lastly spectacular young playwright — Steinbeck brought his 'Of Mice and Men' into the stony heart of the nation's metropolis. The 'best-laid schemes went a-gley' in a very touching way, and we saw ourselves as authors see us. The poor George of the play, like every man, killed the thing he loved, but few men achieve this at such a handsome profit. 'An' live off the fatta the lan'.' Ironic echo of the outcast's dream, on Lennie's little acre there now was Standing Room Only.

Yet, if 'Of Mice and Men' dealt somewhat boyishly with the abnormal, if its effect sometimes reminds us of a pathological fraternity house, here nevertheless was a young writer of unquestioned power creating an exciting show — and not half so good a one as 'The Grapes of Wrath' which two years later did for the nation what the little play had done for the metropolis. In the smart set 'The Grapes of Wrath' was acclaimed the American novel 'of the season, probably the year, possibly the decade.'

Was Mr. Fadiman's sense of symmetry betraying him? The more sober Louis Kronenberger hailed Steinbeck's novel as homeric, breathless, comic, and heartbreaking. A chorus of other critics spontaneously recalled 'Uncle Tom's Cabin,' 'Leaves of Grass,' and obviously, 'Moby Dick.' Besides, fulfilling the virgin's and the author's desire, 'The Grapes of Wrath' appeared to be as popular as it was good. While a score of other books skyrocketed and darkly fell, it stayed. It was not only great literature, it was enjoyable. In ecstasy, the publishers became inarticulate. Burned and banned, borrowed, smuggled, but above all, bought, 'The Grapes of Wrath' began to cause a sort of national aesthetic frenzy without parallel in our time; belles-lettres had turned bellicose.

Labeled as 'vile filth' which incidentally frightened tourists away from California, Steinbeck's novel was read by thousands of indignant American families. Articles, surveys, investigations centered around it, and the motion picture rights went for seventy-five thousand dollars. 'Too hot for Hollywood?' demanded the magazine *Look*, while the magazine *Life* was nodding, but never outdone, the entertainment magnates poured a million dollars into this epic of the penniless. Governor Olsen, Walter Winchell, Secretary of Agriculture Wallace, supporting the picture, were opposed by Ruth Comfort Mitchell, President of Pro-America (who could deny her patriotism?), and Emory Hoffman of the Kern County, California, Chamber of Commerce — which was producing a movie itself, rather ominously entitled: 'Plums of Plenty.' 'The Grapes of Wrath' was now number one of the best-sellers, and sales were mounting steadily. Was it frightening away tourists from California? The literate nation was visiting Kern County.

Tens of thousands, and then hundreds of thousands of eager Americans thumbed a ride in the engrossing pages of Steinbeck's novel, took a literary hitch on the Joads's jalopy, struggled west along Highway 66, perhaps the most historic route in contemporary literature. Clarksville and Ozark and Van Buren, down from Tulsa and up from McAlester, ten pages of suspense while Al is changing a tire, through Texas, Oklahoma, and there's an end to another chapter. Thunder of tractors plowing under the solid American farming classes, the twisting winds that beat across the Dust Bowl, the whine of dry bearings in the ears of America's millions reading and sharing this tale of their own dispossessed. In Bronx dining-rooms and Main Street barbershops, in college study-halls and on Bar Harbor beaches, from the coast of Maine to Louisiana bayous, they are reading the epic of America's disinherited.

A unique modern literary pilgrimage had begun. A twisting draft across a Long Island neo-Tudor reception hall, the heat of middle-western suburbs, the roar of trucks in city streets, and there's an end to chapter twenty of 'The Grapes of Wrath.' From Massachusetts, Tennessee, and Virginia the American readers swept onward, from Minneapolis, Minnesota, and Tampa, Florida, and Reading, Pennsylvania, and Oklahoma too they came, their eyes sweeping along the pages of Steinbeck's novel, knocking off the miles along Highway 66. Resting, stopping, stretching, talking to Minnie and Susy and Mae behind the roadside lunch counters of a continent, starting up again on this bitter journey to the modern Promised Land, the Americans read 'The Grapes of Wrath.' In frilled boudoirs and in army bivouacs the eyes of America swept along the pages of Highway 66.

Thus, by her own tokens the United States of '39, recalling now the gilded glories of Lardner's '29, had marked John Steinbeck as her favorite literary son — this impassioned radical who exploited the ruling classes, who introduced the proletariat to a multitude of model homes, and brought Marx to Hoover's doorstep. Jerking along to California's shores, the Joads's jalopy had become America's new bandwagon — but the true destination of Steinbeck's novel lay incalculably beyond these geographical boundaries.

2. THE CURSE.   Considering this fabulous Success Story of '39, one could hardly have prophesied such a future for the young man who in 1932 wrote 'The Pastures of Heaven,' still perhaps Steinbeck's finest novel. If here he first revealed his talent, his promise seemed to extend in the direction of Edgar Lee Masters rather than Marx. The core of 'The Pastures' is a nostalgic sense of joy turned bitter, of grief that is the only consequence of gaiety, a sorrow invariable and acrid. Here possibly most purely among his works Steinbeck has gained a subtle and affecting fabric of emotion. A lyric pleasure, frustration, resignation are woven delicately into one, into the tone of 'The Pastures,' and each of these feelings carrying with it its other selves, so to say, its swift sea-change. Wit redeems the sorrow which holds within it the sweetness of late joy.

Reminding us of Masters, or perhaps of Winesburg rather than Moscow, or of a Thomas Gray, for in the California community as well as in the English village no 'flattery soothes the dull cold ear of death,' Steinbeck's view in 'The Pastures' is nevertheless strongly his own. If these western townspeople are in the eternal view merely a moving row of shadow-shapes that come and go, they move, however, with actuality, their familiar desires freshly their own, their 'passing tribute of a sigh' so genuine, that their tale, told indeed a thousand times, is new in its telling. In the elegiac tradition, the essence of 'The Pastures' is recognizably that of the ephemeral, but not its effect.

To the lovely California valley country whose quality Steinbeck catches here so well — these meadows floored with rich pasturage before the presence of whose beauty the first bearded savage Spanish explorer whispered, 'Holy Mother! Here are the green pastures of Heaven to which our Lord leadeth us' — come a variety of weak and beaten human souls. In these rich valleys they hope to conquer the forces breaking them, to find in this soil the strength for life again. Such a figure is Bert Munroe, garageman, grocer, contractor, always a failure and now tired of fighting the malignant fate which seems to stop each avenue of his success. But when as a last try he takes over the

deserted and, so the villagers say, 'cursed' Battle farm, it seems
to work. He feels free again. The doom is gone. 'Within
a month his shoulders straightened, and his face lost its
haunted look.' Bringing new life to the ruined farmstead, Bert
finds in each day a new excitement. 'Every seed sprouting
out of the ground seemed to renew a promise of immunity to
him.'

To the cautious villagers who remind him that lots of funny
things have happened to the owners of the Battle farm, Bert one
day explains his happiness. He's also had, he tells them, a lot of
bad luck. 'When I came down here, I had a kind of an idea
that I was under a curse.' Maybe, Bert continues, smiling at his
joke, my curse and the curse on the Battle farm 'got to fighting
and killed each other off.' The men laugh and Storekeeper
Allen counters with another suggestion. Maybe, he cries, 'your
curse and the farm's curse has mated. . . . Maybe there'll be a lot
of baby curses crawling around the Pastures the first thing we
know.' The gathered farmers roar again, and Allen memorizes
the scene, in detail. 'It was almost like the talk in a play, he
thought.'

Like Bert Munroe other desperate personages, torn by defeat
or filled with foreboding, settle in the Pastures — Shark Wicks
the miser, Helen Van Deventer who treasures her unhappiness
as Wicks his money, the aristocratic Richard Whiteside, the
young schoolteacher Molly Morgan (one of Steinbeck's best
portraits), the dreamer Junius Maltby, a sort of Californian
Bronson Alcott who creates a charming new Fruitlands idyll,
the Lopez sisters who sell their tortillas and their bodies with the
same redoubtable respectability. With a graceful warmth
Steinbeck builds a community of decent folk, driven as they are
by the bad past and the nameless future, struggling to make
the present good. Here in the Pastures are no very ruthless
actions, no conflicts of harsh wills, nor tales of corruption.
Thievery is small, lying is harmless, and for a moment the
normal brutalities of Nature herself are subdued by this little
group of seekers finding in the pleasant valley their temporary

heaven. Even the insensitive Raymond Banks slaughters his chickens mercifully, and the idiot Tularecito is welcomed for whatever he may bring to the common welfare.

Why is it, then, that one by one these happy little existences must perish? Shark Wicks, young Molly Morgan, Pat Humbert, Junius Maltby, the pious prostitutes Lopez, each of these lives in turn is ground down in bitterness, the brief release from fear terminated, the aspirations toward joy tumbling. Wondering a little at the uniformity of disaster which befalls these valley people, we come to see that it all springs from this same Bert Munroe. In every instance (though it is very delicately done) the impetus to tragedy proceeds from him or his family. His curse, although Bert is quite unaware of it, has in fact, mated or not with the haunted Battle farm, overrun the valley.

At first glance, of course, this seems a clever but all too theatrical device, one of those neat flowerings of the imagination which are to distinguish the later work of Steinbeck in sufficiency — a semi-mystic, sort of supernatural motif to which a young writer might easily enough succumb. Yet done well as it is here (most subtly for Steinbeck), this 'curse' does in fact add an effective symbolic overtone to the fine realism of 'The Pastures.' With all of its human ramifications the novel becomes the dramatic projection of a single basic question: Dwelling in these green pastures of the world, humanity, which as the young Steinbeck views it is potentially good, finds itself constantly thwarted, its little visions of peace endlessly crushed. What is, then, the curse which defeats us? The doom of the people in the Pastures doesn't after all proceed from the meek and mild Bert Munroe. He is merely the poetic vessel of vengeance. But of whose vengeance?

The significance of this question is apparent when we realize that the subsequent novels of Steinbeck are an attempt, at least in part, and however imperfect, to answer the dilemma of 'The Pastures.' Steinbeck himself is rather like one of the sightseeing tourists who, toward the close of his book, come to gaze into the valley.

The land below them was plotted in squares of green orchard trees and in squares of yellow grain and in squares of violet earth. . . . Cowbells were softly clashing in the valley; a dog barked so far away that the sound rose up to the travelers in sharp little whispers. Directly below the ridge a band of sheep had gathered under an oak tree against the night. 'It's called Las Pasturas del Cielo,' the driver said. 'They raise good vegetables there — good berries and fruit earlier here than any place else. The name means Pastures of Heaven.'

Ignorant of the chronicles of tragedy which fill the valley, these new voyagers look down from their ridgepeak and make new visions. The prosperous man sees in the valley a millionaire's playground, the young husband thinks of a home for his wife, the old man wants to settle there and think his life through. 'I've never had time to think. I've been too busy with troubles ever to think anything out. . . . and maybe I could make something out of them, something all in one piece that had a meaning, instead of all these trailing ends, these raw and dragging tails.' Down there, the priest in turn reflects, there might be a little church. 'No poverty there, no smells, no trouble. My people might confess small wholesome sins that fly off with the penance of a few Hail Marys. It would be quiet there; nothing dirty nor violent would ever happen there to make me sorry nor doubtful nor ashamed.'

Doomed as it seems to be, the vision of the good life recurs with each new generation. With the smell of the inferno on him, man meditates on heavens. The broken Wolfian angel recalls his paradise. The most improbable circumstances give rise to the most utopian concepts, as in the midst of a Europe bleeding through nationalistic dissension men are today talking of peaceful union. Like these tourists of 'The Pastures,' other strangers, standing endlessly on the edge of valleys overflowing with calamity, have fashioned their own ignorant hope. Humanity, gazing down into dying and evil civilizations, builds new ones. And looking across his pleasant valley which covers so much anguish, the young Steinbeck asks himself: What is the source of this human frustration — this curse? A question in truth for the writer to build his work around, indeed a haunting question.

3. PIRATES AND PRIMITIVES.   Three years before he had thus formulated, in 'The Pastures of Heaven,' the question which was to underlie the body of his work, Steinbeck had perhaps prematurely attempted an answer. The year was 1929, the novel was the 'Cup of Gold,' the 'solution' was appropriately enough a veiled form of the Success Myth, and the attempt was not successful. Tracing the glamorous career of Sir Henry Morgan the buccaneer — his childhood in the gloomy Welsh glens, slavery in Barbados, and his final tyranny over the 'blustering brotherhood' of Tortuga — Steinbeck's first novel is poor but illuminating.

Morgan's career offers a promising canvas for a young romantic author, and Steinbeck misses few chances. He packs the Welsh glens with morbidity; he loads Morgan's ships with treasure; and he floods the streets of Panama with rivers of blood. Cruelty, perversion, lasciviousness abound in these early pages of Steinbeck's career. In the midst of such bullion and brawling, moreover, stands the typical romantic heroine, Ysobel, La Santa Roja, more entrancing than her title, inaccessible yet inviting, sensuous but strangely spiritual, and withal quite a philosopher. For, we notice, it is she who stimulates Morgan to his finest utterances.

> You are afraid [he tells this Ysobel]. . . . There is in your mind a burrowing apprehension of the world; the prying world, the spiteful world. But do you not be fearsome, for I say to you that this world is a blind, doddering worm, knowing three passions only — jealousy, curiosity, and hate. It is easy to defeat the worm, so only you make the heart a universe to itself. The worm, having no heart, cannot conceive the workings of a heart. He lies confounded by the stars of this new system.

Yet Morgan's definition of life is more interesting to us than to Ysobel; she is cold. When he complains that, after all, he took Panama to take her, she is sorry, but —

> When I heard of you and your blustering up and down the ocean, I thought of you, somehow, as the one realist on an earth of vacillation. I dreamed that you would come to me one day, armed with a transcendent, silent lust, and force my body with brutality. I craved a wordless, reasonless brutality. . . . I wanted force — blind, unreasoning force — and love not for my soul or for some imagined beauty of my mind, but for the white fetish of my body. . . . I thought richly of you once; you grew to be a brazen figure of the night. And now — I find you a babbler, a speaker of sweet, considered words, and rather clumsy about it.

The trouble is, Ysobel explains, that men don't say what they want. They feel it necessary to justify their passion. 'They, like you, must convince themselves, as well as me, that they loved me.' 'But I will force you, then,' cries Henry, and Ysobel answers, of course, that it is too late. If Morgan, however, has been too considerate in the case of Ysobel, who along with Henry has here been stating the general thesis of the book, this is hardly true of his conduct in other areas. What a harsh, dominating, violent character is this hero of the author who was a little later to attack these very traits as they appear in the context of the capitalist system! How the average people are scorned and crushed by the ambitious Henry, more predatory than any piratical California landlord!

Naïve as its thinking is, and its intellectual mould filled in with a stilted and rash romanticism, the 'Cup of Gold' is nevertheless a valuable index to the young Steinbeck, an author almost as different from his later self as Morgan from his later heroes. This early author is individualistic, advocating the free life of adventure, the bold man, scorning the 'blind, doddering worm of the world' which cannot conceive the workings of a noble heart — an author in this very individualism reflecting, in part at least, the values of the era which had nourished him.

For what is the career of Henry Morgan but the Success Story of the twenties attired in the more lurid robes of the seventeenth century? Excessive ambition, great personal power, inordinate wealth, these are the ingredients of Morgan's 'good life,' just as they were the dominating beliefs of the boom period. The percentage of slaughter is somewhat greater in Morgan's case, the percentage of wealth he could accumulate somewhat less, the percentage of wisdom about the same in him and the industrial barons who were his American heirs. For it is interesting to note that Sir Henry's rise to power brought him no dividends in pleasure, and that Steinbeck, although retaining his admiration for certain of Morgan's qualities, does not again advocate the pattern which they formed. It is almost as if, in these glittering pages, Steinbeck were working out of himself the values of his time which he inherited but did not actually accept. The 'Cup of Gold' was a sort of literary cathartic.

While the purge was effective, certain symptoms of the ailment persisted. 'To a God Unknown,' in 1933, brought Steinbeck's focus up to the present. But the past persisted in his thoughts if not his locale, and here the mysticism and violence which were the background of Henry Morgan's life became the central action. Indeed, moving up in time Steinbeck moved farther backward in theme; from the piratical he slid to the primitive. He again continued to emphasize the unique individual. The hero of 'To a God Unknown,' Joseph Wayne, is so superior, Steinbeck informs us, as to 'lack the ordinary feelings of life,' which I am afraid is true. The direction of Joseph's ambition, however, is fresh. While Henry Morgan sought happiness through dominating the world, Joseph seeks his in a diametrically opposite fashion: through renunciation, through sacrificing himself to this very world which Morgan scorned as a 'blind, doddering worm.'

The manner of Joseph's renunciation is somewhat curious. He leaves his puritanical New England family, voyages west, establishes himself in the Nuestra Señora valley (one of those lovely California scenes which Steinbeck does so well) and

builds his home there. Establishing his farm; calling his brothers to live around him; marrying and surrounding himself with
new life, adopting the tone of the patriarch as well as the farmer;
the guardian of the childlike paisanos, of the multiplying live-
stock and the rolling acres of wheat, Joseph is apparently content. And Steinbeck treats this early part of his tale with the
grace which distinguishes 'The Pastures of Heaven.' Perhaps
here, indeed, the studies of nature are richer, the little details on
the casual events of life very sensitive; in its rural and more
realistic moments, 'To a God Unknown' is unquestionably a
good early novel. Yet this land, so fertile and lovely too, is also
'queer,' and the second half of the novel develops some of its
oddities. The source of all this is the great oak tree under which
Joseph has established his home, and in which dwells the spirit
of the land. Joseph establishes a mystic relationship with the
tree, and this is the prelude to the druidic and pagan practices
which from this point onward fill the book's pages — haunted
glens and recesses, ancient Mexican orgiastic ceremonies, pro-
pitiatory sacrifices, ceremonial sexualities, the letting of blood,
the calling of race, and, in short, all the various other appurte-
nances which seem in our age to mark the return of civilized
minds to primitive emotions.

Such a summary is perhaps somewhat unjust to the novel
itself, for Steinbeck's talent can carry such situations, as he is to
demonstrate more than once, without making us more than
uncomfortable. I am doing, however, no great injustice to the
fallacious thinking which marks 'To a God Unknown' and the
entire range of neo-pagan literature to which it belongs, a school
distinguished by such names as D. H. Lawrence, Jean Giono,
and in a slightly different sense Sherwood Anderson, talented
artists also and often putting their talent to a tepid use. We
don't reach maturity by returning to childhood. It's no good
throwing over the superstitions of today for those of yesterday.
If this return to the primitive answers certain deep, dark needs
in our nature, as Steinbeck implies, so does larceny. Of this
calling of blood and race which in modern literature has at-

tracted some noted artists, and in politics whole cultures, the best that can be said is that we may use it to perceive and chart the social sickness of man, his weakness, the bonds which link him to his savage past. To use this pagan return for itself alone, as Steinbeck does here, to be held by its drama, as a politician by flashing rhetoric, to advocate it moreover as a goal — this is, rather than diagnosing our disease, exploiting it.

It's interesting that such dallying with the primitive and the occult, as in the time of Mesmer, occurs most sharply before social cataclysms, as if men, confronted with extreme demands upon their mature intelligence, fall back upon the instincts of their infancy.

Closely related to his neo-paganism is Steinbeck's concern with violence, the wholesale sadism of the 'Cup of Gold,' and the sacrificial slaughtering of the 'God Unknown.' In the course of his wanderings young Joseph meets an intriguing little old man who every night kills a bird, rabbit, squirrel, or some other thing, and Joseph, exalted, remarks: 'This man has discovered a secret.... He must tell me if he can.' This 'secret' Steinbeck, like Joseph, was to brood over and develop under various names in his future work. In the 'Red Pony' and a variety of other stories, sacrifice, and always bloody, was to be nature's law. In 'Of Mice and Men' the 'secret' was to assume the guise of a lovable pathology, crushing and being crushed. In tales like 'The Raid' and 'In Dubious Battle' it becomes the baptism by fire, proving by pain. In 'The Snake' the 'secret' assumes a sexual overtone. In 'To a God Unknown' itself it is a primitive parallelism to survival's harsh logic. Life must be sacrificed to life, and God, the unknown God of Nature, is as bloodthirsty as his creation.

Yet beneath these varied interpretations, it seems that violence in itself has an inherent fascination for Steinbeck, that its appeal lies merely in the glitter of the knife, the tearing of the flesh, the hangings, shootings, mutilations with which his work is filled; and this violence is used for effect more often than edification. In each of his books, though the best of them suffer from it the least, Steinbeck is the sure conductor for the currents of such barbarism, and this will not do. No such talent as his is necessary to release the monkeys and tigers within us, and the charmed word is hardly worthy to advocate the jungle.

Still, he was also, if never quite losing these early interests, at least to form a better pattern for them. In the space of these four years he has already made significant gains. If both the 'Cup of Gold' and 'To a God Unknown' share common failings, Steinbeck has this early discarded the egocentric individualism of Lardner's age for the identification, if a somewhat odd one, of the individual with his world. Indeed, the 'Worm-world' of Morgan has become the vision of the mystic Joseph, for at the end of 'To a God Unknown,' Joseph sacrifices his blood to the land. And is this sort of abnegation so diametrically opposed to Morgan's power urge as to be hardly better than it? We must notice that the evolution by such sharp reactions, the dialectic of extremes, will be peculiarly characteristic of Steinbeck's career. Between these two weak books, moreover, Steinbeck has written 'The Pastures of Heaven,' an excellent one (though perhaps from internal evidence, rather than the date of publication, we might suspect that 'To a God Unknown' was written earlier). And 'The Pastures of Heaven' indicates his future more accurately than the 'Cup of Gold' and 'To a God Unknown' — though rather like common humanity, Steinbeck may seem to go farthest out of his way to reach his near destination. We cannot, moreover, scrutinize these early novels too sharply, for their worst excrescences of fancy share an appealing sort of excitement, a sense of discovery which, however indiscriminate, shields them. Steinbeck's dabblings with the mystic, his researches into primitive rites, his concern with pathology, all have about them such an air of young, pleased and breathless wonder! Even his massacres are perfectly marvelous! It is this sense of discovery, and of curiosity, like Dreiser and like Wolfe, a passion for experience, which marks him as American, however naïve and strange his experience until this point has been. It is the receptivity to new ideas which will mark him as

the barometer of American public opinion he was shortly now
to become.

In his concern with his new 'secret' of violence, however, what
has happened to Steinbeck's 'curse'? What is the source of human frustration? Morgan in his piratical power urges, Joseph
in his mystic renunciation, had each sought the good life in
diverse ways. But there was a common denominator to these
apparently opposite concepts. In the course of Steinbeck's
early explorations, the basic problem had become more sharply
defined. The source of our troubles is modern civilization. In
his return to the past, in the advocacy first of the lawless adventurer, and then of the pagan seeker who renounces his culture,
Steinbeck makes clear his opposition to the restraints of society.
Yet apparently both Morgan and Joseph Wayne had failed, and
Steinbeck was now to define his thesis in new terms, express his
defiance and opposition to society in new forms. Close to his
hands were the paisanos of California, ignorant, lazy, obviously
'immoral,' childlike, starving, slovenly, lacking, in short, all the
marks of American Progress — and obviously very happy.

Dealing with the paisanos before this, Steinbeck has treated
them with a revealing tenderness. The Juanito of 'To a God
Unknown' who professed himself a proud caballero and lived
his penniless life on a dashing scale belonged to the same engag-
ing family as the Lopez sisters who became the pious prostitutes
of 'The Pastures.' Forbidden to more civilized mentalities was
lasting content; yet here were the fertile lands of California rich
in joy for those who might seize it; and here were the true children of the earth who did. Drinking, chatting, loving, cheating,
making what they could of their moments' lasting, fashioning
of their meager existence a fine life of the imagination, these
paisanos — angels who rushed in where fools feared to tread —
were certainly and exactly the protagonists of the good life
Steinbeck had been seeking. In the sequence of his quest
'Tortilla Flat' is inevitable.

In many sections it is also delightful. Reminiscent of a merger
of the folk epics of John Henry and Paul Bunyan, fusing the

negro's ease with the lumberjack's exploits, 'Tortilla' has its fine moments — and its moral. For these marvelous paisanos gain their happiness by refusing the dominant values of our vaunted American civilization: they scorn equally our competitive motivation and our individualistic power-rewards. Danny, who is rather the paisano King Arthur of a beggars' round table, inherits two tumbledown shacks, and at first feels all the grandeur of the man of property. When he leases one of his huts to his friends Pablo and Pilon, however, the shadow of the rent (which is never paid) lies over their relationship. Owing a man money imposes on him a false distinction and on you a false obligation, even when he doesn't expect to get it and you have no intention of paying it. When his friends set fire to his hut Danny is genuinely happy. The fire is an aesthetic experience into which all may again enter equally. Pablo and Pilon move into Danny's remaining hut, along with Jesus Maria Corcoran, the Pirate, his five dogs, and a few other odd paisanos who have come to enjoy the select company of Danny's circle. Amorous escapades, metaphysical conversations, gossip and gluttony fill their days to overflowing. They work for no man and will have no man work for them. Pagan anarchists they yet practice an odd form of Christian communism in which each according to his ability steals from his neighbor according to his needs.

Developing his thesis with a nice humor, Steinbeck makes his story acute by catching the actual, subtle, and quite formalized code of ethics which underlies the apparent 'immorality' of the paisanos. Relating such a code to the ethics of the power age, Steinbeck is very close to an illuminating comparison of social values. But in the enthusiasm of his discovery, he forces joy beyond its legitimate limits. Harping so constantly on the gargantuan drinking of the paisanos, their love-making, their glorious brawling, Steinbeck imparts a faintly adolescent tone to his native epic. And if in 'To a God Unknown,' he had descended into the depths of primitive mysticism, now, and as if again following the pattern of sharp action and reaction forming his evolution,

he glides rather too easily along the surface of his paisano life.
Even the epic of 'tall-tales,' as in 'John Henry' itself, has beneath it the undertones of tragedy and human loss, and for the
most part Steinbeck avoids this in his narration. The more
mature author of 'The Grapes of Wrath' might, indeed, have
found a few disturbing factors in the life of 'Tortilla Flat.' Isn't
our Danny, in sober truth, being exploited somewhat? His rich
land taken from him by the white 'imperialistic' robbers, his
culture crushed under these same bandits' scorn, reduced to his
ramshackle huts, drinking steadily to escape from his tedious
tragedy — poor Danny! And if Danny, when he is sober
enough to grasp the fact, doesn't seem to mind, is this serenity
or stupefaction? In all this sexual activity which marks the
paisano life, what is the proportion of social disease? And
would the church itself, to which the Pirate, stealing his meals
from convenient garbage cans, contributes his entire fortune —
would this church be perhaps viewed by the later Steinbeck as
another oppressive and reactionary institution? To the Pirate's
utopian garbage cans, however, are relegated only the juiciest
of steaks; and whenever, indeed, there is opportunity in 'Tortilla Flat' for more serious social appraisal, Steinbeck avoids
reflection by the use of an intellectual conceit. Just as he might
have deepened his book by the illumination of the positive
human values in the paisano society, as compared with our
own, he again ignores the more realistic significance of the
paisano existence. His folk epic becomes rather too strongly a
fantasy.

Yet if our author is trapped by a sentimental concept of poverty, through it he has begun to introduce himself to a new
world — and the false manner of his introduction is typical of a
score of other modern American writers, as we may see in the
earlier work of a Cantwell or a Leane Zugsmith, or in the work
both early and late of a Saroyan. In order to gain sympathy
for man's suffering we must generally delude ourselves as to its
nature. We act through illusion in order to act at all. However
eccentric Steinbeck's view of the dispossessed in 'Tortilla Flat,'

if its origins are dubious and its quality inaccurate, here for the first time he has related himself, not with a mystic or piratical life of the past, but with the more immediate social issues of his own world. The importance of 'Tortilla Flat' in Steinbeck's evolution as a characteristic American writer cannot be minimized.

In this sense it is the last of the young novels, the farewell to the entire fabric of ideas which in his early work form a pattern of romantic withdrawal, the closing of Steinbeck's apprenticeship. And a curious apprenticeship; how curious is our training for the work we yet do. Seeking the good life, Steinbeck has eliminated the power-bent individualism of the 'Cup of Gold,' and then the selfless renunciation of 'To a God Unknown,' and now finally the uninhibited but impossible natural life of 'Tortilla Flat' itself. For the fate of paisano Danny has an appealing prophetic quality as we view it in Steinbeck's evolution. The burning of his rented shack doesn't solve Danny's problem either. Still a landowner he is burdened by the responsibility of his remaining hut. Though there are apparently no taxes to pay on it, no income from it, no repairs for the roof over his head and indeed very little roof to repair, Danny continues to feel the blight of its demands on his hitherto carefree life. Miserable and sullen, he undertakes in the end an orgy of pagan pleasures in the desperate hope that he may cast out the specter of civilization within him — and in this final frenzied effort dies.

Very much like the despairing mad orgy of Danny, 'Tortilla Flat' may be seen as Steinbeck's last pagan excursion before he too assumes the responsibilities of his craft in an age of crisis. For the good life of 'Tortilla Flat' was ultimately as inadequate as the answers of his earlier books. Liberty is a larger concept than the mere evasion of civilizational restraints. At certain periods of history we are forced to make our freedom, rather than relax in it. And though Steinbeck might revert at times to the themes of his young novels, his direction after 'Tortilla Flat' was fundamentally changed. The paisano paradise was, after all, only the novitiate's vision. If the pressing social

problems of his time, like poor Danny's huts, would henceforth
cast a sort of blight on Steinbeck's free life, he must nevertheless
dwell in them.

4. FROM HOBGOBLINS TO HUMANITY.   Oafish,
savage, poetic, moronic, the Lennie of 'Of Mice and Men'
seems rather more like a digestional disturbance than a social
problem, and at first glance Steinbeck's fabulous little play
hardly reveals the change in our author's direction. Exploiting,
as it does, the familiar early passions of Steinbeck — the supernatural, pathology, violence — the drama appears indeed to
be a retrogression into the weird spheres of Steinbeck's earlier
novels. And these themes are here coarsened and commercialized, grown almost as gross as Lennie himself. The artist who is
shortly to illuminate America's future seems here to be catering
to its infantile past.

In part this is unhappily true. How thin 'Of Mice and Men'
is after all, how full of easy sensations it appears upon a little
reflection! How we were stirred by such an extravagant drama
of sentiment — a testimonial, as it were, to our American
'willing suspension of disbelief,' or perhaps our devout suspension of disbelief. Slim, the muleskinner, is a case in point.
Slim, who moves in robes of such native splendor, recalling the
natural life of 'Tortilla Flat' — this Slim of the 'calm, God-like
eyes' who has understanding beyond thought, who stands once
again for Steinbeck's simple truth triumphant, who is, in short,
the Wordsworth peasant in cowboy dress. And we notice again
the sentimental qualities of the play's heroine, Curley's wife, this
tragic courtesan, Steinbeck would have us believe, fragile, easy,
and bold, yet her heart innocent beyond the allure of her body;
this polluted harlot who is yet of a somewhat unearthly purity.
In her, we suppose, Sappho calls to Little Nell, and she reminds
us of the philosophic but enticing witch of Steinbeck's 'Cup of

Gold.' 'Of Mice and Men' is a tribute to Steinbeck's narrative power, to the brilliance with which he clothes such mechanical literary types, to the intensity which somehow gives breath to these poor scarecrows. We see here the dominance of the creative fire over common sense, so that we are held by such apparitions as these characters who, when removed from the framework of the play, crumble under the weight of their own improbability.

Half fairy, as it were, and half elephant, Lennie is of course the chief of the impositions upon our literary tolerance. Steinbeck, to be sure, has been interested previously in these grotesque and delightfully demented beings. Tularecito, the talented gnome of 'The Pastures of Heaven,' is one of them. There is again Johnny Bear, who, combining with the weird ancient of 'To a God Unknown,' becomes our own Lennie. Lennie, in fact, is merely Steinbeck's 'Secret' embodied in a rather perverse hobgoblin. What is the meaning of this line of mystic brutes? Do they, like monkeys, obscene but illuminating, perform in public what we consider in private, the materialization of our inner desires, a little more in evidence, perhaps, but no more queer? There are other possible significances, certainly, but there is little evidence that Steinbeck means them to be other than what they seem, and we are forced to conclude that, in terms of Steinbeck's past, Lennie and his brothers are again more theatrical than evocative. The peculiar, like the ordinary, is the legitimate province of the writer, but it is precisely his function to make it legitimate, to portray it for its illumination on the entire context of human activity. As the writer on human oddities, Steinbeck, rather than meditating upon his creations, merely exhibits them. Rather like the barker in a side-circus, he exhorts us to enter and do no more than gape upon poor Lennie; a barker, I am almost obliged to add, himself rather enthralled by the abnormality, and who, after the last sightseer, comes in to gaze in person.

In 'Of Mice and Men,' moreover, Steinbeck uses Lennie to carry his familiar element of violence, the semi-sadism which, appearing most clearly in 'To a God Unknown,' now fills the play: of which the shooting of Candy's dog is a crucial example, and that of Lennie himself is the climax. Both of these executions are wonderful stage and logically unnecessary. The dog would have probably preferred, like most of us, slumber however fitful to eternal rest; and the more civilized solution of the play would have been to take Lennie to an asylum, where indeed, some may argue, he belonged before the play opened. If I seem to stress this infantile and illogical brutality, which is the core of the play, it is simply because Steinbeck himself does. And where these elements were restrained in the early work of Steinbeck, here they are exploited, made commercial and theatrical; here, in brief, is Steinbeck's past pushed to its limit, the end of the road.

And simultaneously, the start of his new direction. 'Of Mice and Men' is happily not the culmination of Steinbeck's career, but its crossroads, for the play has a curious alternate focus and holds another tale. Lennie is not only the apex of Steinbeck's primitive past, but the origin of his more mature future. It is Lennie who typifies the little acre of land on which these outcasts will raise their chickens, and one day have their own house — the acre which gives these exiles their home, their sense of place, as Thomas Wolfe pointed out to us, which every human being needs, their feeling of belonging; the acre which for a moment draws them together under its spell and gives them dignity. 'We'd jus' live there. We'd belong there.' The ancient derelict Candy, who offers his savings to help buy the farm, the negro Crooks, who for a moment loses his bitter racial hatred, as well as George and Lennie themselves, without anchor, drifting, 'the loneliest guys in the world' — the plot of land gives a direction to all these shattered destinies.

In the course of his evolution from the past to the present in time, from nature to society, from an individual romanticism to a communal realism, however sentimental it was still to be, Steinbeck here identifies himself, not merely with the pleasures of the dispossessed as in 'Tortilla Flat,' but with their needs.

He sees in the new outcasts of 'Of Mice and Men,' not a way of evading civilizational restraints, but a measure of their inadequacy. And how great a change is hinted at here, in this merely preliminary view of the artist's social function, how much more fruitful Steinbeck's talent becomes! Just as he uses his powers in the play to make the more or less absurd melodrama credible, so he also endows Lennie's plot of land with equal dramatic intensity. The theme of the outcast's home — in itself a simple, a 'bourgeois,' and perhaps even a banal concept, yet carrying with it, as it does, the broken destinies of this group of men — assumes under Steinbeck's talent a poignancy, a reality which we must accept. (The concepts which we must accept to make our America fruitful are in themselves very likely as simple, as banal, and perhaps even as 'bourgeois' as Lennie's little acre.) And in the double exposure which redeems 'Of Mice and Men' from its own histrionics, Lennie also has his alternate focus. In the hulking, half-mad, infantile giant, building his apparently purposeless life around a dream he only imperfectly understands, his brute strength so far ahead of his wit, we may then see a sort of ironic portrait of humanity itself — the inarticulate, uncoordinated mass of humanity for whom Steinbeck, like the George of the play, would now do his share in guiding and controlling. In this sense 'The Grapes of Wrath' is Steinbeck's Lennie-load. So that if our Lennie starts the play as a sort of mystic Bear, he ends it as a sort of Bunyan in the historic Pilgrim's Progress of modern economic life. The weird freak is after all the average man. This hobgoblin is humanity.

As a matter of strict chronology, however, Steinbeck had moved in his new direction a year before 'Of Mice and Men,' which so concisely summarizes his past and future directions, had appeared. His first labor novel, 'In Dubious Battle,' is a prelude, along with such stories as 'Vigilante' and 'The Raid,' to 'The Grapes of Wrath.' As a study in growth, moreover, 'In Dubious Battle' is perhaps unique among Steinbeck's novels. For to this point the characteristic tone of his work has been a comforting, but actually rather curious and perplexing, appear-

ance of serenity. Simplification, so to speak, has been the source
of his inspiration, assurance has been his métier. In his pursuit
of the abnormal — this modern wonderland which is surely no
sphere for certainty, and in which so many literary Alices have
lost themselves amidst fantasies to shock a Freud — Steinbeck
has ventured only far enough to fashion a tale. So too in his
druidic and mystic peregrinations, no sacred grove has held him
trapped for longer than a chapter. Handling complex material
rather too easily, he has been marked by the popularizing gift
— this indigenous American blessing which has, however, in the
case of so many literary figures (a William Lyon Phelps, a
Woollcott, a Louis Bromfield, as well as Steinbeck himself) become a blessing not altogether unmixed. In Steinbeck's work
the false starts and turns, the thwarting problems of material
and of the artist in the process of penetrating it, which usually
mark the effort to portray truth, these are singularly lacking.
If Steinbeck has reminded us of a Thomas Wolfe rejoicing in the
mournful questioning of youth which wants no answers, he has
never, like Wolfe, found himself disturbed by the final enigma
of existence itself. For Steinbeck, Wolfe's famous stone is a
stone, a leaf a leaf, and the door is sure to be found.

Here is an urbanity of psyche bought a little easily, a certainty whose cost is truth, the understanding which passeth
over knowledge. In this sense, his belief in himself dominating
his intelligence, Steinbeck is an example of Lardner's American.
And if, as we said in respect to Lardner, such a faith is central to
all living and particularly pertinent to the creative process —
the writer being indeed better off with too little intelligence than
too much — this self-belief also demands a certain moderation
in its practice.

In Steinbeck's case until 'In Dubious Battle,' his self-assurance
being somewhat excessive, it seemed, the growth of his thinking
has suffered. Experimenting in a variety of books with the
meaning of the good life, he has not, however, extended the
depth of his experimentation. In the Lardnerian tradition
again he has advocated a change of scene rather than a chang-

ing perception. Being too sure he has tended to be as shallow. Little has seemed to baffle this daring young Lochinvar and there was too little in him to baffle us. To a certain degree, moreover, this tendency continues in 'In Dubious Battle' itself. Mac, the leader of the striking apple-pickers in Torgas County, is simply another of Steinbeck's brave new natural men, brother to the muleskinner Slim of 'Of Mice and Men.' There is again Steinbeck's familiar passion for big theatrical scenes; Mac gains his power over the strikers by performing a startling bit of obstetrics. With optimism as his only technic, Mac risks all, including mother and child, on his gynecological intuition, seizing the moment, and fortunately the infant too. Marked by this apparent nonchalance as to the origins of human life, 'In Dubious Battle' proceeds to much shooting, rioting, burning, and various other forms of brutality. In these instances the struggle for a better life simply affords Steinbeck a better chance for his now familiar violence. Here again is the rather debonair delight in bloodshed, marked by little genuine feeling of either necessity or tragedy, but by a sort of naïve enthusiasm which almost recalls the mood of the Rover Boys. Farmers' crops are destroyed, a bewildered middleman is caught in this battle of business man and worker, a worker himself is maimed, bullets, barricades; it all makes for a better story, or it seems to. And these Rover Boys have visited Moscow, for we see that Mac, in the tradition of Steinbeck's natural supermen, has seen the vision of Communism. The Rousseauistic Eden of Steinbeck's early novels has become Marx's Utopia, and the divine cannibal is now the devout comrade.

Yet beneath these familiar certainties of Steinbeck, there is a new uneasiness which profoundly affects 'In Dubious Battle.' What he attempts so blithely to portray, Steinbeck can't altogether accept. For this picture of labor struggle which Steinbeck here gives us, almost despite himself, is ugly. We see the California workers crushed by the big absentee landowners, terrorized, intimidated, deprived of any value as human beings, sacrificed to the capitalist faith (fanatic and truly mystic) in profits.

These apple-pickers, in short, are reduced to the terrifying industrial concept: 'cheap labor.' And on the other hand the workers are exploited in a not dissimilar fashion by their own labor leaders. For Mac and his fellow revolutionaries also ignore the individual for the abstract, the present needs for the future's problematical good, use terror and cruelty in their preoccupation with an ideal state, sacrifice the workers to their own faith, just as fanatic and mystic, in the communist cause. Mac in turn reduces the apple-pickers to his own concept, almost as terrifying: 'the masses.'

Human life is in both cases wasted for the sake of dogma, and the strike — portrayed on the surface of 'In Dubious Battle' as so glamorous — emerges indeed as horrible. Lie fights lie, radical power struggles against capitalist power, blood is used by the landowners to intimidate, and blood is used by the strike leaders to stimulate. The average man (the London, Anderson, Al, Dakin of the novel), caught between these two extremes, suffers and makes his fellows suffer for no purpose of his own. But this average man himself, theoretically deserving all our sympathy, a subject, Lord knows, of utmost compassion is revealed, beneath the sentiment that Steinbeck hastily daubs on, in an equally depressing light. The average humanity of 'In Dubious Battle' is irresolute, vain, calculating in the individual case, and with his brothers forming the arrogant, stupid, and cruel mob.

How much of this is intentional on Steinbeck's part, or accidental, the product of carelessness, design, or of his own confusion? Difficult as it is to estimate, it is precisely the rawness, the ugliness of the labor struggle and of the human spirit involved in it, this final feeling of bleak misery which gives 'In Dubious Battle' its strength. Through what it reveals when apparently most determined to conceal (and yet we are never quite sure whether the effect is altogether unintentional), it becomes among our contemporary labor novels a powerful and uncomfortable document. Representing, as I think it does, the victory of Steinbeck's repressed realism over the ro-

mantic serenity which he has hitherto assumed as his tone, it
makes us aware, and a little uneasily so, of his undeveloped
powers. For this master of illusion has produced here a sort of
masterpiece of disillusionment. In dubious battle, indeed.

5. OF WRATH OR JOY.   Pausing to collect his shorter
works in 'The Long Valley,' Steinbeck brought together the
varied strains of his past. Of the stories, the 'Red Pony,'
'Chrysanthemums,' and 'The White Quail,' recalling the sensitive lyricism of 'The Pastures of Heaven' and Steinbeck's
earlier relationship to D. H. Lawrence, are perhaps the best,
and are fine. Steinbeck, moreover, achieves a genuine folk
humor in 'The Harness' and an authentic sense of human
horror in 'The Snake.' But he also indicates the purely theatrical origins of Lennie in 'Johnny Bear,' and a work like 'St.
Katy the Virgin,' reprinted in special editions as a collector's
item, achieves the distinction of being at once rather precious
and vulgar. The same uneven quality and fusion of his earlier
themes marks, of course, his next and most famous work. A
great deal has been said about 'The Grapes of Wrath' in the
heat of partisanship; it has been defended by radical critics
with as little literary feeling as it has been attacked by our con-
servative and vested interests; we attempt here to view it as a
writer's work, and as the present climax of Steinbeck's history.

In this sense, knowing what we do of the earlier Steinbeck, it
must become clear how much of Steinbeck's famous novel is borrowed from the past, how many of the characters and themes
in 'The Grapes of Wrath' are reflections of Steinbeck's younger
interests, and of the uneven temperament we have already seen
functioning. The inequalities of the American social system are
affecting thousands of fine American families. Hence the
Joads must be a fine American family. Around them Steinbeck
weaves his typical fantasies, so that the Joads emerge as ideal-

ized in their own way as those smooth personages who dwell everlastingly in the pages of the *Saturday Evening Post*. Of them, of course, Ma Joad is the guiding spirit, the soul of American motherhood, her home in the kitchen but her spirit in the heavens. Like Slim and Mac she is wise, courageous, indomitable, though in tatters:

> Her hazel eyes seemed to have experienced all possible tragedy and to have mounted pain and suffering like steps into a high calm and a superhuman understanding.... And from her great and humble position in the family she had taken dignity and clean calm beauty. From her position as healer, her hands had grown sure and cool and quiet; from her position as arbiter she had become as remote and faultless in judgment as a goddess.

Steinbeck's sentimentality has overwhelmed him, his reliance on rhapsody rather than reflection, the violence which characterizes his temperament here turned into idyllic abstraction — these traits which as yet prevent our considering him fully among the writers whose talent he perhaps equals. And if Ma Joad is thus portrayed, what can we say of Rose of Sharon, with her ripe voluptuousness, her drowsing aroma of universal fertility — except that this is again sentimentalized projection. Connie Rivers, in turn, reminds us of Curley's wife, and the philosophic witch of the 'Cup of Gold' as a symbol of Steinbeck's sexual fascination. Noah Joad belongs to Steinbeck's hobgoblins, and Grampa is a fusion of this and the paisanos of 'Tortilla Flat':

> He fought and argued, told dirty stories. He was as lecherous as always.... He drank too much when he could get it, ate too much when it was there, talked too much all the time.

And with his 'little bright eyes,' his cantankerous, mischievous little old face, Grampa Joad is too much of a typical Steinbeckian whimsicality for us ever to believe, as, in short, are most of the Joads. As in 'Of Mice and Men' we have in 'The Grapes of Wrath' the joining of the old and the new Steinbeck, and the older themes are marked with the deterioration which comes when an author retraces without belief the patterns of his past. It is hard to believe that even Steinbeck himself accepts the Joads as people, or that he has thrown in the variety of pagan, weird, earthy, violent concepts for more than their picturesque value. 'The Grapes of Wrath,' in short, often represents the dubious nuptials of 'Tobacco Road' with the *Ladies' Home Journal*. But the marriage is one of convenience.

For as with 'For Whom the Bell Tolls,' we cannot deny the force and sincerity of the novel which break through the moulds of its presentation. The descriptions of the migration, of the highway caravans, of the used-car markets, of truck-drivers and roadside stands, the geographical panorama of the Western States, the evocations of their socio-psychological temper, and those of the strain of industrial conflict, the repeated affirmations of faith and respect in average humanity, the anger at social injustice, and above all the novel's will for life coming in an era of sickness and death — these again and again capture and arouse us. In tone much like Zola's 'Germinal' (in our own tradition, the later Steinbeck seems to descend from Frank Norris and Jack London) with very similar Zolaesque flaws, lacks of taste, debatable excesses, ridiculous sensations, 'The Grapes of Wrath' has also the same urgency which in Zola's novel holds us some fifty years after its inception, and hence it will be condemned only by those who, in the end, prefer perfection to importance. Before the significance of the book in Steinbeck's own history, and in the history of his society, before the power of it, rough as it may be, we must yield up our reservations to our praise. Lacking the art of 'The Pastures of Heaven' and the realism of 'In Dubious Battle,' marking, as it also does, a return to Steinbeck's glamor, theatrics, and simplicity of view after the conflicts of his earlier proletarian novel, thus sentimentalized, often distorted, 'The Grapes of Wrath' is not at all Steinbeck's best novel. But it is, all in all, his biggest novel.

And in it, what a change has come about in the young author of Morgan's piratical adventures! Urging us, in the 'Cup of

Gold,' to emulate the individualistic power-drive of the buccaneer, this more glamorous portrayal of the values of '29,
Steinbeck is now writing of man's communal good. The bloodthirsty mystic who dwelt among the druidic groves of 'To a
God Unknown' has settled among the disinherited workers of
his land. The advocate of immolation is now protesting the
needless sacrifice of human lives. The dazzling playwright of
'Of Mice and Men,' busying himself there with theatrical abnormality, is here portraying the drama of the most ordinary
lives. The Steinbeck who sought in 'The Pastures of Heaven'
the causes of human frustration finds its true origin in the social
pathology of an economic system both incoherent and inex-
cusable. The 'Curse' is indeed civilization. But the writer who
fled from it in 'Tortilla Flat' now argues for social controls!
Devoted, as we have noticed, to hobgoblins, Steinbeck at least
hasn't treasured the famous one of Emerson's little minds —
'consistency.' Having come to realize, however, that our true
happiness must derive, not through any mystical and mythical
freedom from society, but through making our society genuinely
free, Steinbeck's extremes become a virtue, and the grace of his
final truth redeems his methodological errors. If indeed Steinbeck suffers throughout much of his work from a sort of belated
spiritual adolescence, if his novels are sometimes full of pangs
and clichés, spotted with the marks, as it were, of literary
puberty, it is also and more significantly true that in the final
result he has come of age.

And the importance of this lies not only, of course, with
Steinbeck as an individual, but in his relationship with an entire range of American artists and with our culture itself. In
the variety of his early 'solutions' — the life of egotistic adventure, and that of bloody daring, the primitive way, the
natural and anti-social life, the return to the soil, the dabblings
with the abnormal — Steinbeck seems almost to traverse the
entire circuit of contemporary artistic escapes. In him are reflected the evasions of his generation. Avoiding the most flagrant of these evasions, and from the first always more American

in tone, Steinbeck seems to speak nevertheless for all his fellow individualists, mystics and primitives, symbolists and experimentalists: for all the discontented heirs of Henry James, seeking one or another exit, Kay Boyles, middle-class bohemians gathered in little villages, those who ran from Toklas to Taos. He speaks for all those as well who jumped from 'Transition' to Technocracy, or bold Menckenites scorning the American mob, scholarly humanists from Ohio ignoring the core of humanism, for all those who, in whatever ways, found their souls in Oxford accents, Spanish bullfights, or in red Russia, as well as in the Californian paisanos. In his early evasions Steinbeck is symptomatic of this whole range of American aesthetes whom, as we saw, Thomas Wolfe took off in 'The Story of a Novel,' those American refugees to whom a wide world might have cried: Why, why don't you go back where you came from?

And if in his young work Steinbeck reminds us of those who fled what they conceived to be a hostile, narrow, and materialistic environment, in his conversion Steinbeck again illuminates another era of American artistic thought. Through the errors which mark his first attempts at dealing with his own day, his lack of sociological knowledge, the haste with which he dropped a point of view essentially naïve, and in the naïveté which nevertheless accompanies his new views also, here again Steinbeck reflects the American writer in crisis. Notice the swift embracing of revolutionary violence in 'In Dubious Battle,' a solution paralleling that of a score of other typical artists, as though by the extremity of our feeling we may excuse its tardiness. Steinbeck's path in this too is the one of his time. He recalls the Halpers, Hickses, Hellmans, the Zugsmiths, and Heywood Brouns, and a range of other literary infants in the ideological woods, and even such major figures as Dos Passos who in their belated efforts to escape from Lardner's dead end found themselves suddenly along the road to Leningrad.

The very imperfections, then, of Steinbeck's issue reveal his society, while those of Steinbeck himself make him more effective with this society. The mirror of typical American sentiment that he is, though applying this sentiment to the relatively fresh field of social welfare, Steinbeck is perhaps closer to the American audience than any other comparable writer. The traits in him which fluster the critic are those which endear him to mankind. If angels do rush in where fools fear to tread, they accomplish after all very little, since they are so seldom heeded. The perfection of first-rate art is in one sense sterile, a high peak in itself yet too remote for the majority of us to exist upon, being unable to breathe in the rarefied climate of pure wisdom. But literature of the second order — and we recall 'Uncle Tom's Cabin' — may sway continents and for a moment seduce Destiny herself from her chores. If Steinbeck's impact upon his society derives in large measure from his very imperfections, his effect nevertheless can be tremendous. And this is what gives him, and not all our critical carpings can alter it, his final, largest significance.

For see what has happened in '39 to Ring Lardner's anonymous Mr. U.S.A. who 'bought a book and threw it away,' this same good citizen who is now rushing so dizzily to read Steinbeck's best-seller! 'The Grapes of Wrath' is a sociological catalyst; in a moment it has transformed and given meaning to the chemistry of a decade of social change. And if Steinbeck's novel evokes once again the brazen symbolism of '29 in the sensational trappings of its own Success Story, it is nevertheless informing us that '29, like Lardner's Miss Sarah E. Spooldripper, is gone too. For certainly to the Lardnerian citizen of '29 'The Grapes of Wrath' would present an unbelievable portrait of the America he had thought so unparalleled, unique, and eternal. Consider this popular novel filled with new and perplexing concepts: mass unemployment, hunger, rioting, armed reaction, and revolutionary urging. And between these last two, a large variety of moderating governmental agencies — AAA and HOLC and WPA and PWA and FHA and RFC and SEC — to the solid, sleek, and unknowing citizen of '29, those whom Wolfe called the true Lost Generation, a whole new alphabet of crisis. And his America, once so rich and pleasure-loving, now so disturbed, sick, full of shifting masses and shifting movements; America like Steinbeck's Western States nervous under the beginning change:

> The great owners, nervous, sensing a change, knowing nothing of the nature of the change. The great owners, striking at the immediate thing, the widening government, the growing labor unity; striking at new taxes, at plans; not knowing these things are results not causes.... The causes lie deep and simply — the causes are a hunger in a stomach, multiplied a million times; a hunger in a single soul, hunger for joy and some security, multiplied a million times; muscles and mind aching to grow, to work, to create, multiplied a million times.... The Western States nervous under the beginning change.

To the citizen of '29 so hideous and ominous a best-seller! In this new, incredible America of '39 the Lardnerian business men, once gliding to their Florida paradise by Pullman, are Steinbeck's 'Okies' pushing along to their vagrant camps in dilapidated buggies. Once so grimly bent on pleasure, seeking new vistas for new thoughts, Lardner's American vacationers are Steinbeck's American dispossessed. 'They ain't gonna be no kinda work for three months.' Lardner's Pullmans, indeed, are Steinbeck's boxcars; and in them huddle the new American citizens without bread, facing their season of want. And now Lardner's sleek, shiny America is violent through fear. 'The sheriffs swore in new deputies and ordered new rifles; and the comfortable people in tight houses felt pity at first, and then distaste, and finally hatred for the migrant people.' For the migrant people? Those who own tight houses in the new America are few. This America is migrant.

Behind the gilded Success Story of '39, then, that of 'The Grapes of Wrath,' these de luxe chromium trumpets which herald the arrival of the Joad's jalopy, there is another story, perhaps just as spectacular. We can't, after all, dismiss Steinbeck's novel as the Mah-Jong of the thirties. Do we associate its popularity with 'Anthony Adverse' or 'Gone With the Wind,' seeing in these evidences of America's collectivist complex rather than her critical acumen? Even this association is provocative. For it is not inconceivable that in the end the United States will bring about its great sweeping social changes as a new sort of popular fashion. If, indeed, the energy with which we pursue our vogues were spent in solving our dilemmas, what 'wonderful cities and free nations,' as Whitman told us, we should fetch as we went!

Chapter Seven

SUCCESS STORY, FINIS

Chapter Seven

SUCCESS STORY, FINIS

'DEAD, '29 IS DEAD,' the solid citizen of the Lardnerian epoch, once believing itself so unique and everlasting, might cry as he saw the new America of 'The Grapes of Wrath,' 'For Whom the Bell Tolls,' 'You Can't Go Home Again,' these disturbing best-sellers of the nineteen-thirties: 'And what can come of this, where will it end?' What indeed will be the tale of '39? Is the death only that of a recurrent cycle, and will '29 rise again, immortal phoenix, mocking all our hopes? The long crisis culminating in another boom: the inflated and obsessed egotism of the Big Money once more, the Success Myth which even when most fully achieved brought no great joy to the American man — is this to be the product of a decade of change? And another crash, another, deeper depression, another, shorter, more frantic boomtime; the rhythm growing more sharply defined now; every decade more sterile, every death more brutal; '29 dying endlessly? Prosperity and panic monotonously pursuing one another, each feeding into the other, and the memory of one making the other more intolerable? The eras of plenty very much like the orgiastic dissipation of a condemned man; the panics filled with the echoes of misused abundance; a societal manic-depressive cycle becoming progressively more desperate, leading downward through its illusory spirals of progress to murderous and then suicidal impulses? Until at last, judged a hopeless case, the culture is to be confined within the gray walls of eternity: 'The American Way'?

In the record of our literary evolution to the nineteen-forties lies the crystallization of a modern temper less hopeless than this, giving us another meaning for our national destiny, holding perhaps a less anguished future. While we have seen the imperfections of the American writer grappling with the problems of his society, we have also seen the writer's increasing sense of these issues. Is it merely odd that in a period of chaos the later work of Hemingway, Dos Passos, Wolfe, and Steinbeck should end on the note of affirmation, the note of life, while the splendors of the twenties brought only negation? In crisis the writer may find courage. In the recognition of his social usefulness, his belonging, the writer may gain a conviction he has too often lacked in the past, a faith in his cultural function which was previously denied him by a boomtime America that considered the writer, if at all, a sort of exotic excrescence. And faith can move men as well as mountains. Our Steinbeck gives evidence of the power that the writer holds in the United States of social change.

We have seen all too fully, moreover, the previous aversion of the American writer to the society moulded by industrialism; and the great age of prosperity ends up in the red. Does the pattern of negation which we have traced in the writers conditioned by the nineteen-twenties extend only to them; would a different selection convey a different thesis? We are likely to meet our theme with variations in the work of most American writers of stature. By now, in fact, the moral of our story has become a cliché, but a cliché may also condemn a culture. 'I took to the opium of dream,' Henry Miller tells us in the excerpts from 'Black Spring' published in 'New Directions,' 'in order to face the hideousness of a life in which I had no part. As quietly and naturally as a twig falling into the Mississippi I dropped out of the stream of American life.' And though with Miller, as with James Joyce, it is sometimes difficult to separate the pathological from the sociological elements of his work, the evocation of the American scene he had abandoned is clear enough. 'American Can, American Tel. and Tel., At

lantic and Pacific, Standard Oil, United Cigars, Father John,
Sacco and Vanzetti, Uneeda Biscuit, Seaboard Air Line,
Sapolio, Nick Carter, Trixie Friganza, Foxy Grandpa, the
Gold Dust Twins...' He recalls the men and women prome-
nading on the sidewalks, 'curious beasts, half human, half-
celluloid':

> Walking up and down the Avenue, half-crazed, their teeth pol-
> ished, their eyes glazed.... Smiling through life with that de-
> mented, glazed look in the eyes, the flags unfurled, and sex flow-
> ing sweetly through the sewers.... The living walked over the
> dead, smiling all the while to advertise their beautiful white
> teeth. It's this cruel white smile that sticks in my memory. I see
> it in my sleep when I put out my hand to beg — the George C.
> Tilyou smile that floats above the spandangled bananas at
> Steeplechase.

In Miller we notice again the accent of almost frivolous despair
which marks the writer's reaction to the commercialized society
of the twenties. As with Hemingway's Mrs. Tracy, who 'losht'
her husband and her dental plate at once, the tragic articulation
which should mark the artist's repudiation of his homeland is
reduced to a sort of grotesque mouthing; as if Miller himself
were now crying with Mrs. Tracy: 'Basards!'

We see the forms of this cultural negation everywhere in the
writing of the twenties, in the early William Carlos Williams's
'A Voyage to Pagany,' in T. S. Eliot and Ezra Pound, of course,
early and late, Idaho seeming to feel its rejection most severely
We see it in the snobbish reflections of Mencken; or Cabell's
Jurgen, with his erogenous land of Poictesme, his 'monstrous
cleverness' needing and being given no confirmation, who perhaps most clearly reflected the juvenile fantasies of revolt which
often characterized these writers. In our own array of authors,
we recall the Lardnerian Saturday nights which always seemed
'like something was going to happen,' the American Nada of
Hemingway, or the Modern Hero of the early Dos Passos. And
in his recession from impotence to inertia, we said, the Dos
Passos hero — representing the innocuous aesthetes of the

twenties who were in one literary form or another the real
protagonists of the Jazz Age — reflected the final separation of
the American artist from his society which began with the industrial domination of the Republic in the eighteen-sixties. We
may recall a Henry Adams, in person one of these modern
spokesman, contemptuous of his age's materialistic conquest,
yet hungering after it also, and so twisted in his feelings, and
realizing his own ineffectual position. Or the Henry James
figures, partially disturbed by the same conflict, paralyzed by
nuances in the vain effort to escape the American vulgarity,
pacing up and down their foreign piazzas, trying to decide
whether to offer each other a cigarette, perhaps, or refrain.
The most vital character in Howells is again, as Ludwig Lew-
isohn notices, the Marcia Gaylord of 'A Modern Instance,'
aggressive, possessive, harsh, in turn one of the first of the devouring modern females we have watched in our studies, making
her raids upon the ineffectual Howells male. And Howells
himself, the polished arbiter of the Boston Athenaeum, was to
admit his final bewilderment before the American societal
realities. Yes, the failure of nerve with which the early Dos
Passos is concerned (here too showing his acumen as social historian) is a very legitimate theme in American life. But it is the
failure of the American artist's nerve. For the time of Howells,
James, and Adams was also the time of Rockefeller, Vanderbilt,
and Jay Gould. In that day, certainly, there was no comparable
disability in the American social structure which bore these
oddly oscillating literary males. In terms of our national
economy, there was rather such a burst of energy as the world
had never seen before. Thus we have in our post-Civil-War
period, the paradox of the defeated American artist in the
midst of a young, bold, and supremely optimistic society: these
despairing cultural voyeurs gazing mournfully at the almost out-
rageously successful American entrepreneur.

The curious contrast, moreover, has continued down to our
own time. Our economic order has continually shown such
untutored and unrestrained power and super-power that we

have been unable to find suitable ways to dispose of the products of this tremendous, transforming cultural energy. Our failure has been that of the intelligence to use our wealth; to create better social goals for it, to make the proper moulds to contain the gigantic flow of America's productive will; so that our society like our geography has been marked by a series of catastrophic floods and droughts. And here, of course, we come close to our problem. The writer is ordinarily one of the factors responsible for this social intelligence, particularly so and perhaps crucially so in a democracy; and we have seen how the American writer was divorced from his function in the period before the nineteen-thirties. The failure of nerve in our literature is not the reflection of cultural decadence, but of a cultural ambivalence. Here is a split between the guiding spirit of our society and its productive forces, a split often so marked as to give our cultural pattern the schizophrenic caste which Veblen noticed. Throughout our fabulous economic exploitation, the energy which conquered a continent has been personified by our industrial barons; an energy which has been almost completely pure, without social direction, that is to say, or a sense of communal responsibility. The writers, on the other hand, who represented, in part at least, the sense of civilizational direction, turned away from the men of economic talent — and thus, turning away in a society dominated by economics, found themselves only too often lacking any goal or function, not merely for their society, but in the end for themselves too. The division between social energy and social intelligence, this basic conflict, as it were, of the American body and mind, harmful as all such divisions are to both organs of the political body, was perhaps worse for the writer. For the energy of the economic man, if it had very little purpose beyond that of material conquest, at least had that. It had the vast immediate untamed natural resources of America to work with. The absence of our ultimate and real social goals was hardly realized until our immediate and practical social goals had been achieved. But the writer after 1860, watching the land of Lincoln become that of Mor-

gan and lose its sense of destiny for the sake of profit, this herculean effort, as we said, which led to Lardner's Augean stable,
had no such similar unexploited fields. An apparently useless,
and hardly even decorative fixture on the American dynamo,
the writer felt his lack of purpose much more swiftly than the
American industrialist, who, after he had amassed his fortune,
usually gave it away, and died.

As we have seen in the sepaɪate studies, the writer was to
show the effects of this division very clearly. Possibly the entire
complex of our writers' sense of cultural rejection is best summarized in the Wolfian search for 'Place.' 'The East Side was a
Place — and that was the thing that made it wonderful,' we
remember that he tells us. 'It was a Place that people came
from, where men were born and lived and worked and sweated
and died.' And the sense of belonging, the sense of roots and
identity, of a home, which was at the center of the Wolfian
quest, is that which is also most conspicuously missing in his con-
temporaries whom we have studied. The writer is often the
radical, we have pointed out; his essence is the civilizing spirit
which criticizes and condemns. He is at once society's irritant
and antiseptic; he will be found to carp among Elysian fields;
and in the context of our merely mortal patterns he must remain
continually sensitive to human imperfection. Or say, if this
sounds rather too flattering, he is the problem child of our
social arrangements, in whom our evasions and dilemmas are
likely to show up most sharply. Yet for the writer to become
wholly this, to lose the sense of a larger and perhaps always
skeptical concern for humanity, is for him and his land equally
barren. And we have noticed in our authors the predominant
lack of such concern, or again of that trite 'loving-kindness'
which, toward the close of his life, Somerset Maugham states so
apologetically as the only reason for it. Against this, we recall
rather the Lardnerian hatred, or Faulkner's cold perversions, or
the fabricated emotions of Steinbeck, and his interest, as Edmund Wilson has told us, with the 'animalism' of man rather
than his humanity. Our Dos Passos, who has the most admir-

able intellectual sense of mature personal relationships, is hardly able in his writing to evidence a single very convincing example of his thesis. We have noticed too in the Americans their inability very often to maintain any sort of 'grand style' in their more direct personal utterances: the harsh and petty accents of Hemingway in 'Green Hills of Africa,' those of Dos Passos in the preface to his plays, or of Wolfe on the disenchantment of his Magic City, these surprising tones of the bitter and biased spirit.

By contrast we may mention another recent work, also of a great disillusionment, the young Hungarian Arthur Koestler's 'Darkness at Noon.' In the midst of equal spiritual distress, the European maintains an emotional balance; compassion still colors his indignation; and beneath his malaise there is still the sense of love, for home, land, and people, which is wanting in the American. And if the European today is also the rebel, and the exile from his native tradition, as Silone and Malraux or Koestler, he may yet, as Koestler does, find his commonality with all the breeds of man linked together by the concentration camp, Le Vernet his new homeland; while the American can often find none with his own free and thriving countrymen. But without a feeling of place, it was difficult for our writers in the twenties to feel any genuine affection for its inhabitants. (We appreciate the danger of using such distinctions as 'American' and 'European'; our excuse is that the distinction seems to be valid.) The work of Thomas Mann, again, also rising out of a middle-class commercial society, is in a sense built around an essentially false conflict of the artist as against the citizen. Where is the difference; and what society could long tolerate it? But the American writer, so often without even the sense of formal obligation to his own social order, has hardly felt the conflict. Perhaps we must add, stressing such positive emotions for our now vanishing age of skepticism, seeming once again like Pollyanna among the Encyclopédists, that we are not advocating a false sweetness of temper in our authors. That, in fact, is what we are attempting to avoid. For while love is not to be denied in the human temperament, it demands much practice, like any other habit. And when it comes, as it has in our new dawning epoch of belief, yet after such long estrangement, as in 'For Whom the Bell Tolls,' or 'The Grapes of Wrath,' or in Eugene O'Neill's 'Days Without End,' modern love is apt to assume precisely this sentimental, artificial, parvenu form. The century of American literary hostility is only the more convincing as now our writers attempt to escape from their long bondage.

Showing the effects of their social rejection, moreover, our authors by an odd irony were to reveal many of the cultural traits they had repudiated. The American individualism, as Van Wyck Brooks has again told us in 'Oliver Allston,' is not a sense of character, the appreciation of personality which venerates eccentricity and bows to lunacy. For as the ancient Hebrews viewed their prophets, and as we must feel about certain modern literary groups like 'New Directions,' the Lord chooses strange vessels for His purposes; and out of the many who are indubitably mad may come the one who is truly inspired. No, our individualism is the superiority of one individual over another, the effort to manipulate rather than understand our neighbors; the sense of character sacrificed in the American social pattern to the sense of power. So Hemingway's artistic safari, poised in opposition to the commercial egotism of '29, was nevertheless in many respects to reflect it. The 'U.S.A.' trilogy is again superior to 'Men of Good Will' as a panoramic study of society, despite Monsieur Romains's protestations of his own profundity. It is superior in every sense but one. Dos Passos's work does lack the concern for character in the French narrative, and the Frenchman's insight into the variations, and, in fact, the perversions of human personality. But Dos Passos is the exception to another trait we have noticed in our authors: the lack of intellectual background, the freedom of knowledge and of speculation which seems to mark the big Europeans as almost a native instinct. In his revolt, the American was still the child of the national pragmatism he disavowed. We have seen the failure of Lardner's negative utilitarianism (nothing worked in '29), the restrictions on Hemingway's portrait of the depths, the absence of discrimination in Wolfe, gigantic, as everything else in the torrents of his literary spring. So too in Steinbeck's later book, 'Sea of Cortez,' our American author arrives at once painfully and a little pretentiously at the theoretical speculations of Darwin, who was hardly a theorist.

What our authors illustrate here, however, is not so much their own intellectual incapacity. We mention this to illuminate rather than condemn. We may, in fact, have some question as to the thinking processes of writers as a group; the creative and the ratiocinative habits do not always accompany each other in the perfect harmony we would seek. If the American often reflects with barely half the result of the European, whom he very often surpasses in talent, it is rather the deficiency of cultural thinking which hampers his work. In our splendid national sense of doing, we have felt no urgency to discover what we were doing. Lardner and Hemingway, Faulkner and Wolfe and Steinbeck, give evidence of the lack of a rational, or merely thoughtful cultural tradition upon which they might draw and which would fill out their creative gifts; as Robert Frost and Vachel Lindsay give evidence. Or as Clement Greenberg remarks acutely about an entire group of American modernist poets:

> It is small-scale poetry, lacking resonance, lacking really culture. ... Its makers have neither inherited nor acquired enough cultural capital to expand beyond the confines of their immediate experience and of a narrowly professional conception of poetry.

So in our modern period, very often the major achievement of the American novelist lay in the field of realism, a superior sort of reportage, like the detailed chronicles of Dreiser; the often superb satirical portraiture of the early Sinclair Lewis; or the more recent work of James Farrell — these massive histories of a Chicago lower-class milieu which might have been the less massive as they were more discerning.

For when it came to analysis or synthesis, when the American writer spoke out, what a falling-off was there. In their utter-ances Dreiser or Lewis could not formulate a respectable view of their material, as apparently Farrell could formulate little view at all. Like our own Lardner, they had no alternative to the scene they were excoriating. For the artist of the twenties, as Lionel Trilling remarked about Sherwood Anderson, it was considered sufficient to break with his society. But we know now that this sheer revolt was in some respects as unproductive as the tribal tabus it defied. It is not surprising that Dreiser has turned toward literal Communism, a ready-made system of ideas for the writer whose work is marked by the absence of ideas; and Robinson Jeffers has cultivated Spengler. Or that Willa Cather, a genuine craftsman, has moved from refinement to religion; where T. S. Eliot, following the same course in a more rarefied medium, moved before her. Ezra Pound, in his turn, could think of nothing more convincing than Italian Fascism. While the later Sinclair Lewis is assiduously wooing the muse of Main Street whom the earlier novelist made notori-ous; now turning for his divinity to the hallowed maxims of Zenith. What a wonderful gemmation of talent, and what strange flowering! The Life of Realization, that great act of daring which marked our literary advance in the nineteen-twenties, was very often do and die.

As the twenties, then, were the last frenzied flowering of our miraculous materialism, the last days of Midas in his Stutz, here too the cultural tensions of our authors were revealed most clearly. With its juxtaposition of the Indian and the Engine, 'The Torrents of Spring' is in this sense symptomatic of the course of American literary expression from the Civil War. Hardly finished subduing the pioneer rigors, the writer was faced with the industrial tyranny. Our persistent counter-tradi-tion of literary revolt came to fruit directly before our own era, with such writers as John Reed, Floyd Dell, Randolph Bourne, and the groups they typified, in Woodrow Wilson's New Free-dom. Yet who could long reflect on virtue when he might be cornering the markets of a continent? Like our Lardner, what the American did in spite of his cultural odds was sometimes quite superb. If a Mark Twain yielded to the raw opulence of the gilded age (at least in his public thoughts), when he too thought of his opportunities he might marvel at his restraint, amongst these industrial nabobs whose new western stratagems put to shame all the wiles of the East. But like Twain and Lardner also, too often the explosive talent of our writers yielded only fireworks. In a world of breath-taking physical transformation, we said, the American cultural spirit could hardly cope with such change, nor gain any sense of continuity or of its own function and integrity. By and large the American rebel continued to see Eternity as a suburb of Detroit. With his ironic yet curiously fervent apostrophe to the Dynamo, Eugene O'Neill in the nineteen-twenties betrayed the ineffectual impact of a century of literary protest.

But now in the nineteen-thirties, the Dynamo had stopped its song, this air-cooled Circe which had been turning our authors into such strange literary beasts. Those who were termed the Lords of Creation were, it seemed, only the merchants in the temple. Heartily know, our New England priest had prophesied, when half-gods go, the gods arrive. Well, Monopoly, at least, ceased to be a national career and became a parlor sport. The omnipotent commercial ethos, with Bruce Barton as its voice in the stock exchange, this ethos as insistent as it was insignificant, halted in its glorification of Christ as the Eternal Executive. The power was off. The American writer could look around him. He could see the deepest depression of the industrial cycle, the depression which signified the close of that cycle, as it had existed without precedent and without restraint, so uniquely in the history of western man. If the writer's mind, like that of Dos Passos's Johnny Moorehouse, was still full of auger-bits, canthooks, mauls, sash-weights, axes, hatchets, monkey-wrenches, if it persisted in still asking him why should our cotterpins appeal more than any other cotterpins, in the midst of these nostalgic memories he was now also wandering among the useless citadels of the commercial superman.

If the writer, moreover, could not quite envision the grass growing in the streets of a hundred cities, as the merchants had warned (hurriedly abandoning the temple as insolvent), he could at least see the people walking in them, as Thomas Wolfe did; the people wandering without direction. 'Everywhere around me, during those years, I saw the evidence of an incalculable ruin and suffering,' we recall that Wolfe tells us. 'And the staggering impact of this black picture ... left a scar upon my life, a conviction in my soul which I shall never lose.' The people, yes, as Carl Sandburg affirmed from the midst of the chaos, but as the end result of our unparalleled progress, the people without their home, as the American writer had been without his for the century. America had never had the sort of life the modern artist had considered good. 'The wealthy deserve every consideration of the people,' Saroyan tells us —

> for they have won that war, they have clung nobly and fearlessly to their statistics. In the hills they have fought the living and won. One of them against a million of men. They are the heroes of our time. Only ... when they groan about money, about expenses, about losses, let someone in the world ask, What expenses? What losses? What the hell are you talking about? What can the mortal lose but flesh? ... This is your world and it is my world, and it is not real estate ... it is this pause in time and space. It is this chance to breathe, to walk, to see, to eat, to love, to laugh. It is not financial statistics. It belongs to this mangled tribe, this still unborn God, man.

Now in '29, America no longer had even that lesser sort of existence which our industrial ethics had proclaimed as divine. Yet now also the war of statistics had been lost, and the hills of high finance would yield to the onslaughts of Saroyan's mangled tribe. If we were homeless in '29, we were all homeless together; in this sense we were free at last to build our home. Like Wolfe, a whole new generation of writers was to carry a scar upon their lives, a conviction in their souls. And like Sandburg from the midst of the ruins, standing amongst idle money, idle machines, idle men (the modern Trinity in the worship of the Eternal Executive), the American writer could feel free to create, where too often before he had mimicked or fled. Since he was still by inheritance the child of the machine age, he might often formulate blueprints of the impossible. Yet by and large, they might also be schemes for a fuller and deeper American life than those ever drafted in the epoch of our purely material splendor.

Against the negativism of the nineteen-twenties, then, which culminated the tensions of the century; the two American nations —

> they have clubbed us off the streets   they are stronger   they are rich   they hire and fire the politicians the newspapereditors the old judges the small men with reputations   the college-presidents   the wardheelers   (listen businessmen collegepresidents judges   America will not forget her betrayers) . . .

— we witness the series of American affirmations which mark the course of our literature in the nineteen-thirties. The age of denial and doubt is passing now, the sands of skepticism are running out. We are present at the start of a unique transformation, the turning of a cultural tide. Now the larger hope, the larger faith, the larger love which gave birth and sustenance to the American Republic and lay behind the deeds of Paine and Jefferson and Lincoln, return, in some measure at least, to our modern literary spokesmen — these morose prophets often with honor in their own land and without conviction. (This is particularly significant in the United States, where literature must assume many of the functions delegated in other cultures to church, school, aristocracy, etc., as the poet told us in 'Democratic Vistas': 'The priest departs, the divine literatus comes.')

Echoing Hemingway's Nada — Hail nothing, full of nothing, nothing is with thee — the Lardner of nineteen-twenty-nine's gaudy hour heaped abuse on his own great talents, obliterating the age in himself. Yet the Nada, traveling to the farthest reaches of exile, merges into the dictum of Golz, 'believing in how things could be, even if they never were': *Bon. Nous ferons notre petit possible.* A strange statement, indeed, for all our writer individualists, despairing spectators of America's fruitless materialism, consigning all our works to the fathomless waters of oblivion, placing their own fox hole of art before the interests of humanity! Now the two nations of Dos Passos, in turn, become one. 'I, myself, believe . . . that this country is getting to be a better place to live in instead of a worse.' Marked still by the estranged artistic emotions of the twenties, this shows nevertheless another similar return of our intelligent author to his society. Here is, we say, the true rather than the formal American conversion of Dos Passos, after the two decades of experimentation and disenchantment during which the pallid youth concealed behind the revolutionary ardor of Dos Passos has wrought such miracles of energy, to culminate in the most discerning study of our culture yet given to us by a novelist. U.S.A! High and impossible destiny (for the descendants of Wash Jones) of the states envisioned by the furious chronicler of Jefferson, Mississippi, lost like his Hightower in the thunder of martial hooves upon a cloud of historical dust, 'that son who grew to manhood among phantoms,' and waiting still for something to pant with, to be reaffirmed in triumph and desire with. Among our writers, Faulkner remains the celebrated exception without which our rule would seem in ill repute. Among the new affirmations of the thirties, the twice unreconstructed rebel, bemused by the tender passions of a sweeter infancy, he stands, the great hater of modern maturity. Yet the American fate is not equally impossible to Faulkner's fellow Southerner, our tumescent yokel with his elaborate plans and theatrical pronouncements, but a torrential youth from a deeper source than '29. Compensating for the melancholia of Mississippi, it is Wolfe who perhaps feels the meaning of his nation most intensely — promise, at least, of the rustling leaves across the American space:

> And everywhere, through the immortal dark . . . something stirring in the hearts of men, and something crying in their wild, unuttered blood, the wild unuttered tongues of its huge prophecies — so soon the morning, soon the morning; O America

What a long way he came, our seething provincial, his story
that of incessant struggle, his last accents those of defiance and
change! Held in reversionary prejudice amidst the gleaming
spires of his Enfabled Rock, in his slow and stunted movement
forward, nevertheless, and in the regressions marking his movement, Wolfe stood for us. As he came in the end to stand most
clearly for the new literary faith of the nineteen-thirties. And
what a long way our American society itself seems to have
moved over the decade, still marked by Wolfe's provincial
errors and false seeking, like Wolfe's Eliza often betrayed by
avarice, yielding up its children for the sake of its property; and
half-consumed like Gant by the cancerous growths of the industrial revolution! For we've noticed what has happened in '39
to Lardner's anonymous Mister U.S.A. who once 'bought a
book and threw it away,' and now is flocking to read the celebrated 'Grapes of Wrath.' This incredible best-seller, to the
Lardnerian citizen of '29, so filled with perplexing social concepts, a whole new alphabet of misery, the catalyst of a decade
of crisis. Traversing the circuit of his epoch's evasions, from
the cannibal to the comrade, reminding us of those who fled
from Toklas to Taos, Steinbeck shows us also the power the
writer holds in the United States of social change, the new
courage the writer has won from crisis, the faith in his function
which can move men as well as mountains. And viewing Steinbeck's popularity as an index of our collectivism rather than our
critical acumen, it was not inconceivable, we said, that America
would at last solve her dilemmas as she has pursued her vogues;
and Utopia cemented in from darkness to dawn, what a fresh
and lovely morning would greet us!

So the larger hope of the American writer, drawing close to his
country in the years of want, contrasts oddly with the hopeless-
ness of the isolated and hostile artist in the years of plenty —
this Ishmael, as Melville knew, in the land of honey. As the
prevailing climate of the post-war years, moreover, was destructive (and we are not denying the specific effect of the First
World War upon our writers, but relating them to a larger

cultural pattern), so the new affirmations of the thirties are again hardly restricted to our own choice of writers. Among the mature generation, the movement of Archibald MacLeish from the introspection of his early 'Hamlet' to the conviction of his public speeches is typical; as is that of Robert Sherwood from farce to faith. Robinson Jeffers himself, paralleling almost precisely the course of negativism we have traced in Hemingway and Faulkner, from tragedy to the depreciated tone of 'Mara' (Spengler sits poorly on a bitter spirit) — Jeffers stirs uneasily on the lonely crags of Carmel, though anxious now for England, not America, and 'freedom' rather than democracy. Turning from Jeffers, Muriel Rukeyser, one of the articulate voices of the younger poets, expressed the typical decision of her generation in the 'Citation for Horace Gregory' —

> Young poets and makers, solve your anguish, see
> the brave unmedalled, who dares to shape his mind,
> printed with dignity, to the machines of change. . . .
>
> We are too young to see our funerals
> in pantomime nightly before uneasy beds,
> too near beginnings for this hesitation
> obliterated in death or carnival . . .
> before they die the brave have set their hand
> on rich particular beauty for their heirs.

And in prose, also, we saw the rise of a generation of writers, turning from the century's 'hesitation' to the new directions of their literary seniors: Erskine Caldwell, Albert Halper, Leane Zugsmith, Robert Cantwell, Richard Wright, Clifford Odets, to mention a few other typical names. We are not denying that these turnings to belief were sometimes conversions to violence; the writer, like Wolfe, compensating for his ignorance by his intensity, and, like Steinbeck, excusing the tardiness of his arrival by the extremity of his declarations. Very often the moral got in the way of the story, and conviction became a substitute for imagination. Having so lately found his faith, the writer was likely to become the zealot as well as the believer, and his excess of moral virtue became an artistic vice. As in the list of our own novelists, this was the price of the American tradition under the urgencies of change. But it is certain, too, that the new direction of the nineteen-thirties was in many respects more aware and mature in its values, in the epoch of crisis more fruitful in its intimations of the future, than possibly any other literary movement of the last half-century.

Stressing the American return, the finale of our artistic individualism, the merging of the 'I' and the 'we' in our literary tradition, we do not wish to be taken as the advocate of collectivism. The strict disregard of the individual which, as the dominating trait of the European totalitarianisms, has become identified in some quarters with the wave of the future, is more likely a backwash. History, we said, will in time outbreed the outrageous egotism of Lardner's '29 — yet must we again suffer new varieties of slavery merely to achieve moderation? The Lardnerian conceit, as we saw, was merely the preliminary democratic reaction to the long sociological array of caste systems it succeeded, and not the final destination of Jefferson's vision, nor of Emerson's 'Hitch your wagon to a star.' Despite the extravagances of General Keefe's monomania, would the bard now modify his aphorism thus: 'Hitch your wagon to a commissar'? The distinctive mark of western evolution, the great gift of the Christian heritage, is that of every leaf on the tree, the meaning of every soul in the myriad spawning of the race. We are merely urging, of course, balance: an integrated individualism, not an infantile one; with social responsibilities as well as rights; marked by the sense of character; viewing other individuals as temperaments to relate itself to, rather than objects to be manipulated. Nor should we see the communal life as a block to the growth of this individual, as the later Van Wyck Brooks, looking back upon the earlier one who spoke in 'The Literary Life in America' of the 'solicitations of the mob,' might now freely acknowledge. For the 'mob' has its vitalizing effect upon the writer as well as its corrosions of his judgment. Man's nature is to belong as well as to be separate, his temperament a

fusion of the 'I' and the 'we,' his total being, indeed, so clearly
an agglomeration of the many that, strictly speaking, we can
hardly say he exists as one. His basic heritage as an individual
is more the race's than his own. During the most formative part
of his existence, he believes himself to be part of his parents.
And for the balance of his uneasy progress he alternates between
these two poles of freedom and dependence until he shortly
returns to the communal anonymity from which he came.

'Man's need,' said the once free-thinking and heretical
Dostoevsky, having indulged also in the mad Nietzschean
escape from humanity, 'is for miracles, bread and authority.'
Nothing could be more acute than this as a statement of our
weakness, our human bondage, the survival of that past heritage
which moulds us always more than we know. And as Erich
Fromm has lately told us, developing this theme in 'Escape
from Freedom,' the appeal of the new totalitarian doctrines lies
in their recognition of our need to be subordinate as well as to
dominate, to sacrifice as well as to glorify ourselves, to be part
of humanity as well as to be free from it. The dog-eat-dog
survival creed of modern capitalism (which was, of course,
mainly for the other dogs, and not for those super-canines who
believed in monopolies) and the false assumptions of man's
rational independence made by the early eighteenth-century
democratic theorists have largely worked together for their own
destruction. Yet the totalitarian doctrines supplanting this
today, catering with such acumen to our weakness, will destroy
all chances of our potential strength. Our need, despite Dostoevsky, is rather for a new democratic mythos, wiser and more
flexible, which will acknowledge our human ills while providing
for our health, which will allow for both our individualism and
our belonging, our freedom and our sharing — our freedom
which will be stronger through our sharing. Toward this the
American writer must work (aesthetic rebel who is revolting
against a rebellious culture, artistic individualist who is protesting the society of the economic individualist, and hence is
twice removed from his communal ties). Toward this, we say,

and not toward a blind and rigid social belief of any sort, nor any submergence in the masses; but rather the most delicate balance again of the 'I' and the 'we' which, with the artist, as with the rest of us, is the probable meaning of his life and art. As we saw with Hemingway, it is through the great and solitary researches of unique individuals that we may gain our knowledge of the boundaries and depths of living. But it is very likely only through our united effort, our communal ties, our common being, that we may hope to use such knowledge, to annex these boundaries and to dwell in these depths. And the writer, perhaps more than any other of the precious adventurers into the unknown, must be at once unique and common to make his discoveries and to endure them. He, like the rest of us, must not only lose his soul to save it. He must go on losing and saving his soul; he must conduct, as it were, a perpetual juggling match with his mortality.

Just so, the stress we have placed in these studies on the American integration of our writers, the return of all these sulking natives, is not intended for any sort of spurious and historically now obsolete nationalism. Surveying our contemporary writing from this aspect, we said, even chauvinism might have its charms. Where are the Whitmans of our world? And Emerson loved his land, though perhaps in the end he loved learning more. Yet is it the high destiny of the United States to rule supreme over a universe of prostrate peoples? Life, like peace in our time, is indivisible. It is only in the common good that the individual good can long survive; it is now only in the international health that national health can endure, as our epoch has proved. The widening circle of man's dominion from cave to clan and clan to continent has surely marked our evolution, however tardy and irresolute our organization is as yet. But the dangers for the writer in ignoring close humanity for a distant one, or his own society for a more abstract internationalism, have been illustrated in our studies, and in the course of American literature as a whole. By another of those logical paradoxes upon which human nature seems to thrive, it is

perhaps only those who have the firmest grasp of things near
who can best envision the distant, who must be in tune with the
immediate to know the indefinite, and having the surest sense
of proximity, so to speak, can feel infinity. Or, like the sick who
best understand health, the writer who loves his own nation
may be our surest guide to that final view of life which will
hardly distinguish between nations. In the widening circle of
man's social organization, moreover, it may be that America
has its special significance, which in their spiritual revolt our
writers have forgotten, as the Lardnerian citizens in their
material complacency.

For is it possible to separate the crisis of the American depression, which we have seen changing the values of our writers so
sharply, from the international crisis we are now facing? They
are part of the same historical movement. We have no longer
any occasion to deceive ourselves that our world is not changing.
What is the meaning, if not this, of continents bursting into
flame, of war upon war, international and civil, the uneasy
armistices themselves marked by the reigns of revolt and repression? Everywhere the older social moulds are cracking in their
effort to contain the new meanings, and the immensity of the
horror proclaims the depth of the change. What we are wit-
nessing, of course, is the culmination of the fantastic era of
technological progress which has altered the direction of
modern society. The test tube has forced us into a new mould,
a new set of frameworks for civilization; we may almost say a
new context for human life; and our modern effort is the long
and tormented adjustment to this. We see the transition from
production to distribution, and from existence to achievement.
Interrupted by similar 'intervals of peace,' here is the Hundred
Years' War of our time between the immemorial past and the
infinite future, toward new meanings or possible obliteration.
Everywhere today we destroy each other in the catastrophic
illusion that we must in order to gain those necessities of life
which lie useless around us. In the past, certainly, all our
human energy was directed toward winning these, to achieve

the bare foundations of existence, to gain some sort of meager human sanity out of the insane elements. But so long the butt of circumstance, man's struggle is no longer merely to survive. Our technology has given us the capacity for infinite wealth. Now what shall we do with our wealth? Who will give us the equal capacity for wisdom? Our struggle is no longer against nature, but ourselves. We compete, not against brutal necessity, but our own brute instincts. We have won the war for survival; but can we make the peace? This is, as it were, the utopian crisis, the halting entrance into paradise; now the two worlds of the ancient myth merging into a potential heaven on earth.

Or shall we rather witness another fall of man? Another betrayal, this time by the transmission belt, and this time a most incalculable, prefabricated Paradise Lost. For the peace, as usual, is harder to achieve. We must compare the few decades of technological change, which today both rapes and replenishes nature in the same standardized gesture, with the innumerable centuries during which we fought to gain this technic — with the total span of our evolution, of which our Palaeolithic ancestor, dwelling among the deposits of the Glacial Period, was the fabulous modern climax. We must realize that this long span of scarcity moulded the human temperament, created from nothing as it was, nourished on want, and enduring by the extremes of aggression. In one way or another, of course, all our feeling and reasoning, our morality, religion, and science, have shown the effect, if they are not wholly the result, of the survival struggle. The Christian ethic itself, supplanting at long last force with love (a great step forward in our historical yesterday, and if accomplishing much evil in its pursuit of good, nevertheless a quite unique vision of our tomorrow) — the Christian ethic often reveals the framework of force from which it sprang. What we are faced with, then, is not merely the revision of societal moulds, but the partial revision, at least, of the human temperament itself: our long accumulating matrix of untold deprivation which is now the master of untold opulence.

We face, moreover, hardly so much a moral obligation as an

evolutionary imperative. If we fail to devise new social arrangements, new forms of communal functioning, and new directions for human activities, it is likely that our entire magnificent technological structure is destined to rust, or we are. And if the possibilities of such change are, of course, unlimited, our conversion to them is commensurately difficult. Seeing before us the expectation of such immense human security and power, have we the wit to cope with it? It will take great intelligence, courage, imagination to inhabit a world without want. Our past of scarcity, indeed, has endowed us with the stamina to bear failure, the capacity to accept defeat. Can we likewise endure such good fortune and bear up under our epochal victory? It would be a final evolutionary irony if the forms of life which had evolved around the survival struggle were unable to adjust themselves to its culmination; and the race of man, from the molecule to the mammal, which had prospered to such an astounding degree under adversity, would now yield to extinction by affluence.

Considering the total crisis of our time, then, we may more correctly see our own epoch of '29 as its prophetic if miniature prelude. The American story we have been establishing is the modern story. In the lavish materialism of the nineteen-twenties and the useless suffering of the nineteen-thirties in the midst of the same natural abundance and technological cunning, we may read, so to speak, the little overture to the immense drama of the centuries. Through our failure to fashion a respectable American Success Story, and our lack of sense, surfeited with prosperity, to avert panic, we were the true contemporary protagonist in the parable of past and future. Yet we see also that by contrast with large areas of our world, the American crisis, however painful, was nevertheless relatively lighter, the American intelligence sharper, the emergence of new societal forms to deal with technological change was accomplished with relatively less destruction. Our own native 'beginning change,' in short, was also a miniature civilizational triumph. Just so, in the new struggle facing us, the utopian crisis of plenty, America in many ways can make herself, if she chooses the laboratory of social progress, as the acute theorist Trotsky, for example, knew; and as the vaunted Russian Bear itself, while our own radicals looked always toward the future in the east, has watched the States with anxious yearning.

As we traced in '29, moreover, the crux of a century's industrial ailments, the vocational disease of the American writer, we must also extend the American era of material aggrandisement outward, and see in it the typical epoch of the machine. Very much in the manner of Dorothy Parker's Jew, the American was after all just like everybody else, only more so. (In 'A Revolution in European Poetry,' Emery Neff reminds us that the modern separation of the artist from his society was heralded in 1770 by Goldsmith's 'Deserted Village' where 'wealth accumulates and men decay.') And the 'more so' in every sense is the distinguishing mark of American society today. If we have often, in fact, seemed to attribute to our writers the faults which are more precisely the possession of all mankind, it is because the American, by reason of both his shortcomings and potential stature, is most clearly modern mankind. Deriving from all countries and cultures, the universal cross-breed which Nature cherishes; dwelling near the center of universal abundance; the anonymous master technician; unconscious artisan of steel, cement, glass, brick; harnessing space and annihilating time as if by habit; the accomplished dilettante of perhaps a million mechanical toys; turning all worldly things inside out for what great purpose as yet unknown; showing us most clearly all that is wrong with us, and all that could be right, the American is the Everyman of today. Like Steinbeck's Lennie, in the fumbling, infantile American giant, moulding his existence around a concept he only imperfectly understands, his vitality so far ahead of his insight, we may see a portrait of humanity itself, if too often an ironic portrait.

So we may say the crass and narrow Lardnerian Success Story is finished — the sterile myth of money which enlisted our passions without our hearts; and which, like a vice, we practiced

with sometimes incurable desire, but could hardly defend our
compulsions. As Dixon Wecter shows in 'The Hero in America,'
over the entire era of industrial expansion the United States
emulated but scarcely admired its financial wizards; there
emerged no portrait of a folk-hero comparable to Washington
or Lincoln. But a new American Success Story is starting,
upon which once again, as in 1776, the hope of the years may
well depend. Toward the achieving of that new life, 'copious,
vehement, spiritual, and bold,' what happens with us may help
to determine everywhere the future of which our poet was
assured, whether we came into it 'today or in ten thousand or
ten million years.' And as we saw with a John Dos Passos, on the
edge of his own big American critique, everything is about
ready. The period of our national apprenticeship is over. All
that is necessary is the view. The view; the vision of our storybook democracy which in us, as in our author, is so often the
chronicle of defeat, thwarted if not ridiculed; the American
fate, nevertheless, which haunts our hearts as it does the pages
of 'U.S.A.' Those democratic vistas which America, traveling
too long Whitman's roads 'all even and peaceful,' must seek
again in her crises of anguish.

We need hardly stress, if we have not made clear, the place of
the writer in formulating a democratic view, as now in the nineteen-forties he accepts once more a functioning relationship in
his society, his true sphere which he had deserted along with
the other inhabitants of Goldsmith's village. Here we reach
the last significance of the American return of our writers in
crisis; their return which is only valid as it illuminates the
direction, not of a class, nor a superior cult, nor a dominating
nation, but of everything alive everywhere. Inevitably, we
move toward a conception of life which embraces all societies,
all peoples, the total common civilizing effort. To whatever is
good in our dwelling together we must henceforth yield ourselves, and to all that is evil stand in joint opposition, no longer
as a matter of moral rhetoric, but as historical fact. The new
Chosen People, shall we fashion, then, the living Jerusalem, or

as the children of light be forced to wander, homeless, amidst the dark centuries, our songs of innocence yielding to those of experience?

But whatever is to come, we know what has gone. Over the historical island of '29 the tides of change are sweeping. And now recalling Lardner's monomaniac, the safaris of Hemingway, the orgiastic dissipation of Dos Passos's Big Money, Faulkner's Mississippi, Wolfe's Magic City, and Steinbeck's Okies, despite the limitations of personality and culture which surround them, with what respect must we regard these evocations: our little American trials of poverty and plenty themselves a foretaste of our troubled future! History has made sport of us. How fortunate were they, believing those years so disturbed, who faced such minor trials, today when Destiny lies open for the transforming human will! Have the American twenties been the villain of our piece? Frantic blossoming of a pioneer order, playtime of monopoly in whose heavens, fixed and immutable, glowed the mystic sign of the dollar, whose evening would never come, and under whose bright artificial sunlight (all vitaminized) Lardner's commercial superman saw no sign in its passing of Time's antique chariot? Time passed for you also, more swiftly perhaps than ever before, and soon was overturning empires in hours.

And looking backward from the other side of an historical chasm which for all his ingenuity even the American man cannot yet bridge, we must admit at last that our villain, as described by Frederick Lewis Allen, had his attractive moments. '29! Mah-Jong and the Outline of History, the Provincetown Players and Station KDKA, Pittsburgh. American Can & Can (Debenture 5s, preferred) ¼. Norma Talmadge and The Constant Nymph. (All alone, I'm so all alone by the telephone ...) The League and the Ku Klux Klan. American Can & Can (Debenture 5s) 76¼. Harding, Dempsey, Babe Ruth, and Bathing Beauties. (The stars shine above you, so linger awhile ...) The Hall-Mills Case, Peaches Browning. When I hear you calling you-hoo-hoo-hoo. If Winter Comes? Will Lindy make it? Barney Google with his goo-goo-googly eyes. American Can & Can (Debenture 5s) 100¼. Day by day in every way. Oh fabulous years of yesterday! Cocktails and rouge. Rising skirts and rising stocks. (I love, I love you, that's all that I can say...) Oil wells. Wells of Loneliness. O tempora, O mores, pyorrhea and plus fours. Ten-year naval holidays in which we promise to build no capital ships. Tea for two and two for tea. American Can & Can (Debenture 5s) 160¼. (Fascinating rhythm, you got me on the go...) Model A and the Mississippi Floods. The Man Nobody Knows. Calvin Coolidge. Al Smith and Al Capone, Balto, the Marquise de la Falaise de la Coudray, and My Bill. Red Grange, Gene Tunney, Irving Babbitt, and Professor Billy Phelps who brought Tennyson and Browning to Main Street. American Can & Can (Debenture 5s) 200¼. (Do I love you? Mnn. Do I mean it? Mnnnnn...) The American Mercury, the New Yorker, and Coral Gables. Sold! The Bridge of San Luis Rey, Gentlemen Prefer Blondes and the Jazz Singer. Vitaphone. American Can & Can (Debenture 5s) 244¼. (When day is done and shadows fall I miss you...) Rising skirts and rising stocks. Love for sale, appetizing young love for sale at Broad and Wall Streets. National City Bank, Corn Exchange Bank Trust (How could Red Riding Hood have been so very good and still keep the wolf from the door...), Bank of Manhattan, Chase National Bank. American Can & Can (Debenture 5s) 277¼. (I'm happy in my blue heaven...) Guaranty Trust, East River Trust, West River Trust, Emigrants Trust, Farmers Trust, Bankers Trust, Farmers and Bankers Trust, Farmers and Bankers Trust Trust. Sold! American Can & Can (Debenture 5s) 299¼. Dow Jones, Fisher Bodies, Standard Statistics, C.O.D., F.O.B. American Can & Can (Debenture 5s) 298¼. Federal Reserve System warns. Herbert Hoover consults. (Nursed it, rehearsed it, and gave out the news...) Business is fundamentally sound. W. C. Durant, Charley Anderson, Charles Mitchell. Business is fundamentally sound! (Dig-a-dig-a-doo!) Samuel Insull. American Can & Can (Debenture

5s) 100¼! Thomas Lamont, Albert Wiggin, Richard Whitney Business is fundamerican Can & Can (Debenture 5s, preferred) ¼. Sold! (I can't give you anything but love, baby, that's the only thing I've plenty of, baby...), Franklin D. Roosevelt. The American Twenties! Oh marvelous era of the plush speakeasy, the rolled stocking, the bouncing bond, heyday of the athlete and the salesman, paradise of the expatriate and the racketeer, blessed time of Irene and the Black Bottom, we greet you. As we advance to grapple with Whitman's direst fate, we hail you, gorgeous moment of our youth, mystic hour of the transatlantic toot, hail and farewell. With what reverence shall we now gaze back and tenderly treat these fragile ashes of a day forever past. For now the era of the historian himself is slipping by. Now we shall make rather than record our history. 'I know things change now and I do not care. It's been all changed... Let it all change.' This Hemingway utterance, like so many others of his, was to stand for the feeling of his generation. With a little more outward moving concern, perhaps, the use of our wits and our will, the civilizing effort which our writer in turn was soon to accept, we were to say this also about our time. Like the later novelist, standing in opposition to him who dwelt among fiestas, we do care what happens, and very much so. Yet there was to be certainly enough regret, uneasy and anxious returning speculation, and affection even for those gilded glories of '29, for after all this was our place. But it's been all changed. Let it all change.

THE END

Index